# A DICTIONARY
of
PASTORAL PSYCHOLOGY

## BOOKS BY VERGILIUS FERM

*The Crisis in American Lutheran Theology* (1927)
*What is Lutheranism?* (1930), Editor
*Contemporary American Theology*, Theological Autobiographies, Volume I (1932), Editor
*Contemporary American Theology*, Theological Autobiographies, Volume II (1933), Editor
*First Adventures in Philosophy* (1936)
*Religion in Transition* (1937), Editor
*First Chapters in Religious Philosophy* (1937)
*An Encyclopedia of Religion* (1945), Editor
*Religion in the Twentieth Century* (1948), Editor
*What Can We Believe?* (1948)
*Forgotten Religions* (1950), Editor
*A History of Philosophical Systems* (1950), Editor
*A Protestant Dictionary* (1951)
*The American Church* (1953), Editor
*Puritan Sage*, The Collected Writings of Jonathan Edwards (1953), Editor
*The Protestant Credo* (1953), Editor
*Their Day Was Yesterday* (A Novel) (1954)
*A Dictionary of Pastoral Psychology* (1955)

# A DICTIONARY of PASTORAL PSYCHOLOGY

BY

## VERGILIUS FERM
Compton Professor and Head of the
Department of Philosophy in the
College of Wooster

**PHILOSOPHICAL LIBRARY**
NEW YORK

Copyright, 1955, by
THE PHILOSOPHICAL LIBRARY
15 East 40th Street, New York, N. Y.

ISBN 0-8065-3049-9
ISBN 13: 978-0-8065-3049-9

Printed in The United States of America

**Specific Articles By**

WILFORD W. BOWER, M.A.

*Recently, a Member of the Faculty in The College of Wooster in the Department of Philosophy; Interim Instructor in Philosophy, Western Reserve University; Graduate Student in Philosophy at Columbia University; Ford Fellow, 1951-1952; Special Studies in Counseling at Columbia and Student of Clinical Psychoanalysis.* (W. W. B.)

VERGIL HARKNESS FERM, M.S., M.D.

*Recently, Preventive Medicine Officer for the First United States Army Corps in Korea; now, Research Assistant in the Department of Anatomy, University of Wisconsin.* (V. H. F.)

DEANE WILLIAM FERM, B.D., M.A., Ph.D.

*Director, Montana School of Religion, Montana State University, Missoula, Montana; Special Studies in Parapsychology.* (D. W. F.)

LOUIS I. NEWMAN, M.A., Ph.D., D.D.

*Rabbi, Congregation Rodeph Sholom, New York City; Author of "The Healing of Modern Man" (1954).* (L. I. N.)

GRANGER E. WESTBERG, B.D.

*Associate Professor of Pastoral Care and Chaplain of the University of Chicago Clinics; Formerly, Chaplain at the Augustana Lutheran Hospital in Chicago.*
(G. E. W.)

JOHN R. WILLIAMS, B.D., D.D.

*Minister of the First Presbyterian Church, Wooster, Ohio (since 1937); Counselor to College Students; Community Leader in Interdenominational, Social and Philanthropic Enterprises.* (J. R. W.)

# PREFACE

The field of Pastoral Psychology has in recent years become a popular area of interest. It may be considered a belated offspring of the parent Psychology of Religion which was widely popular during the first quarter of this century. Psychology of Religion suffered an eclipse in interest when psychologists turned their backs upon the essential qualities of the human spirit and resorted to the more scientifically promising field of animal studies and behavioristic psychology. With the rise of what is now known as depth psychology, Freudianism in particular, during the World Wars, the return of interest in the recesses of the human spirit became strong for psychological explorations, even though the ways and means to their understanding were fraught with theories rather than objective measurements. Pastoral Psychology has arisen very largely as a part of this interest although it is not confined to the inner life alone. Its purview encompasses the whole psychological field as it relates to the work of the minister.

It is the legitimate assumption of this book that there is no special psychology that may be called pastoral psychology. Psychology remains the basic subject; the pastoral only a phase of it. It is taken for granted that the human mind operates the same—whatever the field of expression. Pastoral psychology is but the application of the general principles of human psychology—in this case in the area in which the professional minister performs his tasks, whether it be counseling, directing religious education, teaching, executing the practical tasks involved in an institutional church, preaching, or promoting the cause of spiritual and social welfare. A minister is a human being dealing with human beings—all of whom are part and parcel of the common relationships of emotions, habits, responses, learning capacities, temperaments, that go to make up the human family and inter-personal relationships.

It is wrong to think of this field as dealing only with special cases or with abnormal reactions. Psychiatry, psychoanalysis, aberrational behaviors, psychosomatic medicine are only a part of the total interest. A minister professionally is a servant of religion and only in practice a psychologist. In the fields of specializations such as medicine, psychiatry and even psychology itself, he remains a layman. A volume on Pastoral Psychology thus is not a special treatment of psychology (normal or abnormal) but rather a treatment of the subject of psychology in those phases which have theoretical or practical bearing on the work of the minister. Terms thus employed by the professional specialists must be defined in the way the professionalists would approve rather than as the minister would prefer to use them by personal preference or prejudice. This is to say that theology and philosophy or a particular religious faith such as Christian or Jewish are not the subject-matter in the treatment of the subject. Here there is no place for validity of beliefs as such or an apology for any traditional set of religious commitments. There is no spiritual psychology as such: only plain psychology.

For bearings, then, in this field one must read exegetically from the reportings of the psychologists without the prejudice of one's own brand of religious faith. One must not approach the subject normatively as is natural in theology or philosophy but rather descriptively, taking into hand the tools of the psychological trade.

This volume makes no pretense of exhausting a complicated subject. It is one author's attempt to select from the general field of psychology those items of interest which have some relevance to the minister's own use of psychological material —to direct his thinking in the acceptable channels of the psychological field. For example, a minister should be aware of what is meant by such terms as sensation, perception, emotion, instinct (horribly confused even by professional people), afferent and efferent fibers, psychoanalysis and its many concepts, psychotherapy and its ramifications, selected medical terms as they are used in the medical profession (in which area the minister is continually plunged by reason of his pastoral relationships), learning and child training, adult characteristics, human genetics, schools of psychology, religious psychology, and the variety of terms associated with the now popular vogue of depth psychology.

It is apparent that many concepts in psychology, however, represent viewpoints of schools and are used in particular frames of reference. Since human psychology deals with complex rather than simple phenomena not capable of easy analytic surgery one may never dogmatize his opinions or conclusions as final—even though they may square with psychological accounts. There are depths of the human spirit which are really depths, and influences in human behavior which are subtle and evasive. There are many areas of dispute in the psychological profession, scientific claims notwithstanding. And what is more: there are many topics in psychology which cross the border into the philosophical area by reason of the small proportion of data that are amenable to controlled observation and single conclusions, not to mention the variety in the use of conceptual material. Such general concepts as success, morality, talents, personality, self, character, conscience, intelligence, genius, abilities, intuition, the religious response, and a host of others—do not readily fall into generally approved slots of classification. The use of such terms can only follow the frame of reference appropriate to them. Psychology and philosophy meet at this point.

The basic pattern of this book has been laid out carefully within the framework of reputable treatises by specially qualified authors in the psychological profession. Many books and professional papers have been consulted but always with care in their selection. These books and papers form the framework of this work. The topics chosen have seemed appropriate to the purpose of a volume intended for clergymen.

Critical readers may rightly wonder as to the proper qualifications of those responsible for this Dictionary. They may make some judgment on the basis of the following data:

The writer of the major portion of this work (indicated by topics appearing without the signature of initials) has been a member of the ministerial profession for thirty-five years, a portion of which carried parish responsibilities. He has counseled with college students for more than a quarter of a century, teaching a course in the psychology of religion almost from the beginning of his academic profession. When religious psychology was in full bloom he had the privilege of personal discipleship under the great pioneer in this branch of psychology, Professor Edwin D. Starbuck, then at Iowa State University and of working along with others then doing research work in the field under his supervision in particular areas. Those of us who were welcomed into the circle of warm friendship with Dr. Charles Reynolds Brown and who sat in his lecture room at Yale hearing words of wisdom on preaching and on the work of the minister in the parish will never wish to lose the inspiration he gave us nor forget the emphasis he laid upon the human element in all religious aspiration and behavior. It has, through the years, kept the eye ever watchful of the dust that is blown about amidst the lofty sentiments and expressions of the spirit. Special contributors (indicated by topics appearing over the signature of their initials) have been summoned to this volume for specialized treatment of terms, concepts and fields relating to their disciplined experience, their qualifications set down with their names in a separate listing in this volume. My thanks to them for their interest and professional help.

For the permission to reprint my article on "The Psychology of Religion," which will appear in the forthcoming volume on *Contemporary Psychology*, my thanks is directed to Dr. A. A. Roback, its editor, and to the Philosophical Library, publishers. To the same publishers and to Dr. Ralph B. Winn, editor of the *Encyclopedia of Child Guidance* (1943) for permission to reprint my article on "Religious Beliefs" of children I also express my thanks.

Cross references have been generously provided in this volume to avoid undue repetition and are indicated in the usual manner at the end of the articles and by the use of asterisks in the texts.

Since this publication, in a sense, is a work of pioneering (particularly in selection and organization) it may easily suffer the shortcomings and inadequacies common to such attempts. Limitation of size has been set from the beginning: a handbook rather than an encyclopedia. Since ministers are practical people

—the exigencies of the time and the character of the work demanding that they shall so be—it will be understandable why there have been included in this volume topics of practical nature (such as visitation, counseling, sermon preparation, preaching, minister as a person, and the like) and some entries obviously of a homiletical, philosophical and exhortative character.

VERGILIUS FERM

*The College of Wooster*

# A DICTIONARY
## of
# PASTORAL PSYCHOLOGY

# A

**ability:** see deliberate effort; genius; mental ability; success; talents; work.

**abnormal conduct and abnormalities:** see analysis; complexes; genius; glands; old age; psychology of religion; psychoneuroses; visions and hallucinations.

**abreaction:** see analysis.

**absolute contrast, fallacy of:** see fallacy of absolute contrast.

**absolutes, the four, in the Oxford group movement:** see group psychotherapy.

**absolution:** see confession.

**acceptance:** see analysis.

**accidental criminals:** see criminal types.

**acculturation:** A term for the process of absorbing the mores of a culture* originally foreign or alien.

**achievement:** see creative thinking; efficiency and time of day; success; talents.

**achromatopsia:** see color blindness.

**acromegaly:** see hyperpituitarism.

**acrophobia:** see phobias.

**act psychology:** see psychology, schools of.

**actual neurosis:** see neurosis, actual.

**adaptation:** see morale; psychoneuroses; psychology of religion; psychology, schools of.

**Addison's disease:** So-called from the English physician, Thomas Addison, who defined it in 1855. An adrenal disturbance, the symptoms of which are severe weakness, **anxiety,**

apathy, lassitude and vertigo.* See adrenal glands; endocrine glands.

**adjustment:** see analysis; Dewey, John; dysphonia; instrumentalism; old age; pragmatism; psychology of religion (J. C. Flower); psychology, schools of.

**Adler, Alfred:** (1870-1937) A follower of Freud,* he departed from the latter's emphasis on sex, holding to the view that the basic feature of a neurosis* is an attitude of inferiority resulting from a frustration of the urge for superiority. He called his branch of psychotherapy "individual psychology." He stressed purposes and goals rather than drives and causes. In 1920 he set up clinics for the training of teachers in the treatment of poorly adjusted pupils.

Adler, originally from Vienna, developed his psychology in the United States. See fiction; inferiority complex; psychology of religion; psychology, schools of (psychoanalysis).

**Adlerian approach to therapy:** A history of the work of Alfred Adler* would show a particular approach to the counseling or therapeutic situation. Adler bases his approach to analysis* upon the social nature of man. Man sees himself as inferior to the social context in which he finds himself—inferior in his ability to make himself felt as a power in his connections with others. It is the frustration of power drives* in the individual which constitutes the source of a neurosis.* A child is frustrated in his ability to compete with the power which adults have over him and, in sublimating the drives to keep in accord with the power of adults, constructs the foundation of social inferiority throughout his life. Adler points out, however, that the facts of existence dictate a social interdependence which man cannot deny save by endangering his ability to survive. A weak man may be denying the power urge and may subordinate himself to the social structure. An extremely ambitious man may succeed at the expense of others in the social structure. Both of these men, *in extremis*, constitute the two sides of a piece of cloth. The solution to the neurotic personality complex will be, according to this school of approach, to integrate the personality with the social order: the weak man not denying his power and the overly ambitious man not denying the social structure by directing his "power drives" in constructive social channels. Adler, unlike Freud,* does not make a great deal of the sexual aspects of neurosis. He sees sexual activity as simply another manifestation of the social inferiority or superiority. W.W.B.

**adolescence:** see hamartophobia; pastoral counseling: case studies; psychology of religion; teen-agers.

**adolescence crisis-experience:** see psychology of religion; teen-agers.

**adrenal glands:** These are endocrine glands* adjacent to the kidneys. In intense emotional states the adrenal medulla secretes adrenalin; the hormone* known as cortin is supplied by the adrenal cortex. Hyperfunctioning of the adrenal cortex in childhood causes precocious puberty in males, in females a condition tending towards masculinity; in adult women, hyperfunctioning brings on virilism, inhibition of sex functions and excess hair on the face. Deficiency of cortin may result in Addison's disease.* See emotion.

**adult, the:** A fully matured organism is called an adult. In a legal sense, a human adult is usually considered in terms of age, viz., twenty-one years or older. A mental hygienist speaks of an adult as one who adjusts realistically to his environment.

The maturing process is, in each individual, one that begins in the embryonic stage and should cease only with death. No matter what one's age may be one is "getting old." One may justly speak of a very young person in years as an adult if the maturing process is of the kind that makes an adjustment proper to the years of experience.

Old age* is also a relative term in terms of adaptation and functioning. People are now living longer. In America by 1980 there will be some sixty million forty-five years and older and some twenty-one million over sixty-five. Unless the proportionate number of increases in birth-rate balances the increase in life expectancy, there will be more old people than young in another quarter century.

In the maturing process more is now known of the physical aspects of the aging process* than that of the mental. Some medical experts explain the aging process as due to the decrease of food and oxygen to the cells of the nervous system. The Russian scientist, Bogomolets, explains the degenerative process of age as due to the deterioration of connective tissues, including the walls of the blood vessels. He claimed to have produced a serum which would revitalize the degenerating connective tissues or to prevent aging by early administration. His belief was that the natural life span is at least five times the period of growth of any organism. Accordingly, if man reaches the peak of growth at the age of twenty to twenty-five he should live one hundred and fifty years or longer. This conjecture is in great contrast to the life expectation of an ancient Roman, which was twenty-five years. Adult age would have come then in the teens. Today older people look and feel younger at "old age" than their counterparts in previous generations.

The difference in the rate of aging makes the conventional time for retirement absurd. A study made by the Harvard Fatigue Laboratory suggests that the theory of rapid decline after forty in quality and quantity of work is without foundation. In a machine age, heavy physical labor is reduced and the need for maturity in judgment and insight increased. Here the adult has the advantage.

It was long held that intelligence increased with life; that the chronological year revealed the intelligence* of that year; a ten year old having a ten year old intelligence, and so on. Psychologists now show that the average sixteen year old and the average thirty-two year old have about the same intelligence although presumably the older in years has more experience, information and maturity. The average intelligence is held by psychologists to reach full growth about the age of sixteen. An adult thus has a mental level in the sixteen year area.

The standard intelligence tests directed for young people are not fully satisfactory for adults. Their mind-set may be less adaptable to both the contents and methods of such standard tests. However, certain conclusions are offered by the professional psychologists: the growth of intelligence is rapid until about the age of sixteen (some at a slightly higher age of about twenty); there is a levelling off process until about thirty; then follows a gradual decline to the sixteen year level at forty-five; a more rapid tug downward with the fourteenth year level reached about fifty-five. These tests are not fully valid. An adult's speed of reaction may have slowed up enough to make the test-results requiring certain tasks appear to show a decline where the decline is not a matter of intelligence. The adult's slower reactions may well be compensated, however, by other assets such as maturity, experience and greater poise. In any age group about one third do better than the average of a group ten years younger which suggests that a study of individuals rather than groups would reveal a higher score in certain tests than for those younger.

In tests involving logic, good judgment, information and discernment of a problem older age sometimes shows advantage. Within time limits set by some tests the results may appear the other way.

There are other features less amenable and even immeasurable to tests, such as drive, motivation, morale.

Again, it is shown that so-called "native intelligence" at a higher degree tends to retain its degree with adult age.

The general picture seems to be this: that intellectual ability during adult years depends on native ability plus training and stimulation. Many adults do not maintain interests which would reveal their intellectual ability and thus decline for reasons other than such ability.

It is important to emphasize the rapid rise to adult stature in the teens and shortly after. A young person may well think of himself as becoming more rapidly adult than the adult becoming "aged." The realization of this lack of discrepancy between the "youth" and his parent may and should off-set the notion that parents are necessarily "old fogies" and thus create better understanding. Young people (so-called) do well to realize their own adult status when making the charge of hopeless discrepancy between themselves and their parents. The difference is largely one of experience, perhaps, which creates the illusion of incompatibility. Physical deterioration does not begin with "old age" as many believe. It begins early (e.g., receding hair line on the head or even baldness, skin wrinkles, and the short life of athletes as professionals). A twenty-five year old son has passed his mental prime and need not look askance on some mental lapses (e.g., memory) of his father. Only those under twenty are not yet "old" and this group constitutes the minority in society.

Older people should rediscover some of the lost interests of younger days or find equally stimulating substitutes. Such rediscovery is the road back to mental health if such, for the time being, has been lost. Social and mutual contacts may stimulate morale among those of equal age groups and bring back the vividness of self reliance. A long life is not a *desideratum* without good living and good living requires its own discipline at any stage of the game. See climacterium; climacterium virile; emotion; in-laws; I.Q.; menopause; morality and psychology; parents.

**advice**: see counseling; in-laws; structuring the counseling situation; teen-agers.

**aelurophobia**: see phobias.

**aesthetic experience**: The name given to certain qualities of objects which stimulate certain peculiar pleasures is beauty. The response is the aesthetic experience. Such pleasures have the characteristics of being pleasurable without satiety, pleasurable in anticipation and in memory, pleasurable without necessary utility and pleasurable in a time dimension which transcends the momentary, the fleeting and the passing fancy. Aesthetic pleasures seem to carry the stamp of universality, a promise of pleasure to all who submit to receptivity (e.g., by disciplined appreciation). The individual tends to lose himself in the experience. He tends to become absorbed in a kind of *rapport* or unity with the object of beauty and to experience a fulfillment and completeness.

Pleasure is a feeling tone, normal to well being (both psychical and physiological). Responses to life which come from desires fulfilled, hopes sustained, free expression uninhibited and gloriously full to the brim, contacts friendly (not hostile) afford the psychological condition of pleasure. Aesthetic experience is constituted of such conditions of pleasure. It is a response that brings harmony and emotional adjustment, the individual with himself and with his environment.

Beauty is the name for a two-way situation: an object and a response in the *rapport* of poise and harmony. There is no problem to be solved, no struggle to endure, no restraint or resistance to overcome. Value and existence become unified. Symmetry, proportion, varieties which blend into some unity —these give pleasure. Imagination and idealization take over when cross-purposes threaten. Here creativity supplies the omission or the gap. Lines which make graceful curves, rhythm which unites fragmentary steps, colors which flash the representations, forms which translate the familiar into the sentimental, melodies which, by means of the auditory medium, touch depths beyond surfaces (transcending the limitations of sight)—these are the media of pleasurable responses.

Beauty belongs to the teleological side of life (rather than the mechanistic). Its language is purpose, achievement, ends, goals, aspiration rather than origins, history and time-space sequence. Hence, contemplation rather than criticism and analysis is its atmosphere. It is because of this character, probably, that Beauty is linked with Goodness and both taken together support the idealization of some Truth (Absolute) which is beyond the full realization of finite achievement. See empathy; smell.

**afferent-efferent fibers:** Afferent fibers are those nerve fibers which conduct a nerve impulse *inwards* from sense organ (receptor) to the cord and brain. They are also called the sensory nerve fibers.

Efferent fibers are those nerve fibers which transmit the nerve impulse *outward* from the brain or cord to an effector. They are called the motor fibers.

Charles Bell (1807) first discovered the functional difference between sensory and motor nerves. See sensori-motor arc.

**age:** see adolescence; adult, the; aging process; children; creative thinking; memory; mental age; morality and psychology; old age; teen-agers; young, the.

**aggressiveness:** see over aggressiveness; peace and war.

**aging process:** see adolescence; teen-agers.

**aging process, the:** The United States Public Health Service in 1947 set up an elaborate medical research project at Baltimore, Md., to study the factors involved in the process of aging. Some popular theories about aging failed to find scientific confirmation. For example: the notion that digestion worsens with age, that an older person does not absorb the full value of food, that the older heart pumps less blood than the younger, that older people have, by reason of age, a vitamin deficiency, that wounds heal slower with age, that the rate of formation of new cells decreases in older folks, that old people "dry up," i.e., a reduction of body water takes place, etc. . . . these ideas, the tests failed to confirm.

On the positive side, the study showed that older people use less oxygen than the young and, during exercise, the older person cannot take in the extra oxygen required as quickly as a younger person. There is a marked change in the kidney functions (a slowup) but scarcely any major changes with age in the main body organs. A person 80 years of age has a kidney function one-half of that of 30 years. Dr. Nathan W. Shock reported that a pyrogen (chemical) could accelerate the flow of blood through the kidneys and that the blood vessels in the kidneys of old people were as flexible as in the young—suggesting that the kidney itself does not deteriorate sufficiently to account for the noticeable loss of function. Perhaps the problem lies elsewhere—probably in the pituitary gland* plus other factors. (It is held that hormones* from the pituitary act as a trigger on the action of the kidneys.)

The aging process appears to be controlled by more than one factor: a combination of endocrine function, diet, and the ability to maintain an active interest in events. Those who seem to age most rapidly (according to Dr. Shock) are those who, in good health, retire and have no interest to take up the slack. It is now held that the retirement age imposed by society at a fixed calendar year is arbitrary and artificial.

There is, however, the fact of brain deterioration from sclerosis* (hardening) or other disease which is quite another matter in the aging process.

Tests (words, arithmetic) conducted under the same auspices by Dr. James E. Birren, comparing three groups (young high school students, normal old people in 60-69 age group, old people of same group with psychoses*) showed the following conclusions: the process of aging does not slow down the mental process (although eyesight impairs speed); aging, however, combined with brain damage (by reason of disease) reduces mental ability sharply; reasoning power is not greatly reduced among the normally old; talking facility and word association usually rise to their peak at the age of 35 and decline thereafter slowly; in arithmetic, speed and accuracy continue beyond the age of 50.

Victor Hugo once remarked that "40" is "the old age of youth and 50 the youth of old age." It is probably true that the health problems of old age begin at about 40 and continue at varying rates in different organs and to a different degree among people. See adult, the; arteriosclerosis; climacterium;

climacterium virile; memory; old age.
*Bibl.* National Conference on the Aging, Washington, D.C., 1950. *Man and His Years.* An account of the First National Conference on Aging (1951).

**agnosticism:** see Leuba, James H.; reality feeling principle.

**agoraphobia:** see phobias.

**agricultural economy:** see pastoral counseling and case studies.

**aichmophobia:** see phobias.

**albinism:** see human genetics.

**alcohol:** see alcohol and efficiency; Alcoholics Anonymous; boredom; juvenile delinquency; visions and hallucinations.

**alcohol and efficiency:** It is not safe to generalize on the subject of alcohol—though the temptation be strong—because individuals vary in their reactions, vary in the amounts in which they may indulge and because experimental studies have not fully succeeded in controlling some of the factors involved (particularly that of suggestion and its induced performances).

Experimenting on simple motor reactions, some findings show that alcohol proves to be a depressant, reducing either the strength or the alertness of a performance (e.g., sensitivity to electric stimulation decreased 14%; speed of eye movements decreased 11%; speed of finger movements decreased 9%; extent of eyelid movement decreased 19%; eye reactions latent time increased 5%; latent time of the knee jerk increased 10%; etc.).

One experiment was developed to test the more involved psychological processes: Six men were tested at half hour morning-intervals, drinking beer of three different strengths and at different intervals. Similar tests were made on other days when the beer contained no alcohol. One subject was a total abstainer, one a regular drinker and the others occasional drinkers. All of them were unaware of the differences in the beers. Results of drinking alcoholic beer were (a few examples): hand steadiness decreased; hand-eye coordinations poorer; tapping slower; color-naming slower; adding slower; learning substitutes slower; etc.).

Another study gave the following results of the effects of alcohol: pulse rate increased; skin temperature increased; eyelid reflex slower; eye reaction time slower; word reaction time slower; visual acuity less keen; finger movement slower; eye-hand coordination poorer; typewriting errors increased; typewriting speed slower; etc.

People in general who use light doses of alcohol testify to the lift that drinking gives (rather than depression). This popular testimony seems at variance with the experimental studies—but only at first glance. Depressing effects at first concern the highest of inhibitions; then follows emotional release. The result: increase of well-being, self-confidence, general sociability. When drinking is further pursued emotional outbursts increase (anger, weeping, loud talk, gesticulations). A person's efficiency is increased only, under these excessive conditions, in certain of his feelings and expressions! His inhibitions are also lessened—if these are to be regarded as signs of efficiency? See alcohol.

*Bibl.* R. Dodge and F. G. Benedict, *Psychological Effects of Alcohol.* Carnegie Inst. Wash. (1915); W. R. Miles, *Alcohol and Human Efficiency.* Carnegie Inst. Wash., No. 333 (1924).

**Alcoholics Anonymous:** A fraternity, loosely organized, for mutual consolation and aid to overcome the alcohol habit. The movement began in 1935 in Akron, Ohio. Fifteen years later its membership has increased to some 120,000 without benefit of a formal organization or organizational propaganda. One friend helps another and friends undergird the alcoholic sick informally. Only a simple declaration initiates membership. There are no pledges or constraints, no records kept. Its purpose: "to help the sick alcoholic recover, *if he wishes.*" Catholics, Protestants, Jews, agnostics and others of no known religious affiliation join with each other in a common fraternity. All types of business and professions are represented.

Alcoholism has been described as "a progressive, incurable and fatally terminating disease." Its arrest is a matter of the sufferer's own desire.

The first two members, Bill W. and Dr. Bob (noted surgeon of Akron) set the stamp of anonymity on the membership, believing that principles outweigh personalities. One-sided preaching was frowned upon as of meagre therapeutic value. One helps himself by helping another.

New York, Cleveland, Chicago and Los Angeles have each over one hundred groups. There are A.A. clubs in some 90 prisons. In Chicago weekly intergroup meetings have attendance reaching a thousand. No hotel in New York has an assembly eating place to accommodate the number who desire a seat at the annual dinner.

Some fifty percent of those members who genuinely try give up drink at once and stay self-prohibitionists. Twenty-five percent, after some relapse, achieve success. The remaining twenty-five percent show improvement. There is no attempt at classifying to eliminate the incurable. There is no such word as "cure": only help and mutual encouragement.

Some 10 to 15 percent are women (although non-alcoholic wives attend meetings). The average age is between 35 and 40 and is tending toward a lower age.

Groups meet in church parish halls or small hotel rooms.

Alcoholics Anonymous speaks of "twelve steps": 1) admission on the part of the alcoholic that he has become unmanageable; 2) belief that only a Power greater than himself (as he understands that Power) can help him in his sickness; 3) a searching self analysis of his moral status; 4) admission to one other person and to God of his dilemma; 5) a commitment to prayer for Divine knowledge and power . . . and 12) with the achievement of some assurance, a declaration of his adherence to the principles of A.A. and to missionate among others in similar need.

There is what is called "The Nickel Therapy." When desire for alcohol becomes strong, the A.A. disciple drops a nickel in the telephone coin box and asks a fellow member to come to help him in his hour of agony and temptation.

The philosophy is to live from day to day—"the twenty-four hour" plan.

The A.A. motto is: "God grant us the serenity to accept the things we cannot change, courage to change the things we can, and wisdom to know the difference." See group psychotherapy.

**alertness:** see success.

**alleles:** see human genetics.

**Allport, Floyd H.:** see marriage, disharmony in; sex differences, psychological.

**Allport, G. W.:** see psychological frames of reference.

**altruism:** see talents.

**amathophobia:** see phobias.
**amaxophobia:** see phobias.
**ambition:** see deliberate effort; fatigue; psychoneuroses; success; talents; work.
**ambivalence:** This term recognizes the presence of two directly conflicting emotions on the part of a person directed toward the same person or object. E.g., the presence of both love and hate within the same emotional structure of an individual. When love and hate are directed by an individual toward the same object, this emotional structure is said to be ambivalence. Inasmuch as both feelings are genuine, ambivalence often suggests the source of guilt as the emotional schemata try to resolve and reconcile the contradictory feelings. An over abundance of the "need to please" will suggest that a certain ambivalence is present. The counselor will not attempt to further this reconciliation by eliminating one of these two feelings at the expense of the other but will help the patient to see that they play a genuinely significant dual role. Accepting the duality of feelings will help to establish and to end ambivalence as a source of guilt. W.W.B.

**American Institute of Mathematical Statistics:** see psychical research and parapsychology.

**American Psychological Association:** see psychical research and parapsychology.

**American Society for Psychical Research:** see psychical research and parapsychology.

**Ames, E. S.:** see psychology of religion.

**amnesia:** loss of memory* either total or partial. Anterograde amnesia is the term for the inability to recall or recognize events occurring directly after an emotional shock; retrograde amnesia is the term for the inability to recall events immediately before an emotional shock.

**a-moral drives:** see children and religious beliefs.

**analysis:** see intuition.

**analysis:** Analysis in psychotherapy is the process used in investigating and adjusting a maladjusted mind. It consists in inducing, by various means, the mind to reveal its remembered content and to bring to memory the forgotten and the unconscious emotional energies which surge below the threshold of conscious life and which bring on complexes.*

# analysis

Analysis is frequently a long drawn out process. Its dividends, however, are rewarding in so far as the subconscious life is discerned; for only by overcoming repressions can relief and cure of such maladjustments come about.

Successful analysis requires that there be a willingness on the part of the subject to cooperate in the process; that the causes of maladjustment be uncovered and their relation to the symptoms be exposed; that some understanding of the maladjustment relative to a wholesome pattern of life be made clear enough so as to reestablish a mental unity; and that a realistic transformation be strong enough to prevent a lapse.

Audible confession* to someone who is trusted and sympathetic and strong in character is a practice of long standing and productive of psychological relief. Confession involves both a remembered maladjustment and a secret. The latter involves the unconscious realm, the deep-seated area of most mental ills. To cleanse this area of its conflicts is the aim of any completed process of analysis. Catharsis* involves the whole depth of mind—the aim of genuine psycho-therapy.

The subject and the therapist must establish a relationship of rapport to bring about effective analysis—a delicate interpersonal communication requiring both common sense and skill (experience). For success the therapist must be a person strong in character, positive in spirit and well equipped for such undertaking. Utter frankness is a *sine qua non* of procedure which usually becomes easier where rapport has been established. Resistance of the subject may be difficult to overcome since resistance is often below the threshold of consciousness (repression*). Such resistances appear as defense reactions and are difficult to recognize. Undermining the defense mechanisms is the frontal attack of the therapist rather than attacking the resistance itself. Successive interviews may be necessary to wear the defenses down—by scattering them, draining off their energies. No subject easily recognizes his own defense mechanisms.* The outsider has the advantage of clearer perspective.

In analysis the professional psychoanalyst may recommend a procedure that is more drastic but nonetheless beneficial. (This, of course, is professional and must not be handled by any one without special qualifications.) Returning to memory by means of hypnosis, dream analysis or other methods of un-

### analysis

conscious and repressed emotions and reliving the original experiences of emotion is the phenomenon known as abreaction. It is an intensive form of the common impulse to tell over and over again some experienced shock until the repetition eases the emotion and a relief is achieved. Abreaction is, however, a more intense release and has been compared to the conversion experience in religion and its release of emotional tensions. Abreaction consists in recall to conscious memory the original emotions in conflict and re-experiencing them in all their fullness. It is the re-experiencing that gives the relief. The use of abreaction is therapeutic but highly limited (e.g., only to specific incidents of recall and for cases of genuine psycho-neuroses).

What is called "transference" is a phenomenon of analysis delicate of handling, the frequent result of analysis. It arises out of the unique relationship between subject and the analyst, a relationship analogous to that of a penitent to his father-confessor. The therapist becomes the channel through which the subject discharges his emotions, the object to which these discharges are directed. Transference is the name for this projection* of part of the subject's unconscious mind to the analyst as a result of the disturbance effected by analysis. It is not necessarily a transference of affection; frequently it is just the opposite. It is a relief from repression. Transference reveals the depths of mental life where emotions are now being tapped. The subject at this point has "chosen" between his symptoms and his therapist, the latter choice now taking the brunt of the attack. Usually the early life of the subject now unfolds itself (for further treatment see "transference"). Conversion from transference requires great skill. Its successful handling issues in the restoration of a normal human relationship with the therapist. It involves enlightenment by skillful guidance and understanding of the long buried emotional conflicts. A new and balanced rationale must be sought and the "cure" or release can come only when the subject has arrived at the point of acceptance. Acceptance moves on to adjustment to the real world where normal reactions supersede the abnormal. See Adler, Alfred; Adlerian approach to therapy; Freud, S.; Freudian approach to analysis; heightened reaction; Jung, Carl; Jungian approach to therapy; problem complex; projective techniques; psychoanalysis; psychoneuroses; psychotherapy; resolution, the doctrine of; sex and the counselee; therapy.

**analytic psychology:** see psychology of religion; psychology, schools of.

**analytical psychology:** see Jung, Carl; psychology, schools of (psychoanalysis).

**Andronicus:** see metaphysics.

**anemias:** see human genetics.

**Angell, J. R.:** see psychology, schools of.

**anger:** see emotion; structuring the counseling situation.

**angst:** (Ger. dread). Having the concern of dread.

**anhedonia:** a state of passiveness in which there is no zest for life.

**animal magnetism:** see psychical research and parapsychology.

**animal pets, lavish attention to:** see marriage, disharmony in.

**animal psychology:** see psychology of religion; psychology, schools of.

**anoetic:** (Gr. *a*, without; *nous*, mind). A term referring to pre-cognitive or non-cognitive state of mind, e.g., pure sensation or feeling state.

**answers to prayer:** see prayer and autosuggestion.

**anterograde amnesia:** see amnesia.

**anthropological method:** see psychology of religion.

**anthropology:** see psychology of religion; race psychology.

**anthropomorphism:** see belief in God.

**anthropopathism:** (Gr. *anthropos*, man; *pathein*, suffer). Sometimes referred to as the pathetic fallacy, i.e., attributing human feelings fallaciously to things or situations lacking the capacity for such feelings.

**anticipation of rest:** see work and rest.

**anti-noise campaigns:** see noise disturbances.

**anxiety, anxiety neurosis:** see climacterium; climacterium virile; divided self; dysphoria; glands; heightened reaction; hypertension; juvenile delinquency; menopause; morale; psychoneuroses; sick-soul.

**anxiety states:** All human beings are subject to anxiety. The basic cause for repression,* according to the later views of Freud,* is anxiety, particularly the dread of becoming helpless and alone in a hostile world. It may be a state of diffusion or it may be directed to particular situations or specific objects.

As youngsters we experience the restraints of society and the world. We may be frightened by a single experience, by some individual or by phenomena such as darkness, thunder or lightning. We come to realize our deficiencies and limitations and may develop, if we are unduly restrained or experience a marked emotional upset, an anxiety state which may take on peculiar expression or modification. Some such anxieties persist—the root element being fear:* fear in general, fear of harm, fear of failure, fear of not being wanted. It is not easy to draw distinctions between fear and anxiety—both are mental attitudes and bring on suffering. (Some psychologists hold that anxieties tend to be without objects and are fears of fears within.) Many people suffer more from their anxieties than from that which brings them on. Fear of loss of sleep may cause more mental disturbance than the loss of sleep itself. Some fears and anxieties (such as persecution) may result from the inability to throw off lesser fears and anxieties.

Often a person suffering an anxiety state is quite unaware of any ground for anxiety. Anxieties may even create the ideas to which they become attached. Such ideas may be discerned, however, to be secondary to the state itself. Even so, anxieties may detach from one set of ideas and create new ones (imaginary).

Accompanying anxiety are many common physical symptoms: headache, insomnia, heartburn, shortness of breath, nervousness, palpitation, pain, pressure feeling, etc. Preoccupation with health may initiate anxiety and the vicious circle becomes complete with the anxiety nourishing concern over health.

Common precipitations of anxiety are guilt complexes, experience of failure in the struggle to win, separation from friends and security (many of which may have a history dating back to earliest childhood). See emotional tensions, release of; fears, conditioned; juvenile delinquency; repression; speech pathology; sex and the counselee; sthenic.

**apathy:** see glands; temperament.
**apeirophobia:** see phobias.
**aphasia:** see speech pathology.
**aphia:** sense of touch or pressure.

**a posteriori:** In general, the attention to effects and from them searching out their cause(s). This is the method of induction.

Sometimes used in reference to "experience." See a priori.

**apperception:** In its broad sense, apperception is the sum of all experiences, both sensory and reflective, involved in meaning. This totality of meaning is sometimes referred to as apperceptive mass.* See thematic apperception test, the.

**apperceptive mass:** see apperception; memory; perception; psychology, schools of.

**appetitive response:** Desire based on animal wants such as hunger, sex, etc. This response along with the affective and ideational constitute the three phases of consciousness.

**application:** see deliberate effort; success.

**applied psychology:** see psychotechnology.

**applied psychology, popular:** see popular applied psychology.

**approval, social:** see morale; motives.

**a priori:** In general, the assumption of a cause and inferring from it an effect. This is the method of deduction.

In religious theory an a priori idea is one that is held to be an innate character of the mind, not dependent upon first having been aroused by or dependent upon the stimulation of experience. An innate idea is then a priori. See a posteriori; children and religious beliefs.

**aptitude:** see genius; personality; talents.

**archineuron:** see neuron.

**architecture, church:** see symbols.

**argumentum ad ignorantiam:** see fallacy of argumentum ad ignorantiam.

**Aristotle:** see metaphysics.

**Aristotle on the senses:** see symbols.

**arteriosclerosis:** The degenerative changes in the walls of the arteries. See aging process; hypertension; sclerosis.

**artistic expression:** see sublimation.

**asceticism:** see saintliness.

**association:** see memorizing.

**association, free:** see free association.

**associationism, school of psychology:** see psychology, schools of.

**association-reaction-time test:** see deception.
**assurance:** see confession.
**astereognosis:** see stereognosis.
**asthenic:** see sthenic.
**astraphobia:** see phobias.
**astrology:** see popular applied psychology.
**ataxia:** see parathyroid glands.
**atheism:** see displacement.
**Atkins, Gaius Glenn:** see minister, the, and his books.
**atmospheric conditions and work capacity:** The air which we breathe has a definite temperature, a definite amount of circulation and a certain moisture content (humidity). How does all this affect the working potential of a person?

Studies in this area show that manual labor is greatly affected by oxygen content, by temperature and by humidity. When it comes to mental work studies reveal a different conclusion. Considerable variations of the atmosphere (e.g., hot, humid, stale and stagnant air conditions) appear to make no significant difference to mental workers.

Conclusions add up to this: When the element of motivation is considered a mental worker is noticeably affected by atmospheric conditions. Hot weather, for example, inclines to lower the motivation due to discomforts. However, the capacity of mental work is not affected by atmospheric conditions. Motivation and ability are not the same and must be distinguished.

Students, accordingly, must reconsider their alibis! See efficiency; efficiency and time of day; work and rest.

**atomic energy:** see human genetics.
**attention:** see autosuggestion; sleep; threshold.
**attention for sympathy:** see marriage, disharmony in.
**attention, shift of:** see fatigue; sermon; sleep.
**attitude:** see belief in God; faith; prayer and autosuggestion.
**attraction:** see sociometry.
**attractiveness:** see marriage, disharmony in.
**auditory sense:** see hallucination; sensations.
**Augustine, St.:** see divided self.
**authority, quoting of:** see learning; truth.
**autobiographical method:** see psychology of religion.
**autoeroticism:** A term for sexual interest focused upon the

subject himself. See homosexuality.

**automatism:** see psychical research and parapsychology.

**autonomic nervous system (sympathetic):** A group of nerves, ganglia, and plexuses which innervate smooth muscle* cells, gland cells, and viscera. Via this system, these end organs are served by two different types of nerve fibers, the sympathetic and the parasympathetic. In general, the actions of these two systems on the end organ tend to provide for a delicate balance in that one is stimulating and the other depressing on that end organ's activity. This system is said to be "automatic" and not under control of the will, although recent evidence indicates that it may be under some control of higher centers. See emotion; hypothalamus; organic sensations. V. H. F.

**autosuggestion:** Emile Coué (1857-1926), French pharmacist, and his disciple Charles Baudouin on the basis of a theory of autosuggestion (self suggestion) founded a school of psychology, called The New Nancy School, in 1910. This school developed a theory and practice of autosuggestion which became widely popular.

Autosuggestion is the same process, it was held, as heterosuggestion (suggestion by others). A thought or a belief or a course of action—so ran the teaching—becomes realized or translated into actuality by the process of autosuggestion. Baudouin distinguished spontaneous from reflective autosuggestion, the former realized spontaneously without any deliberate cooperation and the latter realized by intention.

An opinion heard often enough tends to become a fixed belief. The sight of fire brings on the feeling of warmth. An illness talked about tends to develop illness. These are instances of spontaneous autosuggestion—induced by attention, surrounded by some powerful effect and held on to by the attention.

The "law of reversed effort" (so called by Baudouin) is to the effect that when an idea is imposed on the mind to the extent of a suggestion, all conscious efforts to counteract it are not only ineffectual but contrary to conscious wish and thus increase the intensity of the suggestion. Walking on a wide plank suspended high creates the spontaneous suggestion of falling; thinking about it only increases the hazards. Volition here helps only in reverse.

Reflective autosuggestion comes with difficulty since deliberate effort tends to make suggestion less possible. Trying to go to sleep\* induces wakefulness. Successful reflective autosuggestion can come only when a substitute is found for volition or a substitute for spontaneous attention.

To achieve effective spontaneous autosuggestion is an art and requires certain disciplines. For example, the state between sleep and waking is a condition highly conducive to spontaneous autosuggestion. Here the subconscious mind may more easily take over, to act as a substitute for effort or will. So also a state of reverie. Keeping the muscles relaxed, the body motionless and comfortable, closing the eyes, imaging vague images, avoiding the external noises—these are preliminary to autosuggestion. Concentration upon one idea without the distraction of conscious concentration is a desideratum. All conscious effort will ruin the success. Mechanical repetition of an idea tends to dissipate reflection and thus promises achievement. Fatigue\* here helps. Prolonged attention tends to relaxation through lessening of conscious interest. This is a state of self hypnosis—fixation on an idea which becomes objectified to the mind.

A pain is not alleviated, in other words, by saying "I want to be relieved from pain." The opposite "I have no pain" is too contradictory to be effective. More effective would be to say "This pain is passing away." The latter is the formula of autosuggestion.

Baudouin held that reflective autosuggestion could work wonders with illnesses such as morbid preoccupation with health, functional disorders and even organic complaints. It increases natural restorative powers of the body, removes bad habits and controls sleep.

The formula "Day by day, in every way I am getting better and better" is the formula recommended to be repeated every night and morning some twenty times to resolve some disturbances. This formula is based on the general principle of the school, viz., that whenever the will and the imagination are at war with one another, imagination always wins. If you imagine yourself well you will be further towards recovery than heaps of deliberate assertions that you must and will get well. See prayer and autosuggestion; psychology of religion; repetition compulsion; resolution, the doctrine of.

**axiology:** (Gr. *axios*, value). A modern technical term for value theory: the nature, criteria and ontological status of value.

**axiom:** see truth.

**axon:** A term for the process of the neuron which carries the nervous impulse from the cell to the next dendrite.*

**Azan, E.:** see psychical research and parapsychology.

# B

**Babinski reflex:** A phenomenon of extension of the toes (in place of flexion) which accompanies the gentle stroking of the sole of the foot. It is a normal reflex* in the infant. In the adult it is indicative of a lesion of the pyramidal tract of the cord (a band of nerve fibers, passing from the motor zone of the cerebrum to the motor ganglia at the lower level).
**bad and good:** see conscience; morality and psychology.
**Baldo, Camillo:** see graphology.
**Barr, Alfred:** see sermons, preparation of.
**Barrett, William:** see psychical research and parapsychology.
**bathophobia:** see phobias.
**Baudouin, Charles:** see autosuggestion.
**beauty:** see aesthetic experience.
**Beers, Clifford W.:** see mental hygiene.
**behavior:** see complexes; psychoanalysis, limitations of; synapses.
**behavior, raw material of:** see drives; urges, elemental.
**behaviorism:** see behavioristic school of psychology.
**behavioristic school of psychology:** see instinct; psychology of religion; psychology, schools of.
**belief in God:** Whatever "proofs" may be set up for a belief in God, people do not rest their beliefs on such proofs.

That God should be an object of reasonable belief rather than proof or evidence may be cause for wonder, especially since there are so many "facts" of life that impinge upon the focus of evidence.

But a little reflection may show that such wonder may well be turned the other way, viz., it would be a cause for greater wonder were God an object of irrefutable demonstration rather than belief, thus in a class with sticks and stones and the audible voices of persons or the visibility of concrete forms. Such a God would hardly be God—but an Object levelled down to below-size. Were God an object of absolute certainty man would, unless he be a fool, be compelled to submit much as one accepts the brute fact that two automobiles coming swiftly head-on will produce a smash-up. To acknowledge a fact is in itself an act of compulsion; in itself it requires no independence of judgment nor any virtue other than acceptance. Virtues are not built out of sheer acquiescence to fact; virtues are built out of adventures, risks, trust, faith. God as an object of belief rather than demonstration makes possible the possibility of doubt, hesitation and any independent judgment.

Thus, the very condition of a belief in God, other than evidence, squares with God's existence—if God is conceived to be more than a Neutral Fact. Evidence, without faith, would present a God who automatically would demand recognition without the honor that goes with trust and adventurous faith, without, in other words, the responses of virtue.

Moreover, God emptied of all beyond-elements of finite experience, confined to the demonstrable facts of commonplace things, is a God after man's own limited space-time images (anthropomorphism: God in man's image). By definition, God is More than all of human experiences and this More must, also by definition, lie beyond the area of proof or demonstration.

Psychologically, then, man comes to his belief in God by more factors than the demonstration that goes with sheer logic, experimentation or the confinements of limited experience. Belief in God is an attitude of trust in the trustworthiness of life at its best. Though there are many adversities to cause a mistrust in this trust, the better side of man's own spirit seems always to keep pointing to a winning side. "Though he slay me I will trust him." Life is always on the side of optimism and growth—whatever the storms. Death is its opposite. Disbelief is the negation of life.

But belief in God is not a belief in God's sheer existence. Belief in God carries with it, at its core, the belief in a character

**belief in God**                                                                       **26**

of God. No one would continue to put his best foot forward on the faith that God is a Devil. (There are, however, such conceptions even in respectable and traditional conceptions of God—though such ideas have a way of being ignored or overshadowed by other and higher concepts of God's nature.) If there be a moral character to God (the usual statement is "God's goodness") and if man is essentially a responsible and a morally destined creation (capable of choices, of freedom, of virtues, etc.), then the relationship between God and man always moves within the area of uncertainty and probability and not of necessity. God, for man, is an Object of belief or disbelief, trust or mistrust, love or indifference, dedication or independence, acceptance or rejection, discipleship or withdrawal —and a host of other moral relationships. Compulsion on any level spells the doom of any moral relationships. (On the other side, God, too, can possess no certainty of outcome by the self-imposed limitations for moral possibilities.)

But there is another phase to this question—one that dips deep into the nature of man.

Many people think that happiness in some form is the goal of human existence. It is what people want most. The fact is, however, that happiness sought is not caught. It is a condition of mind (beyond specific pleasures which are transitory) which comes as a by-product and not as an end-product. A happy person may well be a person who had had many scars and knows intimately the rough edges of life. And, yet, his happiness is genuine and deep.

Now, how is such a frame of mind achieved? The negative answer is: never by concentrating upon it. Concentration upon oneself (introversion*) is a sure way of finding unhappiness. (Those suffering inner conflicts know this full well.) Concentration upon objects or people other than oneself (extraversion*) is only the beginning; such concentration must move in realms of values beyond one's finite perspectives in a kind of all-out adventure (faith) since only then is the self-concentration dissolved and only by a new focus (outside) of enduring values can the response of happiness arise and become sustained. God is the symbol of such higher values of life as bring man to his most satisfying depths of being in the absorption of worth-while goals beyond self. God is the ultimate resolution of man's inner conflicts as 1) an object of devotion to values outside oneself and as 2) the most sustaining symbol of those values which survive the little and the transitory values. God, thus, is a psychological need for man. There may be false gods. Such are recognized, in the long run, by their failures to bring out deep satisfactions. The ideas of God which have persisted are the ideas which bring man his deepest happiness: viz., a God imaged as More in character and ideals than the best in human personality (where ideals are best known). The fatherhood of God is a symbol not merely of Jewish origin. It is a psychological symbol: since fatherhood represents the virtues of both sexes, the masculine as well as the feminine: strength, initiative, provider, sympathy, love, sacrifice, etc.). "Man," the generic, is both man and woman. This does not mean that God is gender nor that God is confined to personality. It means that the symbol in use is the best symbol of the highest virtues known: there may be many others unknown to our finite perspectives and, by definition, there must be.

Belief in God may come through teaching in a family circle, church or synagogue. But such belief is nourished not by the authority of tradition but by a faith in the ultimate trustworthiness of life itself in its widest outreaches. Only by such faith does man find his psychological fulfilment (his psychic health*). It is not an argument, nor a proposition for proof, nor the result of evidence of brute, stark fact—rather it is the reflection of life itself which is adventurous and heroic.

By the same tokens, belief in a life beyond rests upon the venture of faith, not scientific evidence. Beliefs in personal survival rest upon beliefs in the ultimate values of persons; and beliefs in the *ultimate* values of persons rest upon belief in a God great and worthy enough to sustain those values beyond their brief span into a larger existence. This implies at least *personal* survival, not survival-in-general. On the score of general values specific values may be lost (e.g., when an individual is completely lost in a crowd). Belief in a continued personal life after death rests ultimately upon a belief in God: the two are interwoven.

Monotheism rather than polytheism has won out in man's maturing convictions since the principle of Unity (integration) solves more problems than that of Multiplicity. Psychologically, we are better off with a unity of mind (not cancelling out multiplicity) and the world takes on meaning if there is a synthesis (amidst its heterogeneities). It is probably no accident that philosophers all through the history of critical reflection have been monists of one type or another (their pluralisms and dualisms at least modified to some degree). Hence: God in the singular rather than in the plural. See God; religion and mental health.

**beliefs:** see autosuggestion; children and religious beliefs; Leuba, James H.; psychological frames of reference; reality feeling principle; symbols.

**Bell Adjustment Inventory:** see personality.

**Bell, Charles:** see afferent-efferent fibers.

**benevolences:** see minister, the, and money.

**Benussi, Vittorio:** (1878-1927) Austrian psychologist. Experimental psychologist working on light behavior and on the psychological problem of deception. See deception.

**Bergson, Henri:** see psychical research and parapsychology.

**Bernreuter Personal Inventory:** see personality.

**bigotry:** see displacement.

**bilious temperament:** see temperament.

**Binet, Alfred:** see I.Q.; mental age; mental deficiency; social maturation.

**Binet-Simon tests:** see mental age.

**biographical method:** see psychology of religion.

**biography:** see minister, the, and his books.

**biological drives:** see drives; instinct.

**Birren, James E.:** see aging process.

**bitter taste:** see taste.

**blindness:** see glaucoma; social maturation.

**blindness, psychic:** see psychoneuroses.

**blood clotting:** see hemophilia; human genetics.

**blood pressure and deception:** see deception.

**blood pressure, high:** see hypertension; psychosomatics.

**Bob, Dr.:** see Alcoholics Anonymous.

**body scars:** see juvenile delinquency.

**body-mind relations:** see mind-body relations; pineal gland.

**Bogomolets:** see adult, the.

**Boisen, Anton T.:** (1876-    ) Well known leader in the recent interest in clinical pastoral training and author of a widely read book entitled *The Exploration of the Inner World* (1936, 1952). A graduate of Union Theological Seminary, a student of religious-social surveys for the Inter-Church World Movement, he is best known for his studies in mental illness both as a patient (at the age of forty-four) and as a disciplined student of religious psychology (a former student of George A. Coe*).

His mature life's work has been given to the preaching of the need for clinical experience in understanding the mentally sick in connection with the work of ministers. He was associated with Elwood Worcester (a founder of the Emmanuel Movement), William McDougall* and Richard C. Cabot* (who took a special interest in his work). At Worcester State Hospital (Massachusetts) he launched (1925) a chaplaincy program for the clinical training of theological students. He is chaplain-emeritus of the Elgin State Hospital and a Research Consultant for the Council of Clinical Training of Theological Students. See hospital chaplain, the.

**book reviewing:** see reading performance.

**books:** see minister, the, and his books; minister, the, and money.

**boredom:** Normal boredom occurs when a person continues to work at set tasks requiring less than one's capacities or demanding no initiative or creative performance.

In pathological cases boredom manifests inertia and depression.

Boredom is often associated with work inhibitions. In such cases, loafing and dissipating time are characteristics. So-called "playboys" are manifestations of work boredom.

Devices for circumventing boredom are numerous: use of alcohol, drugs, excessive eating, joining numerous clubs, TV or movie mania, etc. See emotional tensions, release of; juvenile delinquency.

**boy and girl:** see sex differences, psychological.

**brain:** The enlarged anterior end of the central nervous system.* The massive size in man is due to the expansion of the cerebral hemispheres, the outer layers of which (the cortex) are folded into many convolutions, separated by depressions called sulci. Voluntary motor regulation, pain interpretation, sight, hearing and speech are some of the functions of the cer-

**brain, the human**

ebral cortex. The cerebellum, a portion of the hindbrain, functions in equilibrium and muscle tonus. The medulla oblongata, the most posterior part of the brain, contains the vital centers for the cardiovascular and respiratory systems. See autonomic nervous system; encephalitis; hypothalamus; pituitary gland.

V. H .F.

**brain, the human:** see aging process; mental deficiency; phrenology.

**breakdown:** see neurosis; psychoneurosis.

**breeding, controlled:** see eugenics.

**Brentano, Franz:** see psychology, schools of.

**Breuer, Joseph:** see Freud, Sigmund.

**Bridges, K. M.:** see emotion.

**Brill, A. A.:** see Freud, Sigmund.

**British psychologists, New Dynamic School:** see psychology of religion; psychology, schools of (psychoanalysis).

**Brooks, Phillips:** see sermons, preparation of.

**Brown, Charles R.:** see visitation.

**Buchman, Frank:** see Oxford group movement.

**Buchmanism:** see group psychotherapy.

**Buddhism:** see sick-soul.

**budget:** see minister, the, and money.

**budgeting of time:** see minister, the, and his books.

**bulletin boards:** see fallacy of over simplification.

**Bunyan, John:** see divided self; sick-soul.

**business executives:** see success.

**business matters and the minister:** see minister, the, and money.

# C

**Cabot, Richard C.:** (1868-1939) Dr. Richard Cabot may be said to be a pioneer in the recent field of pastoral psychology. Born in Brookline, Massachusetts, he became a Harvard graduate in 1889 and a Harvard M.D., in 1892. He became a professor of clinical medicine at his alma mater and a founder (1905) at the Massachusetts General Hospital of a department of medical social work. In 1920 he began a teaching career in social ethics and later gave special attention to the education of theological students in matters of the relation of religion and health. With Russell L. Dicks* as co-author, he published the well-known volume entitled *The Art of Ministering to the Sick* (1936). Psychosomatic medicine became his interest long before this branch of medicine became a recognized discipline. In 1935 he was professor of practical theology at Andover-Newton.

Clinical pastoral research and training under the auspices of the Institute of Pastoral Care at the Massachusetts General Hospital (and elsewhere) have been financed by a fund left by Dr. Cabot designated for humanitarian purposes. See hospital chaplain, the.

**caffeine, psychological effects of:** Caffeine is the potent ingredient in coffee, tea and certain other drinks. It is generally agreed by those who indulge that the stimulation afforded increases general fitness.

Controlled experiments show that caffeine does stimulate simple motor performances. With some few exceptions in terms

**calling, pastoral**                      **32**

of amounts of doses the psychological functions were definitely stimulated (experimental effects such as speed of typing, color naming, naming opposites, adding, discrimination reaction time, cancellation). In the period immediately following, the use of caffeine definitely heightens efficiency. Incidental to the experiments it was noted that there was no case of a secondary reaction of let-down.

Caffeine is habit forming. Those who use it frequently find a strong urge to continue, even complaining of headaches, dizzines and other discomforts when their usual dose is interrupted.

**calling, pastoral:** see visitation; visiting the sick.
**calm:** see learning.
**Cameron, Norman:** see neurosis.
**camps, summer:** see summer camps.
**cancer:** see carcinophobia; human genetics.
**Cannon, W. B.:** see emotion.
**capsule thinking:** see fallacy of over simplification.
**carcinophobia:** see phobias.
**cardiac patient:** see psychosomatics.
**cards, ESP:** see psychical research and parapsychology.
**careers:** see motives; success.
**Case, S. J.:** see psychology of religion.
**case studies:** see pastoral counseling and case studies; pastoral counseling: case studies.
**catagelphobia:** see phobias.
**catatonia:** A mental disorder*—classified under schizophrenia*—in which the voluntary muscle systems retain positions in which they are set. The disorder involves odd postures, muscular spasms, indifference to environment, flexibility and negativism.

**catch phrases:** see fallacy of over simplification.
**catechism, memorizing the:** see memorizing.
**catharsis, mental:** see mental catharsis.
**Cattell, James McKeen:** see social maturation.
**cells:** see cytology.
**cenophobia:** see phobias.
**censor:** A term used in psychoanalysis* (by Freud*) for the selective agency which acts as a barrier to prevent impulses, memories and ideas from emerging from the unconscious* into

the conscious mind. More particularly, it is the active influence of the ego and the super-ego to restrain the impulses of the Id.* Thus barred from expression circumvented expressions appear as dream* symbols, displacement,* etc. See free association; mental catharsis; psychology, schools of (psychoanalysis); repression.

**central nervous system:** The brain* and the spinal cord.
**cerebellum:** see brain.
**cerebral cortex:** see brain.
**certainty vs. belief:** see belief in God.
**chance element in ESP:** see psychical research and parapsychology.
**change of life:** see climacterium virile; menopause.
**changed life, fruits of:** see Oxford group movement.
**chaplain:** see hospital chaplain, the.
**character:** Character may be defined as the quality of the total self which includes a person's sentiments* and dispositions* plus the ideals or moral code he consciously pursues.

Character is the result of many psychological factors: some with hereditary origins, others of environmental conditions. Among the predisposing factors of heredity are those of temperament (*see* temperament) and the biological drives* (which older psychologists called "instincts"*). These are the raw material out of which personality and character are built.

Psychologists are now emphasizing the great importance of the early environment in the development of a person's character. A single event in early childhood may bring about the determining attitude of life and the quality of the self known as character. A bitter disappointment may eventuate in a bitter character; a sexual assault may produce sexual frigidity, hysteria or sexual fear. It is, however, in the area of the general atmosphere of the period of childhood that determinants of character are largely set. Subtle suggestions work over a long period of time. Deep impressions are made upon young and impressionable minds.

Many psychologists hold that during the impressionable years of childhood a person unconsciously creates his whole attitude towards himself, towards others and towards life in general: whether life is looked upon as a struggle to attain, or an easy game that is played, whether people may be trusted or mistrusted, whether goodness is a worthy goal (however conceived) or whether life can be cheated upon, whether the person will develop in himself confidence, self-assertiveness, selfish ends as primary, inferior feeling, thrift, responsibility, modesty, personal integrity, slothfulness, or their opposites. Disorders of character follow upon those ingredient factors which through the years have fostered maladjustment with a person's own self or in relationships with others.

The character of a person as distinguished from personality implies to many some moral standard or norm of evaluation. Another common usage of the term implies an actor on some stage, in the sense of role or symbolic representative. In this sense a character is more identical with a personality.* See children and religious beliefs; child training; deceit (and character); phantasy; self.

**Character Education Inquiry:** see deceit (and character).

**Charcot, Jean Marie:** (1825-1893) A celebrated French neurologist who identified hypnosis with hysteria. His views made a deep impression upon Sigmund Freud.*

**charity:** see saintliness.

**cheating:** see deceit (and character); deception; motives; peace and war.

**chemoreceptors:** see taste.

**child training:** Almost everyone has some special theory of child training—ranging from the "laissez faire" method (let the child be absolutely free to develop as he chooses) to the most rigorous codes of Puritan ideals. Both extremes are hazardous.

Of course, it is axiomatic that every person is an individual and to try to squeeze him into some narrow mould is to induce vices which are both psychological and social. On the other hand, complete self-expression is the open high-road to maladjustment in the complexities of inter-personal relationships.

Influences of parents on children are mostly indirect and atmospheric rather than the effect of any set rules.

A family of more than one child is fortunate if the oldest child is a well balanced individual who may, by subtle influences, influence his brothers and sisters. Big brother or big sister plays a more determinative role in his own generation than is commonly recognized. The "only child" is a problem in itself—since there is the absence of those subtle directions which come only by age compatibilities.

Most parents are concerned over child training. What is commonly called "success" in such training has come by way of common sense and ordinary decency than by the reading of psychological texts. Parents of generations ago got along quite well without reading up on the "rules" and they succeeded very largely on the basis of common sense behavior and practical psychology, being quite unaware of any theoretical methods.

Some of these unconscious and directive influences may be set down here as suggestive to child training, not as fixed rules but rather as general principles which may be re-adapted without losing their fundamental and underlying worth.

Absolute integrity and a sense of fair play observed in the home will create a pattern of behavior in a child "brought up this way" with far more effect than "lessons" on honesty and generosity. The respect for money as representing the fruits of real labor and not as gifts showered indiscriminately from the sky will suggest thrift far better than any exhortations to conservatism in spending. It is a questionable practice to hand out "allowances" without the child's awareness of the symbol of labor which money represents. A child should, it would seem, share in some labor performance to realize what such tokens mean. There are services in the family circle he may render which appropriately may be symbolized as money in which he may have the sense of and joy of earned participation. Not that all services should be in monetary terms—far from it; not that there should never be gifts bestowed—far from it. But . . . the child should associate in his mind the symbol of money as labor expended—as it is for most people in the common business of living.

Promises of parents should be given with discretion. And once given—the parents' words should be irrevocable. It is a sign of mistrust to hear a child ask for a parent's promise with insistence on some token of pledge.

In a schedule so complex as is required by a present-day normal family for things to run smoothly there must be some norms of conscious mutual cooperation and sharing. One meal a day where the family leisurely sits together should be inviolable. Here the *esprit de corps* of a family is best nourished.

It should be at a stated time with each member definitely accounted for. For most American families this is the early evening hour. Along with this there should be days spent together: Sundays, holidays, birthdays, festive seasons of Christmas, Easter and the like—in which the family as a unit belongs to itself, each member to the other. Our present work-a-day rush is the great threat to this disintegration—with disturbing results. Even the churches tend to encroach on sacred family ties by the unwise scheduling of a multiplicity of organizational meetings. To all this, wise parents must respond by a firm negative. The family *esprit de corps* is a foundation stone to good child training. Loyalty to one's own inner circle is the training ground to greater loyalties as the years wear on.

Absolute respect for elders is a "must" in child training. This does not mean parental czarism but rather the training to respect experience and to develop caution and restraint in immature pronouncements. "Honor thy father and mother" was one of the great ten commandments of Israel—a virtue being lost by careless training. A wise parent will realize his limitations but he will nevertheless try to undergird his directiveness with a temper of discretion and wisdom. Many cases of delinquency in children may find their cause in the failure to respect authority, be it legitimate family mores or reverence for elders. Morals are related to good graces and to the limitations of acceptable decorum. Morals are not mere cases of manners, but manners rooted in fundamentally acceptable attitudes. Firmness and consistency breed respect; vacillation and inconsistency breed disrespect. In the fear of causing frustrations in very young children many parents, reading the literature of neo-psychology, refrain from administering physical punishment. But there are times when a brisk application to Junior's *derrière* will set right a situation where vocal reprimand has lost its sting. Where parents express fear of frustration in their child they may really express the fear of frustration in themselves to discharge their sacred duty as parents.

Parents will be greatly rewarded in the satisfaction of successful child training by remembering that no influence is greater than the love and security of the home. Where parents entrust their children frequently to vicarious substitutes—e.g., baby sitters—they have in their own indulgence invited potential difficulties which need not have developed. The child raising period is a time of parental self-denial. To come home to find parents usually gone is to set off the trigger for many maladjustments. Meals, particularly, are to be events of daily importance—not merely to satisfy elemental hunger but to instill in the young mind a sense of belonging and being wanted as a participant of a hallowed circle.

It is not necessary to lie to children. A lie breeds mistrust. Truth should ever be a virtue issuing from parental lips. But truth may be handled with discretion as, e.g., in the acknowledgment to a child of the needless pursuit of further answers to some of his queries. Sex education is not a matter—as are other matters—of blunt encyclopedic information. Sex education belongs with the maturing process and needs never to be a forced issue.

Obedience is an integral part of self discipline. A child need not understand the grounds for every necessary obedience any more than an adult must understand the laws of physics or nature before he will be obedient to them. To try to explain the whys and wherefores of every requirement of obedience is as ridiculous as to wait upon understanding before one submits to a physician's prescription. This is not to imply, however, that obedience must be an act always of indiscrimination. In many cases reasons will be obvious to any requirement of obedience—where the child is capable of following them.

An encouragement toward the development of imagination is a normal and necessary requirement to good training. No one ever succeeds without an imaginative mind. Fairy tales, Santa Claus, poetry and the like are fertile media in developing the imagination. It is wrong to induce into a child's mind the notion that this is a prosaic world, that things are what they simply are or appear to be. The mind must be kept fluid if adjustments are to be made to the shifting sands of circumstance—which is life. The imaginative mind adjusts more easily than the stereotyped and frozen-patterned-mind of mere encyclopedic information.

And with all this goes a sense of humor without which life often becomes intolerable. There should be plenty of laughs, games and home-made fun. These memories of happy childhood days will carry through many hazes of misfortune.

**childhood, second**          **38**

    Fortunate is the child who has had the influence of both parents. Life is rugged enough to have both masculine as well as feminine virtues. A boy who has been mollycoddled by an over-devoted mother will be handicapped immeasurably if he has not had the more rugged influences which may be expected from the father—if he is a real masculine father. What is, of course, of greater influence (often unrecognized) is the circle of playmates who are bound to induce infections of influence to the good or bad beyond any that may come from the overprotection of any parent. To insulate a child from these is to avoid society and to avoid society is to become maladjusted. The most difficult area in child training is the area of age-level companionship since this area is most often beyond control. But such is life. A checking and rechecking of this companionship should be the vigil of all parents—not as a matter of isolation and protection but rather as skilled and subtle direction. Such companionships must somehow be geared into the meshes of home relations if they are to fall into some harmonious pattern. See deceit (and character); fears, conditioned; juvenile delinquency; learning; morality and psychology; personality; reading performance; role playing; sentiments; success; talents; teen-agers.

    **childhood, second:** see learning.

    **children:** see Adlerian approach to therapy; adolescence; anxiety states; character; child training; children and religious beliefs; deceit (and character); emotion; fears, conditioned; Freud S.; in-laws; juvenile delinquency; morality and psychology; pastoral counseling: case studies; peace and war; personality; psychology, schools of (psychoanalysis); readiness, principle of; reading performance; role playing; sex differences, psychological; social perception; speech pathology; talents; teen-agers; visiting the sick; young, the.

    **children and religious beliefs:** A child comes into this world according to the general pattern of the biological processes. This pattern reveals a fundamental kinship with the world of organic nature. The child is truly a product of nature as is any living thing. But it is a pattern more complicated than that of most living creatures. Possessing a brain capable of developing the high powers of consciousness, selfconsciousness, reflective thought and speech—nature's crowning thrust of creativity—

the child's reaction to its world is replete with a heterogeneity of possibilities.

It has long been held that a child is born with a religious nature. Some theologians and speculative philosophers have held that he possesses an *a priori*\* awareness of God, or that God is an original datum of the human mind. Psychologists no longer speak of the mental equipment of children as being so prolific of innate ideas or of specific reaction patterns. The word "instinct," and with it "religious instinct," is so weighted with dubious meaning and supercharged connotations that it has become almost taboo in scientific circles.

It is now said that the child possesses, besides the normal physiological modes of behavior reactions, drives\* all of which have to do with survival and adaptation to its world. But it is always a matter of scientific principle, the law of parsimony,\* to look for the simplest of reactions, to reduce the apparently innumerable drives to the fewest number in consonance with the facts. Fear, love and rage are regarded by some psychologists to be the three most elemental responses. Without entering into the controversy among the psychologists, it is sufficient here to affirm that the child begins as a going concern bent on survival and making adaptive reactions to the world in which it unwittingly finds itself.

Although for each child there is a common world of biological needs (e.g., food), the world of the social nexus into which he is born varies infinitely with the cultural, economic, and what is called the spiritual surroundings. Very subtly these earliest influences mark the child. Some psychologists hold that the mark is indelible: that a child entering upon the period of his formal education is already an oak tree of prejudices and sentiments which will not bend with every breeze.

It is this social world to which the term "religious" appropriately belongs. One may define the religious attitude as that mental adjustment which a child makes, consciously or unconsciously, to the wider social world. By "social" we do not mean social intercourse with other people present. We mean here, rather, the world of societal relations which reach out beyond his grasp, a world of fancy or dream, a world peopled with unseen spirits akin to his own, to angels or demons, to gods or heroes, to ghosts which stalk in the shadows. Only when he reacts to such a wider social environment, either by being afraid or by friendly commerce, can a child be said to be truly religious.

Such a religious attitude is not in itself instinctive. It is but the widening of the horizon of interests based fundamentally upon the (unconscious) will to survive in a world that is strange and baffling. The shape of his ideas about such a world will vary with his cultural motivation. God may be a man in the sky; the devil may lurk in closets and dark places; angels may be sweet little children flying unseen in space; Jesus may be a kind man who comes visiting with shepherdly interest at twilight before sleep, watching over games or is the Visiting Presence during the Sunday Bible lessons. It all depends upon what ideology has been implanted by the particular social environment. The child's religious response does not consist in the possession of such ideas; it consists in his adaptation to what is for him significant in this larger social world.

A child may possess so-called religious beliefs without being religious. He may be religious without the possession of even the most elementary theology. He need not be in company with others in visible presence to experience the religious frame of mind. His company may be visible only to himself.

As his social world widens, the child's religious spirit will remain the same—it is always fundamentally the same. But his social world to which he reacts religiously will take on new personalities, new ideas, a new framework of reference according to the maturing of his vision. "When I was a child I spake as a child, I felt as a child, I thought as a child; now that I am become a man I have put away childish things"—this is a classic expression of the laws of biological and social growth.

Is then a child fundamentally religious? The reply is that he is not religious by a special instinct nor by any *a priori* pattern. He is religious as an organism reacting to an ever widening social world. The same biological and psychological laws operate in religious matters as they do in the give-and-take of everyday living. The difference is plainly the awareness of a beyond-environment which somehow holds for him the strings of fortune upon the world of every day. Does a child possess an innate idea of God? The reply is that the concept of God is in itself not a clear-cut concept even for adults. Nevertheless, for him God is That in the wider social world which matters supremely, in matters of fortune, good luck or destiny. It is also the God, similar on religious terms, of adult religious life.

The worshipful attitude toward heroes or toward a parent or nurse is but the presaging of the religious attitude. The child soon enough finds out that even the wisest whom he knows is not wise enough and he looks out beyond, when need impels. Thus the prayerful attitude is close to the religious; it, too, is the making of an adjustment to the wider environment.

The religious education of children has traditionally followed the method of dispensing a conceived set of truths regardless of the pattern of psycho-biological development. Children have been taught concepts which could have little or no reality for them at their level. "Plans of salvation" have been repeated by the rising generation of little disciples without religious feeling. It is one thing to learn ideas; it is another thing to experience them.

The ideology of any person is always significant. But ideas must fit into one's purview. There is no use of talking about the marvels of symphonic arrangements and of musical scores to one who has no apperceptive mass in such matters. He may develop such apperception; but the development requires that he first begin to study the staff, the notes and the fundamentals of rhythm.

The problem then shapes up to this: What religious beliefs should be taught a child? The answer will vary with age and cultural circumstances. It will not be an academic lesson as such. Children like grown-ups do not learn by mere conscious repetition. They learn by those subtle influences which come by way of the behavior of others, by actions which speak more eloquently than words. Our likes and dislikes are the cumulative additions of many influences of which we are no longer conscious.

The religious beliefs which are valid to be taught a child fall into two classes, both of which are fundamental: first, the moral elements and, second, the metaphysical elements. By the former is meant the kind of behavior-reactions which (if good) makes the best adjustment in the give-and-take social world of human relationships. By the latter is meant the kind of world of the child's fancy and imagination which will best (if good) sustain him in his unconscious struggle to make the most of his potentially best. We shall consider each phase separately.

First of all, whatever else a valid religion should contain, it should be thoroughly moral. Not all religions, unhappily, can measure to this standard. Immoral ideals and practices have been approved by followers of all religions by whatever the name. Among such vices we may name: hatred toward those not of the same household, ungrounded suspicion, bigotry, foul-play, conceit, false humility, hypocrisy, inhibitions of one kind or another. There is no end to the naming of vices. Religious faiths have sinned here, unwittingly or wantonly.

The matter of moral experience raises the corollary question: Is the child fundamentally moral? Theologians and speculative philosophers have run riot in their theories as to the origin of morality. At one extreme it is said that morals are but expedient mores; at the opposite extreme it is said that each child possesses an innate, *a priori* conscience\* which acts as the tyrannical censor lashing the whip of remorse upon actions contrary to it. Again, it is best to turn to the psychologist for an answer. Although scientific opinion is never unanimous in all matters, it is safe to make certain generalizations.

Each child, as indicated in the previous discussion, comes into this world with a biological inheritance. Among the requirements for survival it is necessary that the human being look to his own interests. Otherwise nature would have whipped him out of existence long before in the struggle. On the other hand, it is necessary to look to the interests of others. If individuals did not look after others, nature would have cancelled out the human species. What has long been called the "maternal instinct" is but one evidence among many of the necessity to look out for the interests of others in the total program of survival. Self-regarding and alter-regarding interests are twin motivations (among others) for the preservation of the species. It is in this struggle that the biological basis for morality may be found. Our drives are in themselves a-moral. But these drives in terms of each other and in terms of the environment where the struggle to live must be carried out are the raw materials for morality. Were there no struggle there could be no morality. Moreover, only where the individual has advanced far enough in his self-development, where there is the possibility of mastering the situation for his own good and the good of the species to which he belongs, only there is morality actually born.

An infant, then, is a-moral. It becomes moral at that stage at which it has attained the capacity for self-direction. He is not a born sinner (nor saint). The doctrine of original sin widely taught in many theological circles is right in its affirmation of man's inherent struggle but wrong in its denial that the struggle contains potential good. That same doctrine has horribly confused an irresponsible morality with responsibility-morality. Man is not responsible for his biological equipment and the charge of sin against him on that score is an immoral charge. An irresponsible morality is no morality or, if it is, is an immoral morality. A child is a moral creature not by inheritance. It becomes moral as its inheritance is brought under the possibility of control. Thus we say that a child with a brain lesion is not a morally responsible creature.

A valid set of religious beliefs will inculcate by conscious persuasion or by unconscious motivation (which the child picks up in the fringe of his consciousness or by sheer imitation) a kind of living which will harness the self-regarding and the alter-regarding interests into a mutual interplay or harmony that will make for his own best interests and the interests of his species. A refusal to cooperate with himself and with others toward this end is, when the way is open, sheer sin. The deliberate failure of parent or guardian to help toward this end, when the way is open, constitutes an even greater sin. The older recapitulation theory by which it is said that each child passes freely through the stages of his ancestors from the primitive to the civilized phases is not only psychologically open to question but when applied to educational procedure wholly negative. Have not the elders the responsibility of directing their children in moral matters as well as in physical, inasmuch as nature has entrusted them to their care for so long period of time? This entrustment implies prohibitions (which the recapitulation theory of education denies) along with the encouragement of independence. Many so-called "problem children" are really the reflection of "problem parents." Children who have not experienced definite prohibitions at home have not been helped on their course. Self-direction remains always an ideal; but often self-direction comes by way of learning the prohibitions.

A religion that is moral thus begins much farther back into the child's life-history than has generally been realized. The responses of a child to the bottle, learning to mediate between the cruel pangs of hunger and the necessary patience in securing the fulfilment of immediate demands is a situation fraught with moral implications. Such is but one among many of the little springs of moral experience from which the channels flow into the wider stream of moral character.

Character* may be defined as that socially ingrained pattern of mind which tends to set the course of specific behavior in specific situations. A character is a disposition,* built out of innumerable experiences over a long period. It is not achieved overnight. A religion can be said to be good only if it, by its teachings and practices, contributes to the kind of character or mind-set which brings to fruition man's best possibilities in the give and take of social living. For we live not to ourselves alone.

The second consideration in a valid set of religious beliefs has to do with the metaphysical. If the child's wider social environment is peopled by immoral beings or fancies which produce in him horror or futility or irresponsibility or mental ill-health, such a religion is bad. Religious faiths have fallen short at this point as well. Scaring a child to be good by the threat of hell and torture, by tyrannical demons and devils, is a case in point. Giving him the impression that God will take care of him without any responsibility of his own is equally bad; for the child will learn by the exigencies of experience that he must learn to take his own initiative and carry his own burden of responsibility. God, indeed, may take care of him; but such a care may depend upon elementary responsibilities.

The world of a child's fancies and imaginings is real to him at a given level. This world should never be crushed. The life of imagination is the essence of the delights and rewards of discovery. Such a world must be populated by the right kind of beings. There is no harm in talking about angels and demons if the angels are properly good and the demons properly bad.

## children and religious beliefs

Even Santa Claus has his mission to perform and a mission that is full of fine potentialities. One need not go into the discussion with the child of their metaphysical reality except to show, when called upon to elaborate, how limited is all of our vision and how infinitely greater is the world about us. No one, even in his maturest years, will ever grow so wise as to dispense with symbols.* All knowledge about that which lies beyond our ken must be symbolically treated; otherwise the beyond is as nothing. Symbols will be recast into new forms as the vistas increase but they are ever the servants in our grasping out toward the horizon, whatever our age-level may be. Unless there is this metaphysical side of our religious beliefs, such beliefs will drop back into a mere code of ethics. But man, and the child more so, will never be content with a pattern of mere ethics so long as there is within him the disposition to struggle to get on with the wider social environment of which he becomes aware. The religious spirit has metaphysical as well as moral implications.

One of the master teachers of religion taught by means of parables and fables. Through these, both old and young were made, and still can be made, to see, however dimly, truths which are sublime. The realm of fancy need not be an unreal world. Fancies may be the mirror reflecting realities over our shoulders or the glass through which we see darkly. He who lives without fancy has not measured up to his full stature. The imaginary world of both old and young need not be purely fictional; it may even be the very means of knowledge. Men of research confess, as do the artists, that flashes of truth came upon them as they played with concepts in the wildest orgies of speculation and imagination.

The good religion will match the child's environment and appeal to his sphere of dreams; but it will be good only so far as his imaginations are themselves good. What makes an imagination good is that it will call out of its possessor the best that is within him.

It is now a truism that the immediate family is the real dispenser of influence during the formative years. The mistake of many sincerely religious adults has been to force their theology and religious practices upon children in ways to bring about deep-seated resentment issuing in the negation, in later life, of all forms of religion. No religion can be weighed as valid on the scales of mere sincerity. Even the Devil is sincere. A religion to be valid must be healthy and normal and natural. The child must be brought into ways of guidance which will make all phases of life normal and natural. The line between the secular and the sacred must not be drawn too tightly. The older conventional practices of many stalwart religious people to exact of their children a definite type of experience (notably that of "conversion") has now become almost universally recognized as malpractice. Indoctrination is always permissible as an educational principle. How, otherwise, shall we learn the wisdom of the past? But indiscriminate indoctrination is tragic. To expect each child to measure his religious stature by a single type of experience, be it doctrinal or emotional, is to make of him what he is not. No two leaves on any tree, although similar, are exactly alike.

A "laissez faire" attitude on the part of many parents in matters of religious education is one that is replete with as many ills as an overdose of indoctrination. It should be evident that the religious attitude without a valid set of beliefs is worse than no religious feeling whatsover. It is as important that a proper sense of values be sought towards the building of a good religion as it is to know the elements which go into a proper diet towards the maintenance of good health. Here is where we must rely upon expert opinion and not upon any one who claims a genuine religious experience, called by whatever sacred name.

Organized religion tends, like all institutions, toward rigidity and fixation. The balance shifts from means to end. Organizations have their genesis as instruments but before long turn toward themselves in maintaining self-perpetuation. In the training of children this tendency has played havoc with the sensibilities of the young. Religion has taken on a formal and unreal aspect. Reactions have set in to make potential disciples look upon institutional religion in any form as artificial and of value only to grown-ups about ready to die. The measure of organized religion in this regard is to apply the standard of pragmatic functioning in terms of the child's own reality-feeling. A good barometer to test any institution as to how far it has gone in an undue emphasis upon self-preservation is the criterion of its ability to adjust itself to a proposed reform; if its response is plastic, the situation is probably favorable for real service to the rising generation.

When all is said and done, the religious training of children will follow the course of secular training. The religious mind is no different psychologically from the secular. Each child brought up within a specific religious household should be expected to respond loyally to that household only so far as its teaching and practices may be found to be fundamentally valid and real for him. Organized churches cannot expect its younger generation to acquiesce obediently to mere tradition; churches must make their traditions intellectually and realistically acceptable and sufficiently plastic for the inclusion of man's ever enlarging vision of his world. A child's loyalty to his church may justly be judged on the principle that it is an instrument made for him and not that he has been made for it. Provincial loyalties thus must move on to those more catholic in scope as the manifold ways of the Divine become more evident with increasing knowledge and understanding. See child training; morality and psychology; religious response, the, nature and origin.

*Bibl.* J. C. Flower, *The Psychology of Religion* (1927); W. E. Hocking, *Human Nature and Its Remaking* (1918); G. J. Jordan, *A Short Psychology of Religion* (1927), ch. 3; J. B. Pratt, *The Religious Consciousness* (1920), chs. 5, 6; H. N. Wieman and R. W. Wieman, *Normative Psychology of Religion* (1935), chs. 14, 15.

**children's court:** see juvenile delinquency.
**chiromancy:** see palmistry and pedomancy.
**chivalry:** see sex differences, psychological.
**choice:** see psychoanalysis, limitations of.
**choleric temperament:** see temperament.
**chromosomes:** see human genetics.
**chronophobia:** see phobias.
**church:** see children and religious beliefs; confession; ministry; old age; pastoral counseling and case studies; pastoral psychology: its governing limitations and qualifications; psychology of religion; sancta of religion; symbols; worship.
**church architecture:** see symbols.
**church membership:** see group psychotherapy; success.

**church unity:** see sancta of religion.

**circumventions:** see complexes; displacement; defense mechanisms; marriage, disharmony in; psychology, schools of (psychoanalysis).

**clairvoyance:** see psychical research and parapsychology.

**claustrophobia:** see phobias.

**clergyman:** see ministry.

**climacterium:** Term for the menopause* or cessation of menstruation in women sometimes accompanied by melancholy. See pastoral counseling and case studies.

**climacterium virile:** A term referring to an alteration in the physiology of men which occurs between ages 50 and 60, accompanied by depression and anxiety. See menopause; pastoral counseling and case studies; old age.

**clinical psychology:** The practical application of psychological principles to cases for the purpose of aiding people toward better adjustments to life situations including themselves. The great asset here is practical experience.

**Clinical Training of Theological Students, Council of:** see Boisen, Anton T.

**clinician, the minister as:** see experimental extinction; hospital chaplain, the; pastoral counseling: case studies; pastoral psychology: its governing limitations and qualifications.

**clinics:** see Adler, Alfred; hospital chaplain, the; juvenile delinquency.

**clubs:** see boredom; neighborhood clubs.

**Coe, George Albert:** (1862-1951) A pioneer in the field of the psychology of religion.* A doctor of philosophy from Boston University, he taught religious education at Northwestern University (1893-1909) and taught in Union Theological Seminary (1909-1922) and in Teachers' College, Columbia. His pioneer work was *The Spiritual Life* (1900), followed by *The Psychology of Religion* (1916). He employed the questionnaire method, aware of its limitations. (Coe summarized these limitations: unintentional selection of data by pointed questions; inaccurate conclusions of introspection; inaccurate memory; and miscarriage of interpretations of answers, etc.) In *What is Christian Education?* (1929) he argued for a creative rather than a transmissive type of education. Transmission of ideas tends to staleness and the perpetuation of errors. See Boisen, A. T.

For an autobiographical account see *Religion in Transition* (1937), edited by Vergilius Ferm.

**coenesthesis:** This term refers to the vague pattern of organic sensations* which give the individual a feeling-tone at any given time (of well-being or malaise).

**coffee:** see caffeine, psychological effects of.

**coherence theory of truth:** see truth.

**collective consciousness:** see Jungian approach to therapy.

**college students:** see pastoral counseling and case studies; students.

**color blindness:** This is a term for the inability to discriminate colors. Achromatopsia (total color-blindness) is rare; dyschromatopsia (partial color-blindness) is found to be higher among males. If the blindness affects green, the term is deuteranopia; red, protanopia. Attempts to remedy this condition by treatment (particular attention being given the problem during the last World War by qualified research organizations) have proven futile. It is possible to coach those wishing to pass certain color tests (e.g., for the military) but the deficiency itself fails to be corrected by any known means.

**color perception:** see human genetics.

**comedy:** see emotion; motives.

**common sense:** see pastoral psychology; pastoral psychology: its governing limitations and qualifications; psychotherapy.

**community interest, principle of:** see old age; sociometry.

**companionship:** see child training; juvenile delinquency.

**compensation:** see dreams; juvenile delinquency; motives; sleep.

**complacency:** see success.

**completion:** see dreams.

**complex psychology:** see psychology, schools of (psychoanalysis).

**complexes:** A complex arises out of a deep attachment of emotional response to certain objects, ideas, experiences, or persons and is not accepted by the individual because of its repugnant character and tends to be repressed. Any experience which brings pain or frustration may become material for a complex. The dominant emotion involved in the response or the dominant object to which the emotion is directed gives name to the specific complex, such as, sex complex, fear complex, inferiority complex,* religious complex or mother complex.

Repressed complexes are such experiences as may have been repugnant, "set aside" and forgotten but which produce, on occasion, emotional outbursts: e.g., giving vent to bad temper, indifference, provoked humiliation, and cowardice. Many of these repressed complexes remain unrecognized, such as a natural avoidance of people who were once offensive. Some repressed complexes become known only by some accidental element or some phase of it. Fixed ideas are such instances. A fixed idea may emerge but the repressed complex underlying it may remain buried and unrecognized.

Repressed complexes, though buried, exert an enormous influence upon human behavior. They belong to the deep drives of emotion. When recognized they may be consciously restrained. A man may be aware of his cowardice and try to overcome it; but if his cowardice is a complex he will find it difficult to forget or overcome.

The term "restraint" is used to indicate a complex that is recognized and consciously held from expression in *conduct*. The term "suppression" is used to indicate a conscious inhibition of a complex that is repugnant. The term "repression" is used to indicate an inhibition which goes on without awareness.

When complexes are repressed, *i.e.*, set aside by unconscious incubation, they may produce effects which lead to psychoneurotic tendencies. They may become expressed in various ways: 1) in dreams, 2) in nervous disorders (psycho-neuroses) and 3) in abnormal conduct. See abnormal conduct; ambivalence; analysis; dreams; fixation; Freud; motives; Oedipus complex; projection; psychology of religion; psychology, schools of (psychoanalysis); psychoneuroses.

**complexities of personality:** see problem complex.
**compulsion:** see belief in God.
**concentration:** see autosuggestion; fatigue; intuition; memorizing.
**concept:** see figurative language.
**condemnation of others:** see projection.
**conditioned fears:** see fears, conditioned.

**conditioned reflex:** see experimental extinction; Pavlov, Ivan Petrovitch; reflex.

**conduct, abnormal:** see abnormal conduct and abnormalities; complexes; psychoneuroses.

**confession:** The awareness of guilt is a universal human experience. All religions which acknowledge man's consciousness of sin have found ways of release from it as the condition of fuller living. Penitence and pardon have in some form (sacramental or otherwise) been regarded as a necessity to saintliness,\* to mental health and well-being. The awareness of guilt is the great disturber of inner peace. The experience of forgiveness (a clean slate) itself is a psychological incentive to an endeavor to straighten out the path—if the guilt was genuinely disturbing. Forgiveness is release from the tyranny of past misdemeanors,—if it is appropriated and deeply felt.

To be set free from inner conflicts\* is one of the most difficult psychological ventures. Confession to some one outside of our selves is the open door for release. Religions have practiced it widely as a deeply felt need of human experience. The churches of the Christian tradition took over the practice of confession (public and private) as a major discipline early in their institutional history but they did not initiate the practice.

There are no genuine friendships without confession. This may apply to the Object of religious faith (God) as well as interpersonal relationships of people. To have a real friend is to have found a confessor; and to have found such a confessor implies confidences which a true friend has no temptation to violate.

Confessions to a minister are both sacramental and personal: sacramental as sacred and personal as trust and confidence. A minister will regard confessions in both ways: as a sacramental act of his office and as a deep relationship of a friendship sought.

Confession, however, is not merely a psychological release for those seeking help—not merely a "treatment" in a cure. It is not mechanical and a ritual to be performed without a genuinely felt need. (This is the danger of perfunctorily planned ritualistic observances set by churches where repetitional practices have weakened the high purposes for which they were meant.) Confession, if genuine, requires a willingness to make restitution (at least to the degree that it is possible). A boy may confess to the neighbor that he broke the window with his batted ball and say that he is sorry. But this is not enough. He must—if he is really sorry—bring the savings from his bank of pennies to offer restitution (and it may well be accepted). Not all sins, however, are thus so easily cleared. Even so—restitution of some kind is a natural counterpart even though (soteriologically) the restitution is itself not the sorrow or the grace "conferred."

Confession of guilt, however, needs more than mere counseling on the part of a minister. Nothing less than assurance, reassurance of pardon will remove the sense of guilt. A minister whose own religious convictions are deep, whose religious convictions hold to the merciful character of a good God will, not so much by words, as by the subtleties of his own personality convey this assurance (through his poise, manner, voice and speech). An absolution he may justly feel in his power as minister to pronounce—an absolution unconditional. It should be one of his own richest experiences as a minister and as a friend.

The confessional is a sacred place and its secrets guarded and protected as an eternal commitment. See analysis; cure of souls; emotional tensions, release of; religion and mental health.

**confessional, the:** see confession; religion and mental health; visiting the sick.

**confessor:** see confession.

**confidence:** see prayer and autosuggestion.

**conflicts, inner:** see belief in God; confession; conscience; emotional conflicts; fatigue; genius; heightened reaction; juvenile delinquency; ministry, the, and counseling; morality and psychology; motives; psychology of religion; psychology, schools of (psychoanalysis); psychoneuroses; religion and mental health; schizophrenia.

**conformity in religion:** see pastoral counseling and case studies.

**conscience:** It was believed by the ancients that man possessed a *daimon* which guided his actions. This inner spirit spoke and advised. The Pythagoreans who held this concept passed it on to Socrates, Plato and Aristotle, each giving his own version but essentially holding to its other-worldly origin.

The "inner-light" or the "still small voice" continued to be looked to in decisions of right and wrong. This is conscience: working positively and working disturbingly when wrong acts were committed.

Conscience has been confused with "moral consciousness," the latter being the bare possibility of distinguishing between right and wrong. Conscience as a unique determinant of what is right or wrong has been discounted by both the traditional churches emphasizing a body of revelation and, what is more significant, by contemporary disciplined psychologists.

It is only too evident that what is a matter of "conscience" to one person is not the same to another, or even to the same person under different circumstances of age, experience and social mores. The church shied away from "conscience" since this was an invitation to the disruption of standard codes of conduct and belief.

One school of depth psychologists* theorizes about conscience in the following manner: Psychologically temptation and conscience are the names for types of suppressed desires. Temptation is the voice of suppressed evil when good is dominant; conscience is the voice of suppressed good when evil is dominant. Or to put it differently: both temptation and conscience represent conflicts between the conscious and the unconscious. In the case of temptation: the conscious is aware of some good but the unconscious drives would express evil. In the case of conscience: the conscious is aware of some dominant bad but the unconscious drives would express the good. Both represent inner states. Nothing is a matter of temptation or conscience which comes not from the inside. Temptation does not come from the world, the flesh and the devil but only from within. Thus what is a temptation for one is no temptation for another. So also conscience. Not outward acts make for conscience; but rather an inner history. Thus conscience varies with varieties of experience, codes, norms and mores.

One can say that he may trust his conscience only when that conscience is allied to valid norms and ideals. The latter are subject to the give and take of social experience and not an isolated norm of the inner and intuitive self. Where there is no drive whatsoever to the good there can be no conscience.

(The "unpardonable sin" situation.)

Conscience is not an entity but a name for a certain inner conflict. All moral aspirants need a map subject to social criticism to steer their moral course. To trust conscience alone is to put faith in what may be an illusory norm. See children and religious beliefs; morality and psychology; psychology, schools of (psychoanalysis); super ego, the.

**conscious, pre-conscious, unconscious:** In psychoanalytic literature these terms are distinguished as follows:

>**conscious:** When one is aware of his mental content, he is said to be *conscious*. That portion, therefore, of the mind's content of which we are aware is said to be the *conscious*.
>
>**pre-conscious:** That part of the mind's content which can be brought to conscious level by associations.
>
>**unconscious:** That part of the mind's content which is unverbalized, unintegrated and often antagonistic. Said to be dominated by emotion rather than logic.

See psychology, schools of (psychoanalysis). W.W.B.

**consciousness, collective:** see collective consciousness.

**consensus gentium:** see truth.

**conservatism:** see motives; repetition compulsion; sancta of religion.

**content psychology:** see psychology, schools of.

**contrast, absolute, fallacy of:** see peace and war.

**conversation:** see hospital chaplain, the; postural response; sex differences, psychological; social perception.

**conversion:** see abreaction; analysis; children and religious beliefs; divided self; psychology of religion.

**conversion hysteria:** see psychoneuroses.

**convictions:** see symbols.

**convulsions:** see hypoparathyroidism.

**correspondence theory of truth:** see truth.

**cortex:** see brain.

**cortin:** see adrenal glands.

**cosmology:** The discipline which treats of the origins and the ultimate fate of the world or universe. See naturalism.

**Coué, Emile:** see autosuggestion.

**Council of Clinical Training of Theological Students:** see Boisen, Anton T.

**counselee and professional help:** see heightened reaction; professional reference.

**counselee and sex:** see professional reference; sex and the counselee.

**counseling:** see Adlerian approach to therapy; ambivalence; analysis; confession; counseling periods; displacement; experimental extinction; fees; free association; Freudian approach to analysis; heightened reaction; hospital chaplain, the; in-laws; ministry, the, and counseling; old age; pastoral counseling and case studies; pastoral counseling: case studies; pastoral psychology: its governing limitations and qualifications; problem complex; professional reference; psychoanalysis; psychology of religion; psychotherapy; readiness, principle of; religion and mental health; Roman Catholicism and counseling; sacrifice, a psychological concept; sex and the counselee; social perception; structuring the counseling situation; success; talents; teen-agers; therapy; transference.

**counseling, general, and psychoanalytic literature:** see psychoanalytic and general counseling literature.

**counseling, group:** see group psychotherapy.

**counseling periods:** The amount of time devoted to assisting a troubled personality in finding solutions to the problem complex* is an important part of the counseling situation. Psychoanalysis* which spreads its counseling sessions over a period of years is usually limited to 50 minute sessions. This would seem to be a generally accepted length of time. The school counselor and the pastor will do well to look at the value of this time limit and use its values. The good analyst will end his session with the patient exactly at the end of 50 minutes regardless of the points being made at the time. This time limit has several values: 1) To impress upon the patient that this hour is set aside for a purpose. Knowing that he is in the situation for help, he will be less inclined to avoid the basic problems or dwell at great length upon the superficialities. The counselor must remember that when a person comes for help he may not be willing to go immediately to the roots of his or her difficulty. In fact, it is more often than not true that the decision to get at the problems at hand will bring forth every device ever used to avoid these very problems. Because of this a patient may be capable of talking for literally days without facing the basic issues. The limit of time set upon the counseling period will tend to make the patient realize that there is only so much time and the more he avoids his problems the less help he will get. The teacher will fully appreciate the frustration of having the class bell ring as he is about to make the significant point of a lecture. He can only remove this frustration by getting to the point with more facility and clarity at another lecture period. So it is with the patient and the counselor. If there is unlimited time there is no need to make the point so clear. 2) A second value of the time limit is simply to make it clear to the patient that he may not make unlimited demands upon the counselor. While it is true of a good counselor that he will go to any lengths to be understanding and helpful, it must be quite clear to the person seeking help that this is a partnership-search for solutions. There must be limits to what the counselor will do; if he does too much in the way of pointing out a solution, the person seeking help will only postpone the use of his own powers. Limiting the counseling time will be one way of setting limits upon what the counselor will do for the patient. 3) There is a very practical reason for the time limitation and this is for the sake of the counselor's energies and other time demands. An endless session of counseling will not only not help the person seeking help but will serve to exhaust the counselor. To keep himself free and able to assist others he must reserve time for himself. To be constantly going out to others in an attempt to help them can be psychologically enervating. If the counselor becomes weary of a problem, he may lose his perspective of himself as well as of the problem of the patient. 4) And finally, there is a fourth very important value in limiting the counseling session to 50 minutes. This fourth value is of primary importance. As a troubled person unfolds his problems and fears, he will tend to become more troubled by them. E.g., if a person is "afraid" of strawberries and cream and has denied the existence of this fear by avoiding strawberries and cream, there is little doubt that as he is confronted, by his own choice, with a large bowl of this delicacy, he will experience the fear he has been avoiding. It is important, therefore, for the troubled person to make contact with the reality of his fears. This cannot always be seen in verbalization of his problems. In fact it is possible and common for a person to "see" his problems in terms of concepts without ever feeling them. By limiting the length of counseling sessions and by having periods of time (even be it a twenty-four hour gap) in between sessions, the patient will react to his surroundings and can bring this "heightened reaction"* with him for the counselor and himself to look at. As the counseling sessions bring the counselor and counselee closer to the emotional problems at hand, the reactions of the counselee will be more readily accessible for appraisal by both of them. The limitation of sessions, therefore, serves to keep the counselor and counselee in constant touch with the counselee's current responses. The material for counseling then becomes alive in terms of current and meaningful feelings and not in meaningless and remote intellectualisms. W. W. B.

**counselor:** see counseling; problem complex; professional reference.

**courtesies:** see manners; teen-agers.

**courts of law:** see deception; juvenile delinquency.

**cowardice:** see complexes; psychoneuroses.

**cramming:** see memorizing.

**Crane, Frank:** see pastoral counseling and case studies.

**creative thinking:** Psychologists distinguish four stages in creative thinking: preparation, incubation, illumination and elaboration. Creative thinking is directed to a goal and as such is to be distinguished from pure imaginative activity. Reasoning, of course, plays its part in the stages.

During preparation there is little organization. Phases come to mind without any coherence. It is the period in which material is assembled.

During incubation no directed work is done. Dominant ideas may develop and take over during this process of relaxed thought. It is a period of mood, with no conscious straining toward solutions.

When incubation reaches some clarity of direction to the goal, illumination may be said to set in. Ideas fall into shape or pattern. Relations become clearer. The essential structure becomes outlined.

In elaboration there is conscious and deliberate effort to turn out the finished product.

These stages may vary greatly in time with the subject matter and the person. They may overlap. Creative thinking frequently is an emotional experience, particularly in the stage of illumination. Often there comes the feeling of passive revelation giving the awareness of "otherness" as if some outside force is involved. Here discovery is taken to be revelation.

Incubation is associated with the unconscious mind which is an active area in spite of suspended conscious effort. Ideas in a relaxed state have a chance to break down their frozen relationships and acquire new combinations (thus making for illumination).

Gestalt psychologists emphasize patterns of thought or forms as being significant to creative thinking as over against specific ideas. Conceivably this gives perspective where details tend to crowd it out. Creative thought is nourished in the area of perspective or "whole" thinking. When an idea is transmuted from membership in one configuration or form to another, therein lies the secret of the type of thinking that is called "creative."

Changing the scenery of thought, indulging in sheer physical exercise to divert the mind from its mental grooves, idleness, half-sleeping conditions, breaking routine—these are said to make for conditions for creative thought.

Psychologists have made observations on the ages of creative thought and have come up with the following opinions: H. C. Lehman declares that the best work of individual achievement is done between the ages of 30 and 40 years by the majority in nearly every occupation (naming such fields as music, drama, literature, physics, medicine, philosophy, invention, etc.; architects and astronomers reach their peak between 40 and 50). Where creative thought involves social factors the age levels are raised (military leaders in the late 40's, political in late 50's, economic and financial in late 50's and 60's). It is held also that since individual achievement (with social factors at minimum) is the same in almost any field of occupation (peak between 30 and 40) the same processes of mind are thus indicated: the substitution of new relations of ideas for old (C. Spearman). See intuition; minister, the, and his books; work and rest.

*Bibl.* H. C. Lehman: articles on Creative Years in *Scientific Monthly*, 1936, 1937, 1939, 1941, 1942, 1943; C. Spearman,

*Creative Mind* (1930). For extended bibliography see "Creative Thinking" by Catharine Patrick in *Encyclopedia of Psychology* (1946) ed. by P. L. Harriman.

**creativity:** see Coe, G. A.; Dewey, John; emotional tensions, release of; sublimation; success.

**cretinism:** see thyroid gland.

**crime:** see juvenile delinquency.

**criminal types:** Psychologically, there are no criminal types. Criminals are those people who break the civil law. Since all people some time or other break the law, the term is reserved for those who because of some infraction are sent or should be sent to a penal institution.

A classification of convenience offers the following types: 1) Accidental criminals. Accidents do occur, without intention of those involved. But the law steps in to levy punishment where harm has resulted. 2) Situational criminals. A crime is committed with willful intent but excuses are offered to mitigate it. The law may accept the excuses and temper the punishment; but punishment is a legal expectancy. 3) The irresponsible criminal. The irresponsible may not be considered guilty by law, although some inhibitions are recognized as necessary punishments. 4) The psychopaths. These are said to make up the bulk of prisoners. Their crime is associated with impulses out of control and emotionally immature. Correctional institutions are their punishment. 5) The psychoid. They are without contact with the world of reality but not sufficiently insane to be restricted to institutions of that class. These people do not see why their crime is committed nor do they resent punishment. Violent sex crimes are more often committed by this group. Often their cases show no suggestion of prognosis of the crime. 6) The neurotic. This type is aware of what he did when he violated the law and was deliberate; but he acted even against his interests. He is the "senseless" person, clumsy and often intelligent. Therapy, in such cases, is promising. He is classified as mentally ill. 7) The professional criminal often is undetected. It is his business to keep out of the hands of the law and cleverly cover his tracks. He understands his business and is cautious. He is a specialist in crime. He has his code of ethics: absolute loyalty is expected of his crowd and the integrity of silence. He may be generous and sympathetic

**criminality**

to those who belong to his circle. To outsiders who block him he is ruthless.

Criminal personality groups are not alike and do not call for the same treatment. Each type will need different methods of rehabilitation beyond their incarceration.

>*Bibl.* Raymond Corsini, "Criminal Psychology" in *Encyclopedia of Criminology* (1949), edited by V. C. Branham and S. B. Kutash.

**criminality:** see human genetics; juvenile delinquency.

**criminology:** see juvenile delinquency.

**crisis type:** see divided self.

**criticism of others:** see projection.

**Crookes, William:** see psychical research and parapsychology.

**cross-correspondence:** see psychical research and parapsychology.

**cross-currents:** see divided self; genius.

**crowds:** see group psychology; psychasthenia.

**cruelty:** see dispositions; sadism.

**crusader:** see displacement.

**crying:** see emotion.

**cult, religious:** see faith healing cults; visions and hallucinations.

**cultural differences:** see race psychology.

**culture:** see acculturation; emotion; psychology of religion; race psychology.

**cure:** see Adlerian approach to therapy; analysis; confession; flight into health; Freudian approach to analysis; Jungian approach to therapy; sacrifice, a psychological concept; therapy.

**cure of souls:** This phrase designates the pastoral function of the minister (as distinct from public preaching). Included in it are matters of religious significance in which the minister acts as father confessor, adviser and shepherd. It may include the administration of the church's sacraments, spiritual supervision, private confession,* personal counseling* and visitation.* German Lutherans employ the German term for this function: *seelsorge.** See cure; pastoral counseling and case studies; psychotherapy.

**custom:** see motives.

**cutaneous sensations:** see sensations.

**cytology:** see human genetics.

# D

**daemon:** see psychical research and parapsychology.
**daimon:** see conscience.
**Dante:** see minister, the, and his books.
**Darwin, Charles:** see talents.
**Dashiell, J. F.:** see personality.
**daughters-in-law:** see in-laws.
**day and night, and efficiency:** see efficiency and time of day.
**day dreams:** see dreams; phantasy.
**deafness:** see social maturation.
**death instinct:** see peace and war.
**deceit (and character):** Hugh Hartshorne* and Mark A. May* undertook to investigate deceit and published their findings under the title *Studies in Deceit*. This study was done as a Character Education Inquiry in cooperation with the Institute of Social and Religious Research (at Columbia).

Deceit was divided into three categories: cheating, lying and stealing. Techniques were developed to measure and evaluate the subject. Eleven thousand children—ages eight to sixteen—were tested. Factors considered were: economic level of the home, cultural level, race, nationality and religion of parents, grade at school, deportment, sociability, teacher influence, Sunday School attendance, etc.

The following conclusions were drawn up by the authors of the investigation:

1) By nature no one is honest or dishonest; 2) urging by teachers or by standards has no relation to the control of con-

duct; 3) the prevailing methods of setting up ideals do little good and may even do harm; 4) situations are more important; 5) the need for a more careful study of personal relations; 6) the need for understanding particular instances of dishonest practice before judgments of value are pronounced.

The sum and substance of these character studies, so far as formal religious training is concerned, was the startling conclusion that such training in moral knowledge of right and wrong had little or no effect on moral conduct. Moreover, there seemed to be no general characteristics of honesty in the children investigated. Rather, the varieties of conduct depended upon factors in particular situations. A slight modification in a situation seemed to modify the conduct. There were, it seemed, no general moral standards which controlled behavior. Conclusion: the moral knowledge of these children was unrelated to situations which required its application and, accordingly, was of little or no effect. Something more than mere instruction or general indoctrination is thus required to bring desired results. See deception; lying.

*Bibl.* Mark A. May and Hugh Hartshorne, *Studies in the Nature of Character*. I Studies in Deceit; II Studies in Service and Self-Control; III Studies in the Organization of Character (1928-1930).

**deception:** Deception is a deliberate and conscious effort to conceal the truth, be it by subterfuge, trickery, sophistry or by any device of misdirection. It is not to be confused with error of understanding or even ignorance; when it issues from a pathological lapse of memory or from pathological motivations its tone and character are altered though the end result (deception) may be similar to deliberate intent.

When deception (as above defined) takes place, the individual often betrays himself by certain verbal responses or bodily movements, or both. Common behavior symptoms are: accentuated defensive responses and expressions of fear (such as guilty look, confusion, inconsistent remarks, hesitation in response, running away). This, of course, marks the type of deception that is more easily detectable. Fear manifestations, however, are not in themselves evidence of guilt of deception. Accentuated defense mechanisms are common methods of hiding deception (acting boldly to ward off suspicion).

There are means of detection which overcome the deliberate cover-up of deception. A deceiver cannot control involuntary movements of the body or physiological actions. Internal bodily responses are mediated by the autonomic nervous system and evidences may in this area lead to exposure of deceit. Glandular secretion, heart beat and breathing may furnish the cue to detection.

The so-called "third degree" method—using force to uncover deception—is now regarded as unreliable proof since fear or pain may elicit any confession which promises relief.

The scientific approach to the detection of deception comes by way of an objective type of procedure which rests upon the premise that deception induces certain bodily symptoms of emotional disturbances.

In the latter part of the nineteenth century the first scientific test for fear type reactions prompted by deception was developed in the separate psychological laboratories of Jung* and Wertheimer.* Called the association reaction time test, the test consisted of reading a list of words, some related to the question involved in deception and some not. The subject under test was instructed to respond to each word with whatever word came to mind. A stop watch recorded the time lapse between the word given and the word which represented the response. A chronoscope was used capable of distinguishing fractions of a second. This test was based on the premise that a delayed response betrayed an attempt to cover up the deception. Crucial words which brought on delayed response conspicuous in comparison to the response to ordinary run of words were taken to be highly indicative of fear of detection.

Other tests were the shifty-eye test and the involuntary movement test. When crucial questions were put and the subject turned his eyes away—this was taken to indicate deception.

Again, a test was set up to detect deception by an attempt to correlate emotions accompanying *dominant* defenses during deception by observing variations of respiration and blood pressure. One series of tests affirmed the correlation of deception with respiration reactions. The ratio of inspiration divided by expiration was found to be greater *after* deception than before but greater *before* telling of a truth than after. Vittorio Benusse* set up these experiments holding also that a successful deceiver showed more pronounced variations than did the unsuccessful.

Systolic blood pressure was found by Marston* (1915) to increase significantly during deception, the increase greater with successful deceivers. Marston interpreted this to mean that blood pressure symptoms of deception constituted a test of dominant emotion which accompanied the increased effort involved in deception with consequent release of added nervous energy. What is called the "peak of tension" is the phenomenon of the rise of the systolic blood pressure curve symptomatic of deception at or nearest the point of greatest effort and the dominant emotion intensely furnishing the motivation.

Injection of scopolamin to compel the deceiver to admit his deception came to be called "A Truth Serum Third Degree." This test was developed by Dr. R. E. House. A sedative drug may increase loquacity but the test does not make certain that what is spoken is true or false. (Since whatever the subject admits occurs in a state of abnormal condition this test does not meet the standards of legal procedure.)

The so-called psycho-galvanic reflex test was developed by Dr. W. E. Summers using a more perfected apparatus. The test involved the use of the same crucial question twice and recording the psycho-galvonometric variations of response. A deception brought on a greater reaction the second time and, if the truth had been told, a smaller reaction the second time. This test has not been verified as reliable by others. It has not been sufficiently pin-pointed to the specific response of deception.

The reliability of the scientific tests for uncovering deception today stands in controversial waters. The association reaction-time test is not in general practical use. The psycho-galvonometer records are used along with the blood pressure and respiration tests by some. The dependability of the blood pressure-breathing test, after a period of divided opinion among professional psychologists, has received, on the whole, and with proper caution, a favorable rating for practical use in criminal and personal investigations. The test is held to be sufficiently reliable only in certain courts of law. At the same time the margin of error is acknowledged by psychologists in the conduct of the tests and therefore a conservative caution is exercised in their use. See cheating; child training; deceit

(and character); defense mechanisms; juvenile delinquency; lying.
>    *Bibl.* John A. Larson, *Lying and Its Detection* (University of Chicago Press).
>    William M. Marston, *The Lie Detector Test* (Richard R. Smith).
>    ————, "Lie Detection," *Encyclopedia of Psychology* (1946), ed. by P. L. Harriman.
>    Fred S. Inbau, *Lie Detection and Criminal Interrogation* (Williams and Wilkins).

**deduction:** see a priori.

**defense mechanisms:** In ordinary usage a defense mechanism is the resort to fiction* to maintain personal integrity.

In psychoanalysis the term refers to the unconscious measures to get rid of by subterfuge (as a measure of self protection) the persistently painful or disagreeable elements associated with some highly disagreeable situation. The disguise, unconsciously assumed, may be assumed in certain mannerisms, repressions,* in forgetfulness, in delusions, morbid fears,* hallucinations,* etc. Those who express these defense mechanisms are not easily made aware of them. See analysis; circumventions; deception; flight into health; marriage, disharmony in; peace and war.

**deficiency, mental:** see juvenile delinquency; mental deficiency.

**degenerative process:** see adult, the.

**delayed response:** see deception.

**deliberate effort:** see autosuggestion; freedom; prayer and autosuggestion; psychoanalysis, limitations of; success; talents.

**delinquency, juvenile:** see juvenile delinquency.

**deliverance, psychic:** see psychoneuroses.

**delusions:** see paranoia; paranoid.

**dementia praecox:** A term for a deteriorating mental disorder affecting the intellectual processes and making its occurrence in the post-adolescence years. This term has been replaced by that of schizophrenia.*

**democracy:** see peace and war.

**dendrite:** The short branch of the nerve cell which carries the impulse to the axon.* See receptor.

**depressant, alcohol as:** see alcohol and efficiency.

**depression, mental:** see anxiety states; boredom; climacterium; climacterium virile; emotion; menopause; old age; psychoneuroses; religion and mental health; sthenic.

**depressions, economic:** see psychology of religion.

**depth psychology:** see analysis; conscience; emotion; genius; psychoanalysis; psychology of religion; psychology, schools of (psychoanalysis).

**Descartes, René:** see pineal gland.

**desires:** see dreams; Freud.

**desires, unconscious:** see conscience; psychoneuroses.

**despair:** see dysphoria.

**detection of deception:** see deception.

**deterioration, physical:** see physical deterioration.

**determinants:** see character; genius; personality; race psychology; talents.

**deuteranopia:** see color blindness.

**devoutness:** see saintliness.

**Dewey, John:** (1859-1952) America's most distinguished recent philosopher. His whole point of view is in the spirit of reform against traditional ideas. His book *Reconstruction in Philosophy* (1920, enl. ed., 1948) perhaps best summarizes this reform in the field of philosophy. In the psychological area he also pursued newer paths against the beaten tracks of his earlier day. He followed the functionalistic school but gave to it his own version of instrumentalism.* Ideas function (poorly or well) and that is that. The mind is not a something but the mental process, teleological in character, of the psychophysical organism. "Adjustment to life situations" is the magic phrase. Truth is but an abstraction referring to specific truths; but these in turn, rest upon the adjective "true" which is a function of a workable adjustment. "True," in turn, rests upon the adverb "truly" which is the activity itself in its process. An idea is true if it *truly* functions.

In education he stood for activity. One learns by doing. Handle, taste and see. An educated person gets on in his environment, participating and recreating. He is capable of adjusting to situations and of recreating them to the better. Dewey's influence on American public school methods (practical arts [trades] and in the whole philosophy of participation, discussion, laboratory emphasis) has been enormous. At

Chicago he carried his ideas into the laboratory of the school room. He is sometimes referred to as the father of recent progressive education (child centered rather than subject centered). Many teachers in high schools and college received their graduate training at Teachers College (Columbia) and were brought into the discipleship of pragmatic theories and functionalistic pyschology under teachers who had been directly influenced by him. The list of his publications is in itself of book length. He touched on most of the phases of human interest: religion, art, education, scientific method, logic, culture, democracy and the numerous phases of philosophy itself. A few of his book titles are: *Ethics* (with Tufts, 1909); *The Influence of Darwinism on Philosophy* (1910); *Democracy and Education* (1916); *The Quest for Certainty* (1929); *Human Nature and Conduct* (1930); and *Freedom and Culture* (1939).

He was born in Vermont, graduating from its state university in 1879. His graduate work was done at Johns Hopkins. He taught first in country schools and then at the universities of Michigan, Minnesota and Chicago. From 1904 until 1930 he lectured at Columbia as a member of its faculty. See positivism; pragmatism; psychology, schools of.

**dextrality**: right handedness or right hand preference. See handedness.

**diabetes**: see endocrine gland.

**diagnosis**: It is often stated that a diagnosis is a label placed upon a condition to designate its current nature. Psychoanalytically, a diagnosis is considerably more than a label. It is too often erroneous to put a neurotic personality into one of the many categories of psychologically labeled pigeonholes. Examination of the various categories of behavior disorders will soon reveal that the overlapping elements are many. Diagnosis, through preliminary interviews and through the use of diagnostic tests, should serve to point out possible avenues of therapy and prognosticate the final outcome. Psychoanalytically, then, we may say that diagnosis is prognosis.\* It is often quite clear to the analyst what the nature of the problem is. He would be likely to be aware of its nature long before the patient sees it. The analyst uses diagnostic techniques primarily to assist him in plotting the path which the analysis will be likely to take. Two of the tests often used are the Rorschach\* ink blot test and the thematic apperception test.* These tests are usually administered by specialists in the testing field and reports are then made to the analyst himself. Diagnostic tests are not proofs of a psychological label but are, rather, suggestions as to means of assistance. See projective techniques; word association test.     W.W.B.

**diastolic pressure:** see hypertension.

**Dicks, Russell:** (1906-    ) Co-author with Richard C. Cabot* of the well known volume *The Art of Ministering to the Sick* (1936) Russell Dicks became in 1933 a first full time chaplain at the Massachussetts General Hospital. He and his students authored the volume *And Ye Visited Me* (1939)—a pioneer case book in this field. His *Who is My Patient?* (1941) is "A Religious Manual for Nurses." He is professor of pastoral care in The Divinty School, Duke University. See hospital chaplain, the.

**diffidence:** see talents.

**digestion:** see aging process.

**Dillinger:** see juvenile delinquency.

**diminishing returns:** see work and rest.

**disbelief:** see belief in God; Leuba, James H.; reality feeling principle; scepticism.

**discipline:** see child training; children and religious beliefs; juvenile delinquency; learning.

**discordancy:** see divided self; split personality.

**discovery:** see creative thinking.

**diseases:** see human genetics.

**disharmony in marriage:** see marriage, disharmony in.

**dishonesty:** see deceit (and character).

**dislikes:** see likes and dislikes.

**disorders, mental:** see mental disorders.

**disorders, moral:** see morality and psychology.

**displacement:** This term is a complex one in its common usage as it is often confused with transference.* Displacement, per se, is the substitution of energy for a more socially accepted idea or person from a less desirable person or idea. We see this device employed readily by those who wish to deny certain feelings and impulses by manifesting, quite overtly, their opposites. E.g., an individual who loses himself in work of a social nature may do so not because he is truly dedicated to society but, rather, to deny before his fellows the very real anti-social feelings he has. A crusader against evil may often be "displacing" his own desire to do evil. Extreme forms of puritanism are often a form of the denial of the attractive state of sexual expression. In purely psychological terms, a person of the puritan type is constantly fighting an inner battle. This same battle may be waged by the libertine who may be displacing the energy he would normally expend in his desire to do good. Many a village atheist maintains such a position out of psychological displacement rather than from an intellectually defensible position. Looking at this term for a moment in light of a theological context, we are immediately confronted with the problem of screening those who dedicate themselves to the calling of theological counselor. It has been the experience of one or two excellent theological seminaries that young men and women who seek training at their doors often do so in order to deny the existence of what they believe to be "evil" thoughts. These seminaries have established counseling programs in order to clarify the motives of those persons entering the ministry. They feel that it is an injustice to those whom these students will later serve, as well as to the students themselves, to permit such confusion to exist. Sooner or later, the displacement device will create its own conflict and the results are often vicious bigotry or complete rebellion against the values involved. It is the opinion of a former seminary counselor that only a happy man may bring meaning to the lives of those he works with. Many would-be ministers are finding their ways to psychologists' couches to clarify the question of why the ministry has been chosen. See censor. W.W.B.

**dispositions:** A person may have several dispositions; but these may unite to form a dominant disposition.

A disposition arises out of a deep attachment of emotional response to certain objects, ideas, events or persons and is accepted by the individual quite unconsciously. A disposition is a person's way of responding and comes spontaneously without conscious effort. It is his so-called "second nature." A person who consciously aims to be religious does not reveal his disposition in that direction; however, if he responds religiously —without forethought or even awareness—his religious response is that of his disposition. A disposition is not an inheritance but an unconscious accumulation of emotional experiences which have through the years been accepted and thus find easy and ready expression.

Dispositions may be bad or good depending upon the character of their direction or attachment. A cruel disposition is an unconscious response that comes spontaneously, a response that is refractory in the relationships of life; and a cruel disposition arises by the long increment of sentiments of cruelty toward others. A good disposition is a manner of emotional response which has come out of many good sentiments; the individual is quite unaware of his possession of a good disposition since a disposition is embedded in the unconscious.

A disposition is to be distinguished from a temperament* in that the former is psychological while the latter is psychophysical. A disposition is acquired while a temperament is hereditary in the chemical glandular structures and functions of the organism.

Dispositions become merged into an organized pattern: the dominant disposition which is the synthesis of them all. Thus a person's disposition is the complex of many single dispositions.

Character* is the larger term which includes not only a person's disposition but his whole qualitative self, including his sentiments and his conscious ideals. See sentiments.

**dissatisfaction:** see success.
**dissipation of time:** see boredom.
**dissociation:** see schizophrenia.
**distraction, fallacy of:** see fallacy of distraction.
**distractions:** see noise disturbances.
**disturbances of noise:** see noise disturbances.
**divided self:** William James* used this term to classify those people who seem to suffer "a certain discordancy or heterogeneity in the native temperament" and because of this psychological basis are unable to achieve, without bitter struggle, a unified moral, religious and intellectual unity. These are the twice-born in religion, the "sick souls."* Some people are born with an inner harmony and balance; others are beset with cross-currents and the handicap of inner inconsistencies. The homo-duplex may take on various forms: aspirations which do not square with actual living (Paul's confession 'What I would, that I do not'); cross purposes of drives, the one set bringing

harmony to the self and social behavior, the other frustration and social maladjustment; etc. Unity may come "at once," a "crisis," or by a long process, a "lysis" (Tolstoy, Bunyan); or it may only be partially achieved or not at all. Both St. Paul and St. Augustine are classical examples of the "divided self" both of whose thinking reveals the undercurrent of dualism (psychological and theological). See healthy-mindedness; split personality.

*Bibl.* William James, *The Varieties of Religious Experience* (1902).

**dogmatism:** An assertion that is made without any appeal to argument or reason is said to be dogmatic. A dogmatist may be said to pound both fists and stamp both feet shouting "It's so; it's so." Opposite from dogmatism is the philosopher who seeks reasons. See philosophy; truth.

**domestic difficulties:** see family; in-laws; marriage, disharmony in; parents; pastoral counseling and case studies.

**dread:** see angst; anxiety states; fears; phobias.

**dreams:** see minister, the, and his books.

**dreams:** In psychoanalysis\* dreams are considered of great importance. They are regarded as the language of the unconscious mind. But the language here is symbolic and needs expert interpretation.

There are, it is evident, difficulties in arriving at a correct interpretation of meanings in dreams. Psychoanalysts naturally will favor their own preferred theories of the unconscious and their own explanation of the most fundamental urges which underlie the conscious mind. One may hold that sex is fundamental (Freud\*) and thus dreams are symbols belonging to that drive. Others may hold that dreams are reversions to primitive urges (Jung\*) or to the expression of the preservative and purposeful character of the species, or as compensations of losses and frustrations, etc.

Dreams may well be the realization of desires for that which the waking life itself does not offer. They may reflect deep wishes and needs; they may complete a life that is otherwise incomplete.

So-called "day dreams" are conscious fancies in which a person images himself in the cloak of his wishes. It is a vicarious gratification of desires. In schizophrenia,\* the day-dream may

**dress**                                                     **72**

be substituted for the real thing.

Complexes* denied direct expression may manifest themselves in dreams. See analysis; censor; psychology, schools of; psychoneuroses.

**dress:** see eonism.

**drinking:** see alcohol and efficiency.

**drinking, excessive:** see alcohol; alcohol and efficiency; drugs; visions and hallucinations.

**drives:** These are the originating and stimulating conditions which give rise to an activity. They are the original sources of energy that prompt behavior.

The lines or directions into which these drives proceed are called "motives."* The former are original or native in human nature; the latter are the acquirements. Hunger, sex, unfavorable skin conditions—i.e., the inadequate exchange of energies that take place through bodily surface tissue or temperature conditions—thirst, reactions associated with sensory apparatus, fatigue and urge to exercise, etc., these are listed by psychologists as original or native reactions, diffuse and non-specific in character. They constitute the raw material of behavior.

Drives, thus, operate over sensori-motor pathways. It is unnecessary to appeal to some nondescript and unanalyzable "instincts"* (as in traditional psychology) which produce no explanations and add only to confusion and vagueness. See Adlerian approach to therapy; children and religious beliefs; complexes; conscience; emotion; learning; motives; original sin; psychology of religion; success.

**drugs:** see alcohol and efficiency; boredom; caffeine, psychological effects of; juvenile delinquency; tobacco smoking and psychological efficiency; visions and hallucinations.

**drugs and deception:** see deception.

**dual personality:** see psychoneuroses.

**dualism:** see belief in God.

**dualism, psychological:** see divided self.

**duct:** A tube which allows for flow of secretion from a gland or for the flow of a liquid, e.g., tear duct, lymph duct.

**ductless gland:** A gland not provided with ducts. There are two classes: the endocrine (e.g., thyroid,* pituitary,* pineal,* etc.) and gland-like tissues (e.g., spleen, lymph nodes, etc.). See emotion; endocrine gland.

**Duke experiments in parapsychology:** see psychical research and parapsychology.

**Durkheim, E.:** see psychology of religion.

**dwarfism:** An abnormally diminutive stature associated with the dysfunction of the pituitary gland\* (anterior lobe). See endocrine gland.

**dynamic psychology:** see Woodworth, Robert Sessions.

**Dynamic School of British psychologists:** see psychology of religion; psychology, schools of (psychoanalysis).

**dyschromatopsia:** see color blindness.

**dyslalia:** A term for disorder in articulation. See speech pathology.

**dysphasia:** see speech pathology.

**dysphemia:** A term for the disorder of speech commonly known as stuttering. See speech pathology.

**dysphonia:** A term for disorder in voice. See speech pathology.

**dysphoria:** A term for gloom, anxiety, despair or any excessive abnormality of emotion which hinders well being and good adjustment.

# E

**early environment:** see analysis; character; child training; children and religious beliefs; Freudian approach to analysis; heredity; juvenile delinquency; personality; psychology, schools of (John B. Watson); sex differences, psychological; talents; teen-agers.

**earning power:** see minister, the, and money; success.

**eating, excessive:** see boredom.

**Ebbinghaus, Hermann:** (1850-1909) A German psychologist known for his experimental studies in memory. His nonsense syllables studies are well known and some of his findings remain established in the psychology of learning. See memorizing.

**ecology:** In biology, ecology is that discipline which deals with the relations of organisms to their environment. In social psychology* it is that phase of human social relationships which concern people in relation to their physical environment (migrations and adaptations to change of climate, soil, geography, and the like).

**economic security:** see success.

**economic situation:** see juvenile delinquency.

**economy, agricultural and industrial:** see pastoral counseling and case studies.

**economy in memorization:** see memorizing.

**education:** see adult, the; child training; children and religious beliefs; Coe, G. A.; learning; memorizing; old age; peace and war; role playing; sentiments; teen-agers.

**educational theory:** see Dewey, John; instrumentalism; memorizing; psychology, schools of.

**effector:** A muscle or gland which carries out a response.

**efferent fibers:** see afferent-efferent fibers.

**efficiency:** see alcohol and efficiency; atmospheric conditions and work capacity; caffeine, psychological effects of; efficiency and time of day; fatigue; noise disturbances; reading performance; sleep; tobacco smoking and psychological efficiency; work and rest.

**efficiency and time of day:** Tradition has it that certain times of the day are more favorable to human efficiency than others. For example, early morning hours have been said to be favorable to clear thinking; high noon favorable to activity; twilight to contemplation; midnight to rascality; etc.

The calendar and clock hours are, of course, not biological expressions. Convention has arranged appropriate activities for time-clock hours which have brought on questionable conclusions of human psychology.

Experimental investigations have been made to ascertain the focal relationship between human efficiency and clock hours—particularly in measuring the expenditures of energy by alternations of eating, working, resting and sleeping. Results showed that the expenditure of energy depends on the times of eating, sleeping, working and resting—regardless of whether the subject tested performed during the day or during the night. This is to say that a person's efficiency is not a function of the time of day nor even of a biological rhythm (as another theory has it). Rather, efficiency is directly related to the individual's own type of day, when he arises, when he eats, when he sleeps, and so on. People can readily adapt themselves to night work (assuming the parallel opportunities for sleep*). See noise disturbances; work and rest.

**effort:** see deliberate effort.

**effort, law of reversed:** see autosuggestion.

**ego, the:** see Id, the, the ego and the super ego; psychology, schools of.

**egocentricity:** see psychology of religion.

**egregorsis:** inability to sleep.*

**Einstein, Albert:** see psychical research and parapsychology.

**elaboration in creative thinking:** see creative thinking.

**elation, feeling of:** see euphoria.

**Electra complex:** see Oedipus complex.

**electric shock:** see shock therapy.
**eleven-year old, the:** see teen-agers.
**Elgin State Hospital:** see Boisen, Anton T.
**Elliott, Harrison S.:** (1882-1951) A distinguished writer on subjects dealing with the psychology of religion,* pastoral psychology,* religious education and the relation of religion to mental health. He taught at Teachers College (Columbia) and at Union Theological Seminary (beginning in 1922). Perhaps his best known work is *Can Religious Education Be Christian?* (1940). Other publications: *The Bearing of Psychology on Religion* (1927); *The Process of Group Thinking* (1928); *Solving Personal Problems* (with Grace L. Elliott, 1936), a work on counseling; etc.
**Emerson, R. W.:** see healthy-mindedness.
**emotion:** An emotion has been defined as "a stirred-up state of the organism" particularly during periods of stress and strain in making adjustments, manifested frequently in a variety of bodily and visceral reactions.

The famous James-Lange theory (1886) of emotion states that emotions occur as an accompaniment to physiological response. The classic statement is: one does not run because one is afraid but one is fearful because of running. Moods thus accompany bodily situations. Emotions are organic in origin.

W. B. Cannon, an American physiologist, (summarized in his *Bodily Changes in Pain, Hunger, Fear and Rage* [1929]) took issue with the James-Lange theory after certain experiments with lower organisms. His view is that emotional behavior is changed only slightly when afferent links between viscera and brain are severed. In some cases where the posterior half of the thalamus* was removed there followed the disappearance of the usual emotional behavior reactions. Both theories have contributed to the understanding of the physiological aspects of emotional activity.

The autonomic nervous system* (including beyond the brain) and the ductless glands are regarded to affect emotional responses. Some psychopathologists hold that many neuroses* and some psychoses* are due to defects of the autonomic responses. Endocrinology* points to the influence of adrenal glands in emotional responses. The interplay of the endocrine system is taken to be significant in emotional behavior.

William McDougall* held that each innate propensity or even learned tendency has its specific emotional accompaniment (escape action and fear, successful strivings and elation, failure and depression, sex and lust, combative action and anger, etc.). In a sentiment* many non-specific motives function together in reference to a particular object or experience. A family sentiment, thus, consists of love of home, fear for its threat, anger toward offenders of it.

In depth psychology* emotions are considered to be expressions of unconscious drives.* A phobia, for example, is linked to a repressed memory. Emotions may be transferred and thus hidden making their cause less evident. Hating someone may actually be an unconscious love. Carl G. Jung* held emotions to arise out of a complex of latent ideas or tendencies linked by common felt associations with common histories.

John B. Watson,* the behaviorist, claimed that there are but three primary emotions: fear, love and rage. Each of these emotional responses consisted of specific motor action and each distinguishable.

Some psychologists hold that early emotional behavior is general and diffuse in character (M. Sherman); others (G. M. Stratton) say that the primary emotional response is excitement which then sprays out into specific kinds and, in the adult, the specific emotion precedes a diffused excitement. K. M. Bridges, observing infants and very young children, says that the primary emotional responses appear first as neutral excitement, second, excitement with delight under certain circumstances, and, third, distressed excitement under other specific circumstances. Stimuli which first initiate only distressed excitement may later produce definite responses such as fear and rage. Learning* promotes differentiation of emotional behavior. Thus emotional development is a part of social development. Maturity brings on a wider variety of emotional responses and greater differentiation.

Weeping has been studied by F. H. Lund ("Why Do We Weep?", *Journal of Social Psychology* [1930]). Weeping in adults, he observes, occurs usually in complex social stimulus situations. It is not characteristic of deep depression of psychotic states. Nor does grief of itself promote weeping. Grief when alleviated by sentiments associated in memory, pity by encouragement, tragedy by some phase of comedy—these complex combinations may bring on weeping. Like laughter, weeping occurs most likely in situations that have the element of the incongruous or the contradictory. Emotion here is a socio-individual reaction.

The total and average quality of emotional responses is said to constitute a person's temperament.* Certain psychologists hold that all mental processes go in within the framework of feeling. A person's mood is thus his specific characteristic emotional framework. Temperament would be the term for that framework which appears most constantly in a person. An emotion, in this sense, would be the dominant, short-lived, and most intense feeling response. Temperament, however, is regarded by many psychologists to be the result of a process rather than a fixed trait. Situations bring on habit patterns of emotional responses.

In animals emotional behavior appears conditioned to momentary situations. With humans, however, emotions are more prolonged and are related to more complex social stimuli. Human hatreds are more complex than animal anger. A definite cultural situation is implied in many emotional responses: what is funny for one in an English court might be unfunny were one an American cowboy. What is tragedy in one instance is a comedy to some one else. Thus happiness itself is involved in the kind of social milieu in which it occurs or is expected to occur. Emotional responses involve more than mere individual reactions of the self-induced type. See adrenal glands; ambivalence; complexes; creative thinking; deception; dysphoria; fears, conditioned; feeling; fixation; motives; sentiments; sthenic; social perception; thalamus.

**emotion and sex differences:** see sex differences, psychological.

**emotional conflicts:** see analysis; anxiety states; conflicts, inner; deception; dysphoria; emotional tensions, release of; juvenile delinquency; motives; old age; phobias; psychosomatics; speech pathology.

**emotional disorganization:** see dysphoria; hebephrenia.

**emotional maturity:** see peace and war.

**emotional outbursts:** see alcohol and efficiency; self.

**emotional tensions, release of:** Emotional tensions may be relieved, it is clear, by attending to the problem of health. Recreation and relaxational activities are incontestable aids to the release of emotional tensions. Even a preacher should indulge in care-free activity, with a wholesome let-down of tightly-knit codes of behavior, each week (not merely on annual vacations) and to this end he may well find his professional brothers good partners since the understanding will be mutually appreciated and shared. If anyone has difficulty in remembering when last he laughed or played silly little games he may now count the days until the day of reckoning of his own health.

The "coffee break" now widely practiced in industry is but an expression of the sound principle of intermittent relaxation necessary to effective work of a routine nature. Prizes for creative work or the principle of rotation in assigned work are methods of relief from routines which bring tension. Going stale is a danger signal.

To overcome *excessive* emotional tensions the formula is simple: the situations which bring them about must be removed or altered or another situation must be provided to set up a different response to divert excessive emotional energy. In some cases the frank acknowledgement and understanding of the stimulus which prompts emotional upset will bring relief (practiced in psychotherapy*). Finding new work, new interests which will be absorbing enough for total response is the pathway to release. Grief is best met by a powerful sentiment* for some task which will weaken the intensity of a grief response. Work may be intensely physical—enough to drain off the intensity of the tensions. See abreaction; analysis; anxiety states; confession; emotional conflicts; motives.

**emotive language:** Terms or words which arouse feelings are said to be emotive. This they do through their meaning. A term calls to mind certain characteristics of things or points up certain memories which are feared or admired or loved. These emotive connotations vary from person to person, place to place. When terms do not stir emotions they are said to be neutral. In logical thinking the emotive force of terms must be carefully discriminated and stripped. Otherwise there are distortions and illogical conclusions.

**empathy:** This term refers to the act of projection of a person into a work of art, losing his identity with it. It is a feeling of *rapport*, associated with aesthetic experience.*

**employment:** see pastoral counseling and case studies.

**encephalitis:** A term given to that group of diseases characterized by inflammation of the brain* and caused by infectious agents, some of which are insect-borne.    V. H. F.

**endocrine gland:** A group of specialized cells within the organism which manufacture a specific biochemical agent called a "hormone." These hormones are secreted directly into the blood stream and transported to their effector cells where they produce a specific physiological action. A delicate balance exists between the rate of production and the rate of utilization of hormones in maintaining the normal physiological equilibrium. Several disease states are directly attributable to an oversupply (hypersecretion) or undersupply (hyposecretion) of one or more of these substances. Diabetes, thyroid* excesses or deficiencies, menstrual abnormalities, certain forms of hypertension,* Addison's disease,* gigantism,* dwarfism,* are only a few examples of the profound effect these substances have on normal function. Endocrine glands in the human organism include: pituitary,* thyroid, parathyroid,* adrenal,* pancreas, ovary, testis and certain areas of the gastro-intestinal tract. See ductless gland.    V. H .F.

**endocrinology:** The discipline which undertakes the study of the structure, functions and disorders of endocrine glands* and their secretions. See emotion.

**endowments:** see talents.

**energies of men:** see drives; fatigue; organic sensations.

**enjoyment:** see fatigue.

**enlightenment:** see intuition.

**enlightenment in therapy:** see analysis.

**environment, early:** see early environment.

**environment, home:** see home environment.

**environment and religion:** see psychology of religion.

**environment vs. heredity:** see human genetics.

**eonism:** This term refers to the adoption of dress and manners characteristic of the opposite sex. d'Éon was a Frenchman who gained notoriety by this behavior.

**epilepsy:** A disease of the central nervous system* which is characterized by various degrees of muscle spasms and twitchings, associated with disturbances in the state of consciousness.

V. H. F.

**equivocation:** see fallacy of equivocation.
**eros:** see libido; Oedipus complex.
**eroticism:** see homosexuality.
**error:** see instrumentalism; truth.
**ESP:** see psychical research and parapsychology.

**Esquirol, Jean Étienne Dominique:** (1772-1840) A French psychiatrist who was among the first to make a careful study of hallucinations* (coining the term). His studies included the relation of mental disorders to criminal behavior and statistical investigations of the incidence of various types of psychoses.*

**essayists:** see minister, the, and his books.
**essential pragmatism:** see pragmatism.
**ethics:** see children and religious beliefs; morality and psychology.

**etiology:** In medicine, the study of the cause of disease.

V. H. F.

**eugenics:** A term coined by Francis Galton (1822-1911) referring to the control of human breeding for the sake of improvement in the species. Research with the establishment of a laboratory in London in 1904 was begun by Galton. Eugenics is based on the view of the importance of heredity in combating ills of society. See juvenile delinquency.

**euphoria:** A feeling of general well being. In psychopathology the term refers to the condition of a high degree of elation, optimism, strength, which accompanies a type of mental disorder.

**euthanasia:** An easy, painless death. The term is employed for the merciful taking of life by painless means (in the case of incurable disease or of "hopeless" mental conditions).

**evidence vs. belief:** see belief in God.
**evil and good:** see good and bad; sin.
**evolution:** see human genetics.
**exacting payment:** see sacrifice, a psychological concept.
**exaggerations:** see phantasy.
**exaltation, feeling of:** see peace and war; visions and hallucinations.
**excitability:** see juvenile delinquency.

**excitement** 82

**excitement:** see emotion; sthenic; synapses.

**executives:** see success.

**exercise:** see physical exercise.

**exhibitionism:** Self display is a natural overt expression, particularly in children and in adolescents. If it is unduly repressed it may become a perversion to which the name "exhibitionism" is given. The exhibitionist may be sexually subnormal but with all the outward signs (exhibitionism) of excessive erotic impulses. The lady who is very dressy, perfumed and "attractive" may be very cool and even frigid.

The term is sometimes used in the narrower meaning of so-called "indecent exposure."

**existentialism:** see psychology of religion; psychology, schools of.

**exophthalmus:** see hyperthyroidism.

**experience:** see a posteriori.

**experience and theological concepts:** see ministry, the, and counseling.

**experience, its complexities:** see problem complex.

**experimental extinction:** The principle which explains the losing of acquired responses in the process of relearning. The term is used by the clinical psychologists to describe the instance wherein, experimentally, there are response losses which are conditioned by the absence of that which originally brought a response. E.g., in Pavlov's\* experiment where the ringing of a bell was repeated at the proffering of food, the dog would salivate with the ringing of a bell. However, should the ringing be repeated time and time again and no food forthcoming, the dog's salivating response will grow weaker until it eventually will become extinct. During any counseling process, the counselee will often give a response designed to produce a desired result. E.g., the counselee will act in such a way as to demand the affection of the counselor. If this action (or actions) is repeated often enough and it fails to bring the desired response the action will be abandoned. The counselor must be keenly aware of the negative aspects of this factor as well of its positive elements. Wherever a neurotic behavior is designed to bring forth a response on the part of the analyst, the rewarding of this behavior will perpetuate the neurotic behavior. Wherever the action is healthy, it should be productive. A counselee who believes that the counselor will dislike him unless he is subservient can be helped to overcome subservience by the counselor's acceptance. Assume that a particular counselee's actions have been formed upon the firm belief that speaking his own mind produces wrath in those he cares for. The absence of wrath on the part of the counselor, each and every time the counselee asserts his own thoughts, will serve to extinguish the subservient response. W. W. B.

**experimental procedure in parapsychology:** see psychical research and parapsychology.

**experimental psychology:** see psychology, schools of.

**experimentation, laboratory:** see pragmatism.

**expertness:** see learning.

**extemporaneous preaching:** see sermons, preparation of.

**extinction, experimental:** see experimental extinction.

**extra-sensory perception:** see psychical research and parapsychology.

**extraversion:** A person is said to be extraverted if he is extremely out-going, social. As opposed to introversion,* such a person is not self conscious and introspective. See belief in God; Jungian approach to therapy; talents.

**extravert and introvert:** see Jungian approach to therapy.

# F

**fables and parables:** see children and religious beliefs.
**faces, reading of:** see deception; physiognomy; social perception.
**factors in learning:** see learning.
**factors in success:** see success; talents.
**faculty psychology:** see psychology, schools of.
**failures:** see anxiety states; success; talents.
**faith:** see belief in God; prayer and autosuggestion; psychology of religion (J. C. Flower); religious response, the, nature and origin.
**faith healing cults:** see psychotherapy.
**fallacy, pathetic:** see pathetic fallacy.
**fallacy of absolute contract:** see peace and war.
**fallacy of argumentum ad ignorantiam:** A common fallacy. If one cannot prove something to be true or false, this inability to do so does not make it true or false. One may know something to be so without being able to show it to be so. Beliefs incapable of demonstration may still be true. When one uses this test of inability as proof of truth or falsity, one commits the fallacy.
**fallacy of distraction:** This is a fallacy involving a neat diversion from the issue by equivocation,\* quibbling and irrelevance. He who indulges this type of fallacy is sometimes called "the grasshopper thinker," the person who interjects a joke to divert attention from the issue.
**fallacy of equivocation:** This is a common fallacy. It has to

do with the change of meaning of a word in discourse, a change of meaning involved in a different context. For example "business is business." The first "business" means the interchange of trade (buying, selling); the second "business" may mean competition of a more or less cut-throat type. An equivocal argument appears good because of the disguise of difference of meanings. Thus conclusions do not logically follow with surreptitious change of meanings.

Quibbling is a special kind of equivocation. When one person gives a reason for a statement using a certain term in one sense and another, arguing with him, gives a reason against a statement using the same term in a different sense, then the second person is said to be indulging in quibbling. Result of quibbling: no real argument but rather a dispute that is only verbal. See fallacy of distraction.

**fallacy of occupation:** see occupational fallacy.

**fallacy of over simplification:** This is sometimes referred to as "capsule thinking," "potted thinking" or "tabloid thinking." In an argument someone may say that "*the* simple, unvarnished truth" is, or "what it all boils down to" is, or "the issue is plain and clear." But this may be far from true. The issue may be highly complicated. The "capsule thinker" likes to indulge in slogans, catchwords. Sometimes he displays himself fallaciously with crisp announcements, sermon themes or catch phrases on bulletin boards. Neat pigeon-hole classifications are characteristic dismissals of the complex. In ethics a fallacious judgment is given by saying that an act is either right or wrong—without the qualification of circumstance. Often a straw man is set up to be knocked down. The outcome is distortion and a dead-end street in the argument.

**fallacy of rationalization:** This fallacy occurs when a set of reasons is given which does not reflect the real reason. A person may say he is a Democrat because of "democratic principles" but this may not be the real reason; he is a Democrat because of parental tradition and of his having been born in a southern area tied to the party. One hears this fallacy also in the field of religion: a person is a Lutheran, he says, "by conviction" whereas he may be so out of certain deep loyalties. See occupational fallacy; occupational prejudice; motives.

**fallacy of the reification of abstractions:** A common fallacy in which a term is treated as if it were a thing. Instinct,\* for example, is a name for a complex kind of unlearned behavior. But to say that one is possessed by an Instinct or that an Instinct prods one to behavior is to suggest a "thingness" to a mere name or term. "Religion does" or "religion says"; these are common fallacious expressions.

**family:** see in-laws; marriage, disharmony in; pastoral counseling and case studies.

**family, influence of:** see child training; children and religious beliefs; old age; personality; psychology, schools of (psychoanalysis); success; teen-agers.

**fanaticism:** see saintliness.

**fancies:** see children and religious beliefs; dreams; imagination; phantasy.

**Faraday, Michael:** see psychical research and parapsychology.

**fasting:** see visions and hallucinations.

**fatherhood of God:** see belief in God.

**fathers-in-law:** see in-laws.

**fathers:** see parents; teen-agers.

**fathers and sons:** see adult, the; success; teen-agers.

**fatigue:** Fatigue may take place after violent exercise or after doing nothing. Both physical exertion and lack of interest produce fatigue. So also physical ills, mental depressions, poor nutrition, worry, lack of sleep, over-indulgence, emotional disturbances, "nerves," foot trouble—all may produce similar reactions of fatigue. Fatigue covers a variety of phenomena. It has not yet become a subject of objective measurement. It is one of the commonest of all complaints.

There is no sharp delineation between physical and mental fatigue.

In physical exertion fatigue occurs, it is believed, because food and oxygen are not supplied at a rate sufficient to meet the energy demands and because the wastes are not gotten rid of rapidly enough. Eye strain, tight clothing, loud noises, and a thousand factors play into fatigue.

The use of added vitamins has been advocated as an antidote to fatigue. Yet a scientific study (University of Minnesota) has concluded that vitamin supplementation has no effect on muscular activity, endurance, recovery from exertion or resistance to fatigue. This, of course, implies the added use of vitamins beyond their normal intake in a good diet.

There is no direct relation between fatigue and amount of sleep. If one experiences a lack of rest this alone does not necessarily induce fatigue although there may result a sense of disorganization (same report). Sleep permits normal repair of physical fatigue and may have a beneficial effect on mental fatigue. However, sleep does not necessarily dispose of fatigue which comes by reason of many mental or physical ills.

Physical fatigue does not mean that disease is present. Normal fatigue may be overcome by sleep (if lack of sleep be the factor), by reducing physical work (if too much work is the factor). The state of worry, however, nullifies these benefits.

Mental fatigue is in evidence where interest is lacking in a performance. Aroused interest overcomes the fatigue. Thinking about some disliked task may itself bring about fatigue. Enjoyment tends to dissipate it. Mental conflicts are great sources of fatigue. The fear of fatigue itself may produce fatigue. This is the most difficult type since it moves in a vicious circle: the one promoting the other endlessly.

William James[*] in his essay on "The Energies of Man" pointed out that under pressure fatigue may rise to a critical point and then of a sudden pass away, leaving refreshment. His theory was that a new level of energy has been tapped.

It is common knowledge that fatigue is successfully fought off very frequently by effort, a change, a new pattern of ideas and by excitement. Interests also have the same effect. Worthy goals and ambition fight monotony, the door to fatigue. Group activity makes fatigue less the master.

Anyone knows that a shift of attention halts the oncoming cloud of fatigue. When one is working at a desk it is to his advantage to get up and move around, undertake for a while some task wholly different. The effect on fatigue is amazing. It may require but a few minutes' change of scenery and attention to restore zest for a return to the task initially undertaken. It is well to have several books going simultaneously—reading a variety of topics wards off fatigue. (This writer, in preparing this volume, does not take the subjects alphabetically but the subjects which offer interest at the time, so that the volume develops quite unmechanically and spontaneously. He has more than one book in preparation at the same time. Such variety of interests and simultaneous diversity cut down the fatigue element to a marked degree.) Most music teachers hold, for the same reason, that practices at frequent intervals is much more rewarding than long sustained periods of concentration. See adult, the; autosuggestion; caffeine, psychological effects of; drives; noise disturbances; psychoneuroses; sleep; visions and hallucinations; work and rest.

**fears:** see anxiety states; complexes; counseling periods; deception; emotion; fatigue; fears, conditioned; glands; juvenile delinquency; menopause; phobias; psychology of religion; psychoneuroses; Roman Catholicism and counseling; sublimation.

**fears, conditioned:** Most of our fears are conditioned. It has been observed by controlled experiments (by e.g., John B. Watson*) that a child shows no natural fear of animals or the dark (a common belief is that there are such innate fears). Misguided parents or others have conditioned us to certain fears.

Fears, thus conditioned, are antagonistic to normal development. When such an emotion gets out of hand it may cause great damage to a person.

Under great care it has been shown by experiment that a specific fear may be reconditioned. A child's fear of a white rabbit was overcome by a gradual presentation of the rabbit while the child ate food which he enjoyed. See anxiety states; psychology, schools of.

**feeble-mindedness:** see mental deficiency.

**feeling:** see aesthetic experience; anoetic; emotion; emotive language; intuition; sociometry; sthenic; truth.

**feeling of well being:** see coenesthesis; euphoria.

**feelings, contradictory:** see ambivalence.

**feeling tone:** see coenesthesis; organic sensations.

**fees:** see minister, the, and money; money; sacrifice, a psychological concept.

**female:** see women.

**female climacterium:** see climacterium; menopause.

**female virilism:** see adrenal glands.

**feministic movement:** see sex differences, psychological.

**fiction:** An Adlerian term which will not be new to the philosophers and theologians of the naturalistic schools. It designates the attachment of a person to an impossible goal. It is synonymous with "old-fashioned" idealism (practical but not philosophical idealism) to which many a pre-naturalistic theologian adhered. This term as defined by Adler* suggests an interpretation of those exponents of the "pie-in-the-sky-by-and-by" philosophies. It suggests that the "pie-in-the-sky" enthusiasts do not wish to attain "heaven" but do wish, in reality, to avoid coming to terms with life (as included in nature) as they found it. Many a sermon has ignored salvation by "fictionizing" only to ignore life and life's attainable goals. Fictionizing seems to have a more profound psychological basis than either a philosophical or theological one. See defense mechanisms.

*Bibl.* Gardiner Murphy, *An Historical Introduction to Psychology* (1932); L. F. Schaffer, *The Psychology of Adjustment* (1936); Clara Thompson, *Psychoanalysis: Evolution and Development* (1950); C. G. Jung, *The Collected Papers on Analytical Psychology* (1916) and other materials cited by these texts. W. W. B.

**fifteen-year old, the:** see teen-agers.

**figurative language:** An image is a term designating reference to some sense experience. A concept is not thus imaged. Images enter into what become "figures of speech." A figure of speech is a comparison. The comparison may be confined to but one or few points and only under certain circumstances.

A figurative comparison may be in terms of a simile ("like," "as," "similar" or "same"). Similes may be "closed" or "open" —a closed simile specifies in what respect the comparison is made; an open simile makes no such specific comparison and leaves much to be supplied. The latter is vague and may mean little.

A metaphor does not give or state a comparison but only suggests comparison. A simile must look to a given context to supply meaning; a metaphor looks to a context only for a limit to meaning.

Figures of speech often lead to confused thinking and are avoided where exactness is required.

**figures of speech:** see figurative language.

**first signs of delinquency:** see juvenile delinquency.

**five senses, the:** see sensations.

**fixation:** A term describing an *excessive* emotional attachment to a person or object. It was said by Freud that this attachment was often affixed to parent images of the patient and sapped the strength of his libido* making it impossible for the patient to deal with reality. W. W. B.

**fixed ideas:** see autosuggestion; complexes; psychoneuroses.

**flattery:** see pastoral counseling and case studies.

**flight into health:** A defense mechanism* by which a patient in psychoanalysis* and in psychotherapy* takes flight from further exposure of unpleasant truths by posing apparent health (normalcy). Its difficulty lies in bringing treatment to conclusion at the expense of real cure. This phrase is attributed to Freud* and is employed in psychoanalytic psychology.

**Flournoy, Theodore:** see psychical research and parapsychology.

**Flower, J. Cyril:** see psychology of religion.

**folk psychology:** see group psychology; psychology of religion.

**forgetting:** see defense mechanisms; Freud; memorizing.

**forgiveness:** see confession.

**fortune telling:** see pseudopsychology.

**Fosdick, H. E.:** see sermons, preparation of.

**Foster, G. B.:** see psychology of religion.

**fourteen-year old, the:** see teen-agers.

**frames of reference, psychological:** see psychological frames of reference.

**Frazer, J. G.:** see psychology of religion.

**free association:** The therapeutic technique of reciting whatever "pops" into the mind with the hope of discovering clues with which to unfold the unconscious. This technique is often employed when there is a blockage or a resistance to revealing the true nature of thoughts. It is useless and perhaps even dangerous to employ this technique outside the context of an extreme wealth of information about a patient. It is doubtful that it has much use when employed by the amateur or uninformed counselor. See censor; mental catharsis; projective techniques; psychology of religion; psychology, schools of.

S. Freud's *General Introduction to Psychoanalysis* (1920);

———, *New Introductory Lectures on Psychoanalysis* (1933). W. W. B.

**free responses:** see projective techniques.

**freedom:** see ministry, the, and counseling; psychoanalysis, limitations of; sacrifice, a psychological concept.

**Freud, Sigmund:** (1856-1939) Founder of the psychoanalytic movement, Freud was born in Moravia of Jewish parents. Most of his life he spent in Vienna. As a student of medicine his interests lay in the field of neurology and later he became an enthusiastic student of Charcot\* in Paris (1885-1886). With Joseph Breuer, a Viennese physician, Freud began to combine hypnotism with mental catharsis,\* a method of free expression on the part of patients. The cathartic method replaced hypnosis. Patients were encouraged to relax, speak freely of anything that popped into mind—using the reclining posture as aid to relaxation. Hesitation in free expression was a signal to some important block which especially needed investigation. Early childhood experiences were looked upon as especially important, so also dreams. The disturbing factor, the complex, was probed—the patient's real difficulty. The unconscious mind\* was held to be the seat of trouble and every effort to uncover it sought out. In 1900 his *The Interpretation of Dreams* was published (in German); *Psychopathology in Everyday Life,* a work which enjoyed wide circulation, appeared in 1904. In this volume, an analysis was given of memory lapses, slips of tongue, forgetting of articles, all indicative of unconscious complexes and hence significant.

He developed an intricate theory of the unconscious mind and its repressions. Behavior (he held) is motivated by desires —nearly all of which are rooted in the sexual drive. Repressed childhood sexuality is the cause of the beginning of neurotic responses. All infants reveal sexuality in narcissism or self love, gratified in pleasurable experiences such as sucking, urinating or defecating. The libido or sex urge comes early in life, to be directed to a parent of opposite sex while the other parent becomes the object of refractory wishes.

The censor which keeps repressions from expression represents the demands of moral and social codes. Unconscious desires often by-pass the censor in disguise, appearing in symbols.

In 1902 Freud founded the Viennese Psychoanalytic Society for the discussion of his theories and techniques. He remains a dominant figure in contemporary psychology and has increasingly been taken seriously by the medical profession. Psychoanalysis, however, did not receive recognition until about 1911. Freud visited the United States in 1909, lecturing at Clark University. It was A. A. Brill, one of Freud's first students, who, as translator and interpreter of Freud's writings, helped to establish the psychoanalytic movement in the United States. Dr. Brill founded the New York Psychoanalytic Society in 1911.

Psychoanalytic literature today is of vast proportions. See Adler, Alfred; anxiety states; censor; conscious, pre-conscious, unconscious; dreams; fixation; flight into health; free association; Freudian approach to analysis; Jung, Carl; juvenile delinquency; libido; masochism; phobias; projection; projective techniques; psychoanalysis; psychological frames of reference; psychology of religion; psychology, schools of (psychoanalysis); religion and mental health; repression; sadism; schizophrenia; sublimation.

**Freudian approach to analysis:** Without making reference here to the historical aspects of Freud's principles of psychoanalysis,* we may cite one rather unique factor in a Freudian analysis. Freudian analysis does not stress a reorientation approach. The Freudian analysis tends to help the individual to express the unconscious* and, for the most part, leaves the counseling process at this point. The individual expresses his problems, his feelings about them and attempts are made to relieve the elements of guilt.* There is not usually an attempt to reconstruct the personality in terms of the aspirations (conscious) of the counselee. A cure may suggest that the counselee express himself in terms of what he finds within himself. It would not, in all likelihood, recommend the negation of what is found. In this respect, a Freudian analysis will concentrate upon the experience of the patient or counselee which constructed the personality. Attention to current activities and responses will be valuable in so far as they shed light upon the early and formative personality. The sexual basis of current neurosis is explored. Therapists do not seem to fit neatly into the Freudian approach in its purest form. Each and every psychoanalysis is indebted to Freud.* W. W. B.

**Freudianism:** see Freud; Freudian approach to analysis; psychology of religion; psychoanalysis; psychology, schools of; sex and the counselee.

**friendship:** see confession; pastoral counseling and case studies.

**Fries, H. L.:** see psychology of religion.

**fright:** see anxiety states; fears.

**frugality:** see talents.

**frustrations:** see Adlerian approach to therapy; child training; complexes; divided self; genius; juvenile delinquency; motives; peace and war; psychology of religion; psychology, schools of; psychosomatics; psychotherapy; resolution, the doctrine of; success; worry.

**functional school of psychology:** see Dewey, John; instrumentalism; pragmatism; psychology of religion; psychology, schools of; truth.

**funeral fees:** see minister, the, and money.

**funerals:** As soon as the pastor learns of a death in his congregation, he calls without delay on the family, or the nearest relative. He extends his sympathies and offers his services.

If the relatives have previously gone through the experience of making arrangements for a funeral service, they have, in all probability, already called an undertaker and have some plans in mind. If they have never before had anything to do with making funeral arrangements, they may be at a complete loss as what to do or where to begin. In any case, they usually will seek the pastor's counsel.

Certain decisions have to be made without delay. The services of an undertaker must be engaged. A decision must be made as to the time and place for holding the funeral service. Most undertakers prefer to conduct their funeral services in a funeral parlor where they are prepared to handle almost any and all possible situations. The facilities of the church are always available to all alike, without charge. A decision must be made as to the place of burial, or as to the possibility of cremation. In any event, arrangements must be made with the proper cemetery officials for burial and with the officers of a crematorium if cremation is planned. Usually the undertaker makes these arrangements. Pallbearers must be selected. Usually

**funerals** 94

these are chosen from among the family's friends. In the event the deceased has few friends or relatives, or is an elderly person whose friends may have passed on or are too old to serve as pallbearers, the minister always offers to furnish pallbearers from his congregation. Usually church officers are available for this service. The undertaker usually assumes the responsibility for notifying relatives and friends by telephone or telegraph and putting the proper notices in the newspapers. He will advise concerning the choice of a casket and prepare the necessary legal papers for burial. The family will find it difficult to think clearly or with judgment under the heavy emotional stress and the confusion of the household. The pastor should advise against excessive or unnecessary expense in the purchase of a casket or in the purchase of flowers. He reminds the family that there is no social stigma associated with an inexpensive casket and that floral offerings are exorbitant in cost and money might better go to some worthy cause intended to relieve the sufferings of the living.

Usually, the family will leave details of the funeral service to the pastor. He will, however, ask if there are any special scripture passages they would prefer to have read, whether or not they have any special poetry or music they wish to have used in the service. With the usual newspaper coverage of details, the custom of having an obituary read has passed almost entirely. If the service is to be held in the church, he will arrange with the caretaker for things to be in order, and with the organist to "play the service."

In the great majority of cases, the people will leave the service entirely in the hands of the minister with the suggestion that it not be too long. Just once in the writer's experience (and he has conducted more than a thousand funeral services) did a family come to him just five minutes before the service was to be held with the request that he preach a sermon not less than thirty minutes long. It happened on that occasion that the deceased was a young man who had died in a federal penitentiary. The family were in no way connected with the church. The pastor had intended making no remarks, nor did he make **any**.

Tradition and custom play a large part in the type of service that is conducted. In the average church community, the pastor usually follows the order of service in his denominational book of liturgy. The Episcopal prayer book is widely used by ministers of all denominations. The Methodist and Presbyterian books of Common Worship are excellent and such books as John Hunter's *Devotional Services* are valuable as sources of appropriate scripture readings and prayers for funeral services. In rural communities a funeral service is often a social event. People will come from afar and spend hours afterward visiting with relatives and friends. Public services are usually held for prominent people and often such services are attended by great numbers of people. In the Catholic church services are always held in the morning. In Protestant churches services are usually held in the afternoon, and often at night. The late hour is set to suit the convenience of the family and friends. In the case of cremation the service is always called a memorial service, but is conducted as any other service would be.

Along with the obituary, the old-fashioned long funeral sermon has pretty well disappeared. The pastor will be expected to offer some appropriate remarks—a funeral talk—in which he will pay tribute to the deceased, aimed to say something that will comfort the bereaved and remind the living that death comes to all men alike and it is well to be prepared for it. Services are often read and consist only of scripture selections and prayers. Occasionally the reading of poetry or hymns will be added. Where the pastor is expected to make a few remarks, he must be thoroughly honest and yet sympathetic in what he says. The occasion affords him an opportunity to recognize and extol certain ideals of character and of spirit. But he must not become reckless in his praise of the deceased for he will be judged by the integrity of his remarks. He must not sit in judgment of the deceased but rather recognize his worth and good works and let the Lord take care of the deceased's shortcomings. It is always advisable for a minister to prepare rather carefully any remarks he makes at a funeral service and the prayer he may offer, for frequently he will be asked by the family for written copies of his remarks or his prayers.

In his closing prayer, it is well for him to use some of the great liturgical prayers of the church, and if the occasion calls for it, he should remember the bereaved, the departed, and

# funerals

others—and he should do this in a dignified, restrained, but friendly way.

At the cemetery the pastor will precede the casket to the grave. The custom at the grave varies widely from the reading of scriptures and the making of additional remarks to a simple committal and benedictory prayer. After the burial, he will often return to the home of the bereaved to offer his sympathy and friendship.

Occasionally an unusual situation arises. For example, a family was notified that their son in the Army had been accidentally killed in one of the camps in the Middle West. He was an only son and the family were well-to-do. The father was sick and unable to travel. The pastor offered to drive the mother to the camp. When he arrived on the scene it was discovered that the young man had been detailed to dispose of some high explosive. An accident occurred which detonated the explosive while he was carrying it. They never found even a small piece of his body. According to U. S. Army regulations, the casket was sealed immediately and a military guard assigned to watch it. The mother tried to have the casket opened without succeeding. Unfortunately the officers and chaplain gave her different stories concerning what happened. It was the pastor's duty to get the facts as near as possible and report them as delicately as possible to the mother.

The pastor went into a nearby city, made arrangements with the resident pastor for services to be held. The services were conducted and burial made in a nearby cemetery. This particular case was complicated by the fact that the young man had married a local girl who lived near the camp; and also by the fact that the Army officials had been drinking to excess and that everyone was trying to "cover up." The pastor did much running around in an attempt to get the whole story straight that the family might have the truth and also the assurances and comforts religion can bring under such circumstances.

Funeral services can be overdone. Every effort must be made to prevent an undertaker from commercializing the occasion. The pastor's aim is to observe the more common conventions, but to keep the service on a high spiritual level to avoid the materialistic note as much as possible. J. R. W.

# G

**Gall, Francis J.:** see phrenology.
**Galton, Francis:** see eugenics.
**gambling:** see juvenile delinquency.
**garb:** see minister as a person; self.
**generosity:** see talents.
**genes:** see human genetics.
**genetics:** see human genetics.
**genius:** What constitutes a genius is a matter of definitions and view-points. A person is said to be a genius (Terman and others) if he has an IQ* of over 140. Some place the IQ point at 180. Whatever the point suggested, a genius here is said to be a person of conspicuous intellectual ability. Such a person is sometimes called "gifted" or "precocious" or simply a "prodigy." Others use the term for a person possessing "special aptitudes" (apart from intelligence tests). Popularly, genius is a term for unique achievement in some field.

Most psychologists simply regard a genius as a person of abnormal mental ability—abnormal in the best sense, that of degree, on the plus side of normality. The "abnormality" is being explained by depth psychologists* as the result of inner conflicts. Tradition has it that the genius was some kind of neurotic individual (Lombroso*). This is a half-truth. While some may be neurotic in terms of inner conflicts and difficulties with the social environment, genius generally is neurotic only in the sense of conflict. Such a person may have conflicts (cross-currents) that are resolved and his behavior accepted socially. It is the motivation arising from these frustrations that makes him do the unusual. Psychoanalytic studies suggest that the resolution of conflicts are in a manner that is acceptable to the genius and very often to society. By sublimation rather than repression is the balance achieved. The person is richer for having the conflicts.

Genius is often confused with talent.* As suggested elsewhere people with "talent" may differ not so much in the initial gift of grace but rather because of stimulated interest and stick-to-it-iveness to a task because of the driving interest. See mental age; psychoneuroses.

>   *Bibl.* J. F. Brown, article "Genius" in *Encyclopedia of Psychology* (1946) ed. by P. L. Harriman.

**geriatrics:** see old age.

**gerontology:** see old age; psychology of religion.

**Gesell, Arnold:** see teen-agers.

**Gesell Institute of Child Development:** see teen-agers.

**Gestalt school of psychology:** see creative thinking; psychology, schools of; reading performance; whole reading; whole thinking.

**gestures:** see physiognomy; social perception.

**gifts:** see child training.

**gigantism:** An abnormally large stature which is the result of the hyperfunctioning of the anterior lobe of the pituitary gland.* See endocrine gland.

**girl and boy:** see sex differences, psychological.

**glands:** see adrenal glands; ductless gland; emotion; endocrine gland; parathyroid glands; pituitary gland; thyroid gland.

**glaucoma:** An eye disease characterized by the accumulation of fluid within the eyeball in greater amounts than normal with resulting distortion of the tissues, leading to blindness if untreated. V. H. F.

**gloom:** see anxiety; dysphoria.

**God:** see belief in God; children and religious beliefs; confession; disbelief; ministry, the, and counseling; religion, theistic; religious response, the, nature and origin.

**goiter:** see thyroid gland.

**good and bad:** see conscience; dispositions; morality and psychology; peace and war.

**Gordon, George A.:** see sermons, preparation of.

**gospel:** see social gospel.

**grace:** see confession; ministry, the, and counseling.

**grandparents:** see in-laws.

**graphology:** A pseudo-science which claims to discern the traits of personality from handwriting. Camillo Baldo (Italy) as early as 1662 published a treatise in this field. Writing which was marked by disconnections was said by some later graphologists to reveal a disconnected type of thinking, upward swing in writing to reveal idealistic inclinations. In 1919 Hull and Montgomery after a careful study reported no grounds for the supposed correlation between handwriting and personality. In Europe, however, there continued more scientific interest in the subject. More recent estimate of some scientific psychologists suggests that writing *taken as a whole* may reveal some *general* characteristics of personality. (G. W. Allport and P. E. Vernon, *Studies in Expressive Movement* [1933]). Handwriting is a form of expressive behavior as are gestures, bodily movements in general or "inter-muscle consistency." Some businesses are employing "hand-writing experts" to determine credit risks. European psychologists continue to engage in serious studies of the subject; but, by and large, the field is crowded with charlatans and theoretical enthusiasts. See pseudopsychology.

*Bibl.* Article "Pseudopsychology" by D. H. Yates in *Encyclopedia of Psychology* (1946), edited by P. L. Harriman.

**grasshopper thinker:** see fallacy of distraction.

**gratitude:** see sacrifice, a psychological concept.

**grief:** see emotion; emotional tensions, release of; funerals; pastoral counseling and case studies.

**group mind:** see morale; race psychology.

**group psychology:** see group psychotherapy; psychology of religion; race psychology; sancta of religion; sociometry.

**group psychotherapy:** This term refers to group activities which are controlled by some leader who acts in the capacity of a therapist. Examples: Alcoholics Anonymous,* Y.M.C.A. and Y.W.C.A. guidance groups, the contemporary Oxford Group movement (once called Buchmanism [after Frank Buchman, its founder], now called simply Moral Re Armament —a life changer group which exalts the four absolutes: honesty, purity, love and unselfishness and extols surrender, restitution and sharing as fruits of a changed life).

When an individual becomes a member of a group there are noticeable changes in his attitudes, motives, feelings and behavior toward society. The leader sets the atmosphere. Group therapy appears to have best results if the number is relatively small. Each member may establish more intimate feeling relations with other members in a group of a dozen or so than if the group is larger. Eight is considered an ideal number for intimate group therapy. Stimulation for active interchange of expression is thus promoted. Mixed groups (both sexes) have certain therapeutic advantages,—e.g., the avoidance of a tendency toward individual fixation. A common ground of experiences solidifies the group structure. Fulfillment of needs with social support enhances therapy. When improvement is achieved the individual naturally tends to withdraw until or if there is a recurrence of the need. Much depends on leadership: the warmth of approach, the ability to suggest sincerity in the purpose of the group and a sense of security established to meet frustrations and criticisms (both within and outside the group). The group leader must have had a depth of experience in the cause for which he stands to lay claim to and to hold leadership.

**guess and ESP cards:** see psychical research and parapsychology.

**guidance:** see counseling; group psychotherapy.

**guilt:** see ambivalence; anxiety states; confession; deception; Freudian approach to analysis; ministry, the, and counseling; religion and mental health.

**gustatory sense:** see sensations; taste.

# H

**habit:** see autosuggestion; caffeine, psychological effects of; emotion; motives; reading performance; repetition compulsion; sleep; talents.

**Hadfield, J. A.:** see psychology of religion.

**Hall, G. Stanley:** see psychology of religion.

**hallucination:** An hallucination is a response which, in the absence of the usual external sensory stimuli, purports to be the perception of some object or objective condition and accepted as such, but a condition which otherwise would be subject to serious doubt under the usual circumstances of awareness. Hallucinations may be had in any sensory area, but their most frequent occurrences are in the auditory field. See defense mechanisms; Esquirol, Jean Étienne Dominique; paranoia; paranoid; schizophrenia; visions and hallucinations.

**hamartophobia:** see phobias.

**hand washing, frequent:** see mysophobia; psychoneuroses.

**hand writing:** see graphology.

**handedness:** see dextrality; sinistrality; speech pathology.

**happiness:** see belief in God; displacement; emotion; healthy-mindedness; pleasure; role playing; self; success.

**happiness and success:** see success.

**harmony, inner:** see healthy-mindedness.

**hard work:** see success; talents; work.

**Hartshorne, Hugh:** (1885-    ) Professor emeritus in the psychology of religion at Yale University. He is best known for his studies with Mark A. May\* of character. Some of his publications: *Studies in Deceit* (1928); *Studies in Service and Self-Control* (1929); *Studies in the Organization of Character* (1930). Also *Character in Human Relations* (1932); etc. See deceit (and character).

**Harvard Fatigue Laboratory:** see adult, the.
**hate and love:** see ambivalence.
**hatred:** see emotion; peace and war.
**Haydon, A. E.:** see psychology of religion.
**healing:** see pastoral counseling and case studies; pastoral counseling: case studies; pastoral psychology: its governing limitations and qualifications; therapy; visiting the sick.
**health:** see adult, the; aging process; anxiety states; autosuggestion; emotional tensions, release of; old age; pastoral counseling and case studies; psychosomatics; visiting the sick.
**health, flight into:** see flight into health.
**health, mental:** see adult, the; autosuggestion; mental hygiene; psychology of religion; religion and mental health.
**health, psychic:** see autosuggestion; belief in God; pastoral psychology, its governing limitations and qualifications; psychosomatics; role playing.
**healthy-mindedness:** A term used by William James* to refer to those people for whom "happiness is congenital and irreclaimable." These are the persons for whom life is good in spite of hardships, optimistic, harmonious, "once-born," those who though they miss their mark get up on their feet and try again. In religious outlook such examples are given by James, as: Emerson, Theodore Parker, Spinoza, Walt Whitman, and in such philosophical and religious movements as New Thought and the various forms of Mind-cure. Healthy-mindedness is the opposite of the chronically worried and anxious people who are termed the "sick-souls"* and to whom sickness and trouble are or have been of great concern. See psychology of religion; temperament.
**heart:** see aging process; cardiac patient; hypertension.
**hebephrenia:** A mental disorder occurring early in life in which the sufferer becomes increasingly detached from reality. Emotions are highly disorganized. Behavior exhibits silly manners and often untidiness in personal appearance. See schizophrenia.
**heightened experience:** see visions and hallucinations.

**heightened reaction:** It is commonplace that during a period of counseling or psychological assistance, the reactions of the counselee or patient will be "heightened." This is to say that the counselee will perhaps over-react to the very slightest real manifestation of the anxiety which he confronts. The disturbed personality, it must be remembered, whose behavior, although even anti-social, is reacting to the world about him, usually avoids his honest reactions. Whatever his behavior may be, he is substituting a more peace-giving (or so it would seem to him) behavior for a reaction which creates anxiety. As this person begins to face the basic conflicts of his personality, he will commence to react in a manner less of a substitution. Where, for example, harsh angry words were sufficient, prior to counseling, to produce a mild anxiety, they may during the counseling period produce a heightened reaction. This is all to the good as it gives both the counselor and the counselee an opportunity to see this reaction "writ large" and to decipher its meaning. The reaction will often be directed toward the counselor. Latent hostility will often manifest itself with unrealistic (in that it is incommensurate with any real justification—or should be) vigour. An analysis* can be a stormy affair and the vague anxiety of the problems which prompted his seeking aid may make the counselee feel that he is getting worse before he gets better. It will be wise for the counselor to realize that the counseling process itself accentuates the reactions of the patient or counselee. See counseling periods. W. W. B.

**help, seeking of:** see counseling periods; readiness, principle of.

**hemophilia:** A disease of the blood clotting* mechanism in which a slight injury will produce profuse bleeding in an affected individual. This disease is known to be transmitted genetically via a sex-linked mechanism, and males are much more commonly affected than females. See human genetics. V. H. F.

**Herbart, J. H.:** see psychology, schools of.

**Herbartianism:** see psychology, schools of.

**heredity:** see drives; early environment; eugenics; human genetics; juvenile delinquency; race psychology; talents; temperament.

**heteroeroticism:** see homosexuality.

**heterosexuality:** A term for the normal sexual interest in members of the opposite sex.

**heterosuggestion:** see autosuggestion.

**high blood pressure:** see psychosomatics.

**history:** see minister, the, and his books.

**hives:** see psychosomatics.

**Hodgson, Richard:** see psychical research and parapsychology.

**holy things of religion:** see sancta of religion.

**home:** see family; sex differences, psychological.

**home and in-laws:** see in-laws.

**home environment:** see child training; family, influence of; juvenile delinquency; parents; talents; teen-agers.

**homo-duplex:** see divided self; split personality.

**homosexuality:** The term refers to the sexual attraction toward individuals of the same sex. The term may or may not apply to erotic contact. In psychoanalysis* the term refers to a stage in the development of personality in which members of the same sex are attracted to each other. This is regarded in psychoanalysis as the second stage (the first being that of autoeroticism* and the final being heteroeroticism). See Lesbianism; schizophrenia.

**honesty:** see deceit (and character).

**honorarium:** see minister, the, and money.

**Hopkins, E. W.:** see psychology of religion.

**hormic psychology:** see McDougall, William; psychology, schools of.

**hormone:** An organic chemical compound secreted by an endocrine gland. See endocrine gland; menopause. V. H. F.

**hospital chaplain, the (Protestant):** During the twenty-five years from 1925 to 1950 significant changes took place in the field of the hospital chaplaincy. During this period a great many articles and books appeared which pointed up the important role that the minister ought to play on the healing team.

The Rev. Anton Boisen,* the father of this movement, was himself for a time a patient at a mental hospital. There he became aware of the absence of a religious ministry. As his own mental health improved he gave himself enthusiastically to encouraging mental hospitals to provide chaplains who could understand and minister to the needs of mental patients. Not long after, he himself became chaplain of the state hospital at Worcester, Massachusetts. This marked the beginning of the modern clinical training movement in theological education, for almost immediately he arranged to have a few theological students spend the summer with him in the hospital. They were made welcome, given the freedom of the hospital and were even invited to sit in on meetings of the psychiatric staff.

Since 1927 hundreds of students and pastors have spent from six weeks to a year in clinical centers at mental hospitals, general hospitals and penal institutions. These students have been impressed with the friendly reception given them by psychiatrists, physicians and prison authorities. It has not only added a new dimension to theological education, but it has contributed immeasurably to the building and strengthening of the interprofessional relationship between medicine and theology.

What Anton Boisen did to show that mental hospitals could be used in theological education, Russell Dicks* and Dr. Richard C. Cabot* did for general hospitals. For years medical interns had been permitted to practice under careful supervision in general hospitals. Now it was seen that at the same time that theological students were helpful to patients in a hospital, they could be improving their ability in pastoral care. Massachusetts General Hospital in Boston was one of the first hospitals to invite divinity students to serve under a chaplain.

These early seminars and internship programs were largely centered around techniques and psychological insights which would aid the student in his approach to and in his understanding of the patient. More recently there has been an increased emphasis on the specific nature of the pastor's role as he ministers in the clinical situation. The theological implications of his work with people have become the center of clinical seminar discussions. In fact most of the students undergoing the clinical experience are doing so under the sponsorship of their own seminary faculty, thus encouraging the integration of theory and practice.

The hospital chaplain has not "left the ministry." He considers himself a full time pastor. In fact he can easily show that he now does more specifically "pastoral work" than he was able to do in the parish. He is no longer bothered by many of the routine problems and irritations of the parish pastor. He need not, for instance, get bogged down with the mechanics of administration and money raising, nor does he have to drive many thousands of miles each year just to get to his parishioners. His "parishioners" are all within easy walking distance. Because of these advantages he is able to spend the greater part of each day in pastoral conversations with individuals. As every pastor knows, he can do his best work in the "one-to-one" relationship and particularly when the person is under the kind of stress that forces him to look deep within himself.

Hospital chaplains have become very much aware of the great amount of talking that is required of them. They are reminded that this is true also of every parish minister. Yet they have come to see that the average minister does only about five percent of his talking from a pulpit or a platform. This means that the other ninety-five percent is carried on in conversations with people. The question that naturally follows is, how much of the minister's conversation can be described as "pastoral" in nature? When the pastor talks with people is something different happening? Or are his conversations just like those of anyone else? These are questions which the hospital chaplain insists need to be discussed. Because the minister spends so much of his time in such relationships he ought carefully to analyze those relationships in order to be a good steward of his time.

The hospital chaplain knew that when the doctor entered the patient's room, a particular kind of conversation took place. Because the chaplain worked so closely with the doctors he became self-conscious at this point and asked himself whether his own conversations could be described as unique. If they were not unique, why weren't they? If there was such a thing as a pastoral conversation he wanted to know how he could carry it on in a way natural to his own personality and at the same time center it around the essentials of the Christian message.

Because the chaplain was working with a team of professional people he soon saw the specific ways in which they went about helping people. When they talked with patients they seemed to know what they were doing. This definiteness gave the patient a feeling of being in competent hands. By comparison, the minister felt that his ways were vague, uncertain and undefined. He wished that he might have a better idea of what he could do for people. With this in mind the chaplain encouraged ministers to come in to use his clinical facilities for research in pastoral care in the hope that this would hasten the development of an undergirding theory upon which to build a better Christian ministry to those who were ill.

In one sense then it can be said that the hospital chaplain became a specialist in conversation. As he, with his colleagues, studied the exceptional opportunities the hospital offered for conversing with people under stress he became convinced that pastors were not using their time to the best advantage. The questions which he and his fellow chaplains have been raising for the past twenty-five years have undoubtedly stimulated some of the present great interest in pastoral counseling. It was due in some part to these hospital workshops that a good beginning has been made in the study of methods and content of pastoral counseling.

The few specific rites which the average minister conducted in the sick room caused the chaplain seriously to question such perfunctory handling of holy things. He sensed that most pastors believed that the reading of Scripture or the prayer were the only important things they could do in a sick room. When asked about their conversations they described them as just so much "chit chat," with the prayer tacked on and totally unrelated to it. The chaplain saw the *entire* conversation, as having the possibility of becoming sacramental in nature. He believed that to think of it as anything less than this was to miss completely the tremendous opportunities of going down to a deeper conversational level with the patient. In order to prove this conviction he then tediously wrote out, as best he could remember them, page after page of conversations he had had with patients. Then with the aid of some of his colleagues he made a careful study of his exact words as he responded to the expressed feelings of the patient. It gradually became clear that he was not accomplishing very much because he was unconsciously centering the conversation around himself rather than the patient. His calls were much more "pastor centered" than "patient centered." When he asked himself why this was so, it brought forth a great flood of psychological material concerning himself and the dynamics in his own relationships to people. This, in part, explains why the minister who is willing to submit his work to such careful analysis must be prepared for what at times may be an overwhelming psychological as well as theological experience.

Seminary courses in Pastoral Theology are going through a thorough overhauling these days and are being taught in a very different manner than formerly. The hospital chaplain is somewhat responsible for this. He has helped to bring clergymen face to face with their inadequacies in the area of personal relationships and has demonstrated that something can be done about it. Some of the specific things chaplains have developed in order to bring new light into the field of pastoral theology may be listed under the following four headings:

1. The art of pastoral conversation.
2. The need for pastoral guidance in crisis situations.
3. The interrelationship of medical and theological education.
4. The role of the nurse in religious ministry to patients.

1. *The art of pastoral conversation.*

The hospital chaplain has seen that the minister must learn to talk to all kinds and conditions of men. Until recently there was no way to teach the art of conversation to ministers. The seminary classroom did not lend itself to such discussion, but the clinical situation did. Then chaplains began experimenting with many different methods of teaching their students. Their classes were small enough to give each student a chance to describe in detail what he said when he talked with individuals. The chaplain as a pedagogue was not bound by any long established traditions so he felt free to experiment with a variety of methods. Five methods which have been found unusually helpful in developing the art of pastoral conversation are:

a. The tutorial method. This is much like the medical internship, for the student accompanies his instructor on "rounds" and observes first-hand the approach of an experienced pastor.

While it is true that "three is a crowd" in most pastoral conversations, much can happen in the early interviews with patients which can help establish the foundation for deeper level talks. The student learns much as he watches the teacher establish the kind of rapport necessary for future contacts. Occasionally the patient is under such stress when the chaplain and his intern enter the room that a full blown counseling experience takes place despite the presence of a third person.

b. The "What would you say?" quiz. This quiz has been developed particularly for group teaching. However, it can also be used with individuals. Here a previously written verbatim conversation is given to the student with all the pastor's statements deleted. He is then asked to write down immediately (under the same kind of pressure present in a conversation) what he would say or do each time the patient pauses for the pastor to respond. What a student writes down reveals amazingly well the type of approach he customarily would use. When this test is used with a group of students, all are interested to see how the others have handled this problem. Such a method can be used with an infinite variety of counseling situations and stimulates the kind of discussion which every instructor knows to be valuable because every student in the class has involved himself in the problem by what he has written.

c. The controlled interview method, or role playing. This is another group device for helping a student study his methods of conversing with people. Here the instructor (or someone else) plays the role of a patient whose problem is such that pastoral care is needed. A first student interviews the "patient" in front of the class. During this interview two other students have remained out of the room. The conversation is tape-recorded. When this first student finishes, a second student from outside the room comes in for his turn. The instructor again plays the role of the same patient with the same problem. The class then can see how a second and finally a third student handles the "same" problem in pastoral care. When the third student has finished then the interviews are played back on the recorder for the class to analyze. In this way the students who were out of the room get a chance to analyze all three. The recorded conversations have the advantage over the written ones in that many feeling tones which do not show on paper come out in one's voice. While this method is somewhat artificial, it, nevertheless, has unusual teaching features in that so many things related to mannerism, voice and carriage can be pointed out on the spot. It is valuable also as a periodic testing technique for it picks up bad habits in bed-side manners which may unconsciously have been picked up along the way.

d. The case write-up. After the student has accompanied the instructor on rounds, has participated in several "What would you say?" quizzes and has satisfactorily passed the controlled interview ordeal, it is considered safe to allow him to call on patients in the hospital. He is asked to see a small number of people each day and write up in detail one conversation which he considers to be significant. It is surprising how much of a call can be remembered when one concentrates on it. As a part of the write-up and in addition to the verbatim recording of what he said and what the patient said, he is required to analyze the conversation both psychologically and theologically. In the psychological analysis he tries to describe what he sees in terms of the inner dynamics at work in this person. In the theological analysis he looks back over this significant conversation to think through the theological implications of what was said as well as the pastoral opportunities which now present themselves. In other words, he addresses himself to the ever present question, "What am I, a minister, doing here?"

e. The case study critique. When a student turns in a case write-up which has exceptional teaching value, the case is mimeographed, with all identifying material eliminated, and given to the students a few days in advance of the class. They are asked to react in a carefully thought-through critique without consulting any other students. These thoughtfully written statements, each coming at the problem from a particular point of view, then become the basis of a two hour rapid fire discussion. For the student who wrote the original case, this is often quite a traumatic experience. Yet he usually comes out of the session with a much better understanding of himself. Some students say they have been shaken up and humbled by it. Others say that their own obvious defensiveness throughout the discussion forced them to see in themselves what previously they had been able to see only in others.

2. *The need for pastoral guidance in crisis situations.*

The hospital chaplain has shown the importance of having a minister available to give spiritual guidance to people in time of crisis. Through the years he has shown that patients are exceedingly grateful for the services of a hospital pastor whose spirit is warm and understanding. He has demonstrated that individualized pastoral care to fewer people is much better than superficial care to many.

Chaplains in the nineteen twenties were expected to "visit" scores of patients every day, to greet them, pass the time of day, offer a prayer or read Scripture and be on their way. These men were kept very busy making their rounds. The average amount of time spent with each patient was about four minutes. If a doctor had visited his patients in the same way it would have done them little or no good. A sense of futility came over many of these chaplains as they realized that what they were doing could be done by any intelligent Christian layman with no formal theological education. Yet for years and years the chaplains did nothing about changing their method of ministry. Looking at it realistically it was probably because most chaplains had already retired from the active ministry and were too weary to fight any more battles. It remained for the young men who entered the hospital chaplaincy as a career to show that such superficial visiting of patients fell far short of the goal of meaningful pastoral care.

As hospital boards of directors began encouraging their chaplains to see fewer patients, but to see them better, new and deep level experiences began to take place between patient and minister. There was now an opportunity not only to sow the seed but to take the time necessary to prepare the ground for that seed. The chaplain now found himself ministering to people who consciously or unconsciously were wanting the kind of care he could offer them. He was no longer distressed by having to spend the majority of each day in small talk. Nor did he have to walk out on patients, due to his four minute time limit, just when the conversation was coming alive.

3. *The interrelationship of medical and theological education.*

The hospital chaplain has helped bridge the gap between medicine and religion, or between physicians and clergymen. While the doctor and the minister have always met each other in the local hospital, their meeting has usually been of the casual type. Although both were ministering to the same patient there was little genuine understanding of how each could aid the other.

A new day now seems to be dawning in this inter-professional relationship. Both doctors and ministers are saying that they ought to know each other much better. They realize that when a patient is ill the whole patient is ill and not just part of him. The strong emphasis today on the wholeness of man is influencing medical as well as theological education. For years some seminaries have included medical doctors as regular lecturers. It now appears that medical schools are willing to consider having an occasional lecture by a clergyman. The hospital chaplain who works closely with doctors every day of the week, who learns to know them as friends in the coffee shop and dining room, is making no small contribution toward a "team" concept of pastoral and medical care. The general acceptance of the chaplain in a medical setting is striking evidence that the gap between the two professions is shrinking fast.

4. *The role of the nurse in religious ministry to patients.*

The hospital chaplain has called attention to the value of the nurse as a co-worker with the pastor as well as with the physician. The church through its many hospital schools of nursing has for years been the primary institution in the nursing education field. But it was not until the clinically trained chaplain came on the scene that embarrassing questions began to be asked about the training of the nurse in understanding and dealing with the religious needs of the patient.

The hospital chaplain was keenly aware of his dependence upon the nurse to help him get to those patients who most need him. This is why he was shocked to learn that Christian hospitals gave no training in the religious aspects of illness. Their nurses were no more prepared to assist the pastor than graduates of a county hospital. He insisted that courses in religion and health be inaugurated. Such courses have helped the nurse to see that there is much more to her work than the technical aspects of caring for the bodily needs of her patients. She spends much more time with the patient than either the physician or the pastor and is often in the room at the very moment when the patient is wrestling with inner spiritual problems. In fact, it is said that there is more solid thinking going on in hospitals than in any other building in the community. To minimize the importance of her conversations with patients during these moments of crisis is to overlook one of the great potential strengths of the nurse-patient relationship. It stands to reason that the mature Christian nurse can bring her religious resources to bear in a way that will add new dimensions to the concept of the wholeness of man.

The next quarter century should see some significant developments in the field of religion and health. While it cannot be said that pioneering days are over, at least a trail has been made and we expect scores of hardy clergymen to set out on it, broadening the trail and then going out in all directions to explore areas related to it. To sum up, we quote from an editorial in the *Journal of Medical Education* for January 1954. This Journal is read widely by deans and professors in medical schools:

"Recently, at the University of Chicago Medical School an interesting experiment has been started. An understanding and experienced young chaplain has been made a member of the staff. He will visit the sick . . . and will work with the doctors studying the patient and going over his social and spiritual problems. All deans of medical schools will be interested in seeing how well this experiment works out. It is a fine move forward. A few physicians may be skeptical at first, but in time they probably will be won over." G. E. W.

**hostility:** see heightened reaction.

**hot tempered:** see temperament.

**hours of the day, and efficiency:** see efficiency and time of day.

**House, R. E.:** see deception.

**Hugo, Victor:** see aging process.

**human behavior:** see behavior.

**human drives:** see drives.

**human efficiency:** see efficiency and time of day.

**human genetics (heredity):** A specialized subdivision in the general field of genetics. The basic laws of genetics were first described by Gregor Mendel, an Augustinian monk, in the year 1866 following his astute observations on the breeding of pea plants. He described the inheritance of certain characteristics of these plants (color, size, texture, peas per pod) as being passed on to the filial generation in very definite and predictable manners if the breeding was controlled (Mendel's Laws). His descriptions were made in spite of the fact that the science of cytology (the microscopic nature of cells) was still in the early embryonic stage. Present-day theories of cellular structure state that the nucleus of each body cell contains minute, darkly-staining bodies called "chromosomes," which have been found to be very definite in number and structure for each species of animal and plant. Further theory postulates that these chromosomes are individually made up of smaller, precisely arranged particles of nucleo-protein called "genes." These genes behave similarly to enzymes (organic catalysts) and each affects a certain biochemical reaction in the organism. Thus such bodily characteristics as eye color, hair texture, bone growth, blood groups and a myriad of others are determined by the action and type of one or more of these genes. The human species has twenty-four different pairs of chromosomes, each one of which is found in every body cell (except in the germ cells where one member of each pair is found). Each chromosome presumably contains several hundreds of different genes. Each gene, in turn, may exist in one or more closely related forms called "alleles," and each of these alleles may affect the gene-determined characteristic in varying degrees from that of the "normal" gene. The mathematical possibilities of differences among members of the same species is thus obvious, but so-called races are set apart from other groups by the retention of a greater percentage of similar or "basic" genes. Progressive fixed differences in individuals and species (evolution) are accounted for on the basis of a definite change in gene structure and expression and the retention of those changes which are beneficial to the organism (natural selection). These gene changes are called "mutations." Mutations naturally occur at an extremely slow rate and in a very unpredictable manner, but certain artificial methods may be used to accelerate their occurrence (rate but not location). Such methods include: heat, certain drugs, ultra-violet light, x-rays, and atomic irradiation. Since most mutations are harmful (recessive) to the organism, it becomes obvious that indiscriminate present-day use of x-ray equipment in medical and non-medical (industry, shoe-fitting, etc.) activities may seriously increase the rate of these harmful mutations. Even more alarming to the human race should be the realization of the potentials of danger that exist with the unregulated use of atomic energy in war or peace. The full effects of the mutagenic nature of atomic irradiation is now under study in the exposed Japanese population. Various unique statistical analyses of genetic data have been devised for the study of human populations since the family size is small, controlled matings impossible, and the generation span so long. The advancements made in the relatively recent history of human genetics have been quite remarkable. Several physical characteristics (albinism, blood clotting,* color perception) and several diseases (certain anemias, certain types of cancer, certain types of neurological conditions, etc.) have been shown to be transmitted through the genetic mechanism. Still far from being settled is the age-old argument of the relative values of heredity and environment in determining such abstract measurements as I.Q., "talent," criminality, etc. Studies on twins, both fraternal and identical, have been helpful. It is quite apparent that in some instances gene "expression" is very capable of being modified by the environment.

*Bibl.* The interested reader is referred to any recent text on the general principles of genetics only a few of which are listed below. There are also listed some texts on the subject of human genetics.

Laurence H. Snyder, *The Principles of Heredity*, 4th ed. (1951).

A. M. Winchester, *Genetics* (1951).

Curt Stern, *Principles of Human Genetics* (1949).

Horatio H. Newman, F. N. Freeman, and K. J. Holzinger, *Twins: A Study of Heredity and Environment* (1937).

UNESCO Publication: *What is Race?* Distributed by Columbia University Press. V. H. F.

**human interrelationships:** see pastoral counseling and case studies; sociometry.

**humanism, religious:** see positivism.

**humidity:** see atmospheric conditions and work capacity.

**humiliation:** see complexes.

**humor:** see child training; sermon.

**hunger:** see drives; organic sensations.

**husbands and wives:** see marriage, disharmony in; sex differences, psychological.

**hydrocephalus:** A developmental abnormality of the cranium and brain in which there is an overproduction (or decreased drainage) of the cerebro-spinal fluid within the cavities of the brain. This results in marked distension of the brain and cranium with the production of a large head. A certain degree of hydrocephalus is compatible with life. Recently, surgical attempts to reduce the fluid-secreting tissues by cautery have been made with some success. V. H. F.

**hygiene, mental:** see mental health.

**hymns:** see symbols.

**hyperhidrosis:** An excessive activity of the sweat glands.

**hyperkinesis:** An intense restless activity. See hyperthyroidism.

**hyperpituitarism:** A condition characterized by a large head, thick lips, large chest, short arms and legs, large hands, etc. Acromegaly is a hyperpituitary disorder, the symptoms being physical abnormalities (enlargements) described as gradual changes after the age of twenty. See pituitary gland.

**hypertension:** In general the term means an excessive mental strain or an excessively nervous anxiety. In "essential hypertension" the principal causes are known to be prolonged worries* and anxieties. Hypertension is also the designation for high blood pressure.* See endocrine gland.

**hypertension:** A physiological state of the cardiovascular system in which the blood pressure is elevated over that of normal. The force of contraction of heart muscle is measured by the distance (height) that a column of mercury may be driven by that force. This is called the systolic pressure.* The heart during rest, i.e., between contractions, continues to maintain a measurable pressure called the diastolic pressure.* An elevated blood pressure may be due to many causes some of which may be: kidney* disease, arteriosclerosis,* hyperthyroidism,* psychogenic* mechanisms, etc. See shock (physiological). V. H. F.

**hyperthyroidism:** Excessive activity of the thyroid gland* which brings on loss of weight, hyperhidrosis* and irritability. The disorder caused by hyperthyroidism, the principal symptoms of which are protrusion of the eyeballs, muscular tension, hypertension* and irritability, is called exophthalmus.

**hypnosis, self:** see autosuggestion.

**hypnotism:** see analysis; Charcot, Jean Marie; Freud, S.; psychical research and parapsychology; speech pathology.

**hypocrisy:** see self.

**hypoparathyroidism:** see parathyroid glands.

**hypophysis:** see pituitary gland.

**hypopituitarism:** A deficiency in the secretions of the pituitary gland.* Psychotic disorders resembling schizophrenia* have been noted in connection with this dysfunction. See endocrine gland.

**hypothalamus:** A specific area at the base of the brain* in which is located the center of the autonomic nervous system,* the thermo-regulatory center of the body, the nerve tracts controlling the pituitary gland* and certain other vegetative functions. See thalamus. V. H. F.

**hysteria:** see Charcot, Jean Marie; conversion hysteria.

# I

**Id, the, the ego, and the super ego:** These pychoanalytic terms will be defined together as they can only be distinguished by comparisons. The *Id*, or the "it," is the equivalent to the "unconscious": the source of the libido,* or "psychic energy." Hedonistic in character, "it" has no contact with reality save through the mediation of the *Ego*.

The *Ego*, or the "I," is partly conscious and partly unconscious. The Ego grows and develops through association and contact with reality. It represses unwanted urges by forcing them into the realm of the unconscious, or Id.

The *Super Ego* is the "acquired" self and is the critic of the Ego, or its "conscience."*

The Super Ego and the Id wage war upon one another. The Ego is the battleground of this conflict. See censor; psychology, schools of. W. W. B.

**ideas:** see a priori; creative thinking; minister, the, and his books; occupational prejudice; reasoning; symbols; thinking.

**ideo-motor theory:** see learning.

**idiots:** see mental deficiency.

**idleness:** see creative thinking.

**ignorance, appeal to:** see fallacy of argumentum ad ignorantiam.

**Ilg, Frances L.:** see teen-agers.

**illness:** see anxiety states; autosuggestion; glands; hospital chaplain, the; menopause; mental disorders; nosophobia; pastoral counseling and case studies; pastoral psychology: its governing limitations and qualifications; psychoanalysis; psychology of religion; psychosomatics; psychotherapy; religion and mental health; sacrifice, a psychological concept; sleep; visiting the sick.

**illumination:** see creative thinking; intuition.
**illusion:** see religion and mental health.
**image:** see autosuggestion; dreams; figurative language; symbols.
**imagination:** see anxiety states; autosuggestion; child training; children and religious beliefs; creative thinking; dreams; memory; minister, the, and his books; phantasy; sermon; symbols.
**imbeciles:** see mental deficiency.
**imitation:** see learning; personality; talents.
**immediate senses:** see symbols.
**immortality:** see life after death.
**impotence, sexual:** see psychoneuroses.
**impressions:** see self.
**impulses:** see censor; drives.
**impulses, neural:** see synapses.
**inattention:** see juvenile delinquency.
**inborn determinants:** see determinants; heredity; talents.
**income groups:** see success.
**inconsistencies of self:** see self.
**incubation:** see creative thinking; intuition.
**independence:** see old age; sacrifice, a psychological concept; social maturation.
**indifference:** see complexes.
**individual:** see personality; race psychology; self.
**individual achievement:** see achievement; creative thinking.
**individual differences:** see mental age; social maturation.
**individual psychology:** see Adler, Alfred.
**individuality:** see Jungian approach to therapy.
**indoctrination:** see children and religious beliefs; pastoral counseling and case studies.
**induction:** see a posteriori.
**industrial economy:** see pastoral counseling and case studies.
**ineffability:** see intuition.
**inertia:** see boredom.
**infants:** see children and religious beliefs.
**inferiority complex:** see Adler, Alfred; Adlerian approach to

therapy; complexes; juvenile delinquency; motives; personality; psychology of religion; psychology, schools of (psychoanalysis).

**inherited factors:** see early environment; heredity; human genetics; talents.

**inhibitions:** see alcohol and efficiency; complexes; sex differences, psychological; work inhibitions.

**initiative:** see social maturation.

**in-laws:** Many family difficulties come about in relation to in-laws. This is natural since there is introduced into the parental family relationship members who are strangers to the family tradition and mores.

A very common mistake on the part of mothers-in-law (and fathers-in-law) is, in their eagerness to continue giving concern and services to their "children," that they tend to forget that marriages establish new units which are other than the old home unit. There is always friction invited when interference comes about with respect to the new family unit no matter how high the intentions of those nestling in the old unit.

A good rule to follow, it would seem, would be for parents* to restrain themselves from giving specific advice, aid and services until such counsel and help are sought by the "children." Over-eagerness begets difficulties. Parents do well to turn to new interests and respond overtly to their married children when that response is genuinely sought. A son-in-law and daughter-in-law must be made to feel that it is up to them now to show a specific interest in the continuation of the relationship (unique with their partner) and to carry it as a definite responsibility on their part. It is no longer the requirement of a parent to cover with its wings the youngsters who have left the home nest, by furnishing them with either money, sustenance, undue favors or advice. If children have any spark of appreciation for those whose concern is emotionally deep they will turn to the parents both in days of joy and sorrow for the continuation of the hallowed relationship of the home of which one of them was an intimate member and for which they both must be grateful.

In our type of civilization the maintenance of separate households is a *desideratum* which can not too strongly be advocated. Children can not expect to begin their own family units at the economic level of their parents, nor should parents regard their remaining years (after the children are grown and married) as other than their own lives in new dimensions and interests, with their right to their own privacy and security.

If in-laws do not seek to foster a happy and even intimate relationship with the parents of their married partner they should only blame themselves if such parents turn to others who appreciate their love and friendship. There are instances where a younger generation of one family becomes the object of more intimate relationships with older people of another family, who are pleased to share with them. This substitution of relationship must be considered normal where the circumstances foster them. One grandparent has declared: "Look about you. . . . and I am sure you, too, can find opportunities to spend your love as grandparents where it will be welcome." It goes without saying, however, that the flesh and blood relationship is sentimentally deep in all involved—both parents and their real sons and daughters—and the in-laws, on both sides, must *earn* the privilege of good relationships where they do not come by them so readily as by ties of blood.

But all said and done, much of the responsibility lies with the younger in-laws since it may be taken for granted that the older generation naturally seeks the good of those who were so much a part of themselves and who through the years have so generously spent themselves for their children in sacrifice and love.

**innate ideas:** see a priori.
**inner conflicts:** see conflicts, inner.
**inner light:** see conscience; intuition.
**insanity:** see criminal types; mental deficiency.
**insight:** see intuition.
**insomnia:** see anxiety states; menopause; sleep; visions and hallucinations.
**inspirational books:** see pastoral psychology: its governing limitations and qualifications.
**instinct:** The classical definition of instinct was formulated by William McDougall\* (*An Introduction to Social Psychology*, 14th ed., 1921, p. 30): "an inherited or innate psycho-physical disposition which determines its possessor to perceive, and to pay attention to, objects of a certain class, to experience an

emotional excitement of a particular quality upon perceiving such an object, and to act in regard to it in a particular manner, or, at least, to experience an impulse to such action."

In the literature of psychoanalysis* the concept of instinct refers to the inner drives* of action which bring about tensions in the human personality.

The list of these innate dynamic determinants was, in the earlier psychology, both popular and academic, a long one (e.g. Thorndike*); but in behavioristic psychology* the list was reduced to zero and in place of instincts three emotional (visceral) responses were named to be elemental (fear, love, rage). Many contemporary psychologists shun listings since the term is itself too broad, covering as it does a complex pattern of unlearned impulses or drives.

Psychologists, remembering the fallacy of reification of abstractions,* realize the danger of ascribing to the generic word "instinct" the category of concrete explanation of specific human behaviors. Such an explanation would be like saying that things fall because of gravity where gravity is only the name for the fact that things fall. To explain religious behavior as due to a religious instinct may be to say no more than that people are religious because they are religious. Moreover, remembering the law of parsimony,* psychologists avoid increasing categories of explanation since such procedure ends only in confusion. To say that a person sings because he possesses a musical instinct, that as a child he manipulates blocks because of a building instinct, that he is an artist because of an art instinct, and that he is religious because he is possessed of a religious instinct, is not only not adding information but multiplying entities (in this case instincts) beyond necessity or beyond clarification. Knowledge is not gained by multiplication of concepts but by simplification.

It is more illuminating to explain the religious response as the result of many drives* and motives* none of which singly furnishes the sole basis for the response. See children and religious beliefs; religious response, the, nature and origin; psychology, schools of (Wm. McDougall).

**instincts:** see death instinct; fallacy of the reification of abstractions; psychology of religion; pugnacious instinct.

**Institute of Pastoral Care at the Massachusetts General**

**Hospital:** see Cabot, Richard C.

**Institute of Social and Religious Research:** see deceit (and character).

**institutionalism:** see children and religious beliefs; pastoral counseling and case studies; pastoral psychology; psychology of religion; sancta of religion.

**instrumentalism:** This term is given to that version of functionalistic psychology represented by John Dewey.*

In brief, mind and ideas are tools of adjustment (like hands, feet, eyes, etc.). They serve as instruments of adjustment. This is their biological function. In the case of thought: we have thoughts much in the pattern of habit but at such level thoughts are not "thinking." Thinking is an active process of adjustment to a new and baffling situation. Ideas are instruments to resolve the difficulty. When resolved, thinking is no longer necessary and routine thoughts take over. An idea is true if in a situation it resolves a problem with success. Conversely, it is false if it fails.

We need no such concepts as the traditional "soul" says Dewey. Mind is a biological tool of the psychophysical organism. It serves a biological purpose such as any instrument of the body. It is an adaptive instrument, teleological in character. It is folly to speculate beyond the vista of our world. (This is positivism,* for which Dewey gave his full self in the attempt to reform traditional philosophy.) Our business is to get on, use our tools, cope with Nature and recreate it if and where possible for advantages of adjustment. All education is thus instrumental (adaptation to life situations); so also religion where it serves this fuller adaptation (not speculation or dogmas about a world unknown or unknowable or falsely knowable); so also psychology in the whole business of getting on with our fellowmen and ourselves by a better understanding of how we tick. His book *How We Think* (1910) is the standard exposition of instrumentalism in the area of reflection. See psychology, schools of.

**insulin shock:** see shock therapy.

**insurance:** see minister, the, and money.

**integration:** see psychology of religion.

**integration of the self:** see psychoneuroses; psychotherapy; self.

**integrity:** see minister, the, and money; self.
**intellectuals:** see symbols.
**intelligence and tests:** see adult, the; I.Q.; memory; mental age; social maturation.
**intelligence quotient:** see I.Q.
**interest:** see adult, the; aging process; children and religious beliefs; emotional tensions, release of; fatigue; genius; sermon; success; talents.
**interrelationships, human:** see sociometry.
**introspection:** see psychology, schools of.
**introversion:** A person is said to be introverted when he is typically self-conscious and given to turn in on himself rather than spontaneously express himself. Introversion may become morbid. It is the opposite of extraversion.* See belief in God; Jungian approach to therapy; talents.
**introvert and extravert:** see Jungian approach to therapy.
**intuition:** An intuition may be defined as a manner of knowing which comes not by discursive reasoning or by the stimuli of sensations (or both) but by an inner grasp or comprehension, directly (without analysis) and with the force of immediate possession. Psychologists have spoken of intuition as "the unconscious notice" taken of things. An intuition may appear to have no relation with the usual manner of knowledge but this is probably a misunderstanding. It has a history: an intuition is the name for the fruition of the many impressions of sensory awareness and the incubations of thought processes which combine in new relationships illuminating the mind, a fruition ofttimes coming with a suddenness that is startling. An intuition is not so much a special way of knowing as it is the re-formation of relationships in experience which present the material in a way that is fresh and enlightening.

A mystic is one who looks to intuitive knowledge as the base of understanding and insight. He often believes he has discovered a special *modus operandi*: using techniques to force the insight (relaxation,* concentration, etc.). His characteristic manner of speaking is his claim to possess an altogether unique source of knowledge. William James* points out four characteristics of mysticism: it is 1) ineffable (quality of superintellectualism); 2) noetic (illuminating in knowledge value; 3) transient (comes and goes); and 4) passive (the subject doing little or nothing about it).

It is undoubtedly true that some knowledge comes by way of a sweep, like the all-at-once grasp of motion in which particulars are submerged. Some thinkers believe that reason itself is too confined to the units of particulars ever to present the total sweep (such as motion) of certain experiences and they therefore claim that intuition is that special quality of mind which transcends analysis.

It probably would be correct to suggest that reason may itself be both analytic and synoptic and that in the latter phase the term intuition is an appropriate designation. There is, of course, no appropriateness in designating an intuition apart from reason (in this broad sense); for, if an intuition were *beyond* reason, there would be no knowledge whatsoever (perhaps, only the vaguest kind of feeling). See aesthetic experience; conscience; creative thinking; truth.

**involuntary movement test:** see deception.

**I.Q.:** IQ stands for "intelligence quotient." This is the figure which is obtained by dividing an individual's mental age* rating by the norm for his particular chronological age. Opinion varies as to what constitutes the norm or "basal year" for adults (whose I.Q. is held not to increase after the sixteenth year). The Stanford-Binet scale, originally standard, gave sixteen as the norm for the average adult (result of studies with several thousand California school children). In the Army entrance examinations, however, the average rating was tested and found to be somewhat less than fourteen years (tests given to thousands of men). Psychologists now feel that the original norm was too high and are using fourteen as the basal year. See adult, the; genius; human genetics; mental age; mental deficiency; social maturation; S.Q.; success.

Bibl. F. L. Wells, *Mental Tests in Clinical Practice.*

**irrationalism:** see visions and hallucinations.

**irresponsible criminals:** see criminal types.

**isolationism:** see peace and war.

# J

**Jacks, L. P.:** see psychical research and parapsychology.
**James-Lange theory of emotion:** see emotion.
**James, William:** (1842-1910) One of the most distinguished psychologists, philosophers and men of letters in America. He taught at Harvard from 1873 to 1907. His two volume work *Principles of Psychology* (1890) is outstanding both in the care of his psychological observations and in the lively imagination employed in useful hypotheses of human behavior. A pragmatist in philosophy and religion, he was more than a pragmatist in psychology: his hypotheses foreshadowed some of the later conflicting schools of psychology, which look back to him as their trail-blazer. His *The Varieties of Religious Experience* (1902) remains a charmingly readable classic in the biographical and autobiographical approach to religious psychology. His *The Will to Believe* (1897) was a call to the adventure of faith in the values of religion in the face of current tempting scepticism. See divided self; fatigue; healthy-mindedness; intuition; minister, the, and his books; pragmatism; psychical research and parapsychology; peace and war; psychological frames of reference; psychology of religion; reality-feeling principle; saintliness; sick-soul; visiting the sick.
**Janet, Pierre:** see psychical research and parapsychology.
**Jastrow, M.:** see psychology of religion.
**jealousy:** see marriage, disharmony in; sex differences, psychological.
**jealousy, sibling:** see juvenile delinquency.
**Jewish question, the:** see peace and war.

**Jewish Science:** see pastoral psychology: its governing limitations and qualifications.

**Johnson, Alvin:** see old age.

**Johnson Personal History Record:** see personality.

**judgment of others:** see projection.

**Jung, Carl:** (1875-    ) An early disciple of Freud,* Jung carried on his activities in Zurich, Switzerland. His type of psychoanalysis* he called "analytical psychology." Jung unlike Freud (departing on his own way in 1911) does not stress sex. Instead, the libido* is interpreted as undifferentiated life energy which expresses itself in many ways, such as food getting, sex, creative strivings, etc. The unconscious mind* carries in it not only the dynamic energies of repressed desires but also the energies of "primordial ideas" inherited from the racial past. Symbols expressed are not the by-passes of repressed desires but the manifestations of primitive thinking. Normal individuals, and not neurotics alone, are of concern to him. He developed a word association test as a diagnostic device which became widely acceptable. (The test consists of a word series to which the patient responds by saying any word which comes to mind following the presentation of each word of the series. His responses are noted as to the nature of the word in response, signs of emotion, alertness or lack thereof in response, unusual responding word, and the like. These responses are subject to analysis, indicative of basic difficulties.)

Jung classified human beings into types. His descriptive terms "introvert" and "extravert" have been widely adopted. He also conducted significant studies in schizophrenia* showing up meanings in the abnormal mental associations of such patients. See deception; dreams; emotion; extraversion; introversion; Jungian approach to therapy; projective techniques; psychology, schools of (psychoanalysis); religion and mental health.

**Jungian approach to therapy:** It is not safe to generalize on the subject of what would be a "typical" Jungian approach to therapy. We may cite a few examples, however, of Jungian concepts which seem to suggest common denominators to the Swiss psychologist's approach to solving the problems of the "neurotic" personality. It may be well to look at Jung's principle of the collective consciousness. Jung* saw man as possessing a mental structure which was in common with all men. Strip man, if you will, of his acquired responses to his environment and you will discover that he has an inherited personality structure which is common to that of his fellows. It was Jung who spoke of the introvert, the man who maintains contact within and the extravert, the man whose primary orientation is to his environment. It is not possible to classify each man thus, but in general we may say that the categories of orientation-within, introversion,* and orientation-without, extraversion,* serve as pointers to the therapists as to the basic structure of the individual personality. Each man is unique in his total orientation despite the common-denominator factors. It is the element of individuality which characterizes a Jungian analysis. If there were such a thing as a "pure" disciple of C. G. Jung, we might suppose that he would seek to encourage the individual to express his uniqueness as a means of personality fulfillment. (I have known well a person who had a complete psychoanalysis* from Jung himself. This person was declared "cured" by the great Swiss. The orientation of this cure is curious. On an abstract level of activity this individual possesses an extreme social orientation. The person in question is a leader in movements which promote well-being for many a downtrodden group. On a feeling, highly personal, level this person is inclined to mistreat members of these same groups as they personally contact her. She is bombastic, totally expressive to a point of anti-social frankness in personal contact and gives vent to whatever feelings are present within her. On a purely intellectual level, she embraces all men and is totally accepting. This person, dominated entirely by family, later by husband and children, had at one point been incapable of making a decision. Suddenly left without an authoritative guide, she could only find peace as she was able to express her own feelings which, because of age and long domination, were confused and inconsistent. While one with an Adlerian* orientation would perhaps question the adjustment of this personality, Jung saw a cure in the happiness which this personality found in expressing its highly specialized feelings and at the same time finding an "acceptance" base in an abstract and intellectualized social consciousness.) A Jungian analysis of the purest form, if one such there be, would tend to stress individuality above sociality.

In this sense the neurotic personality might find salvation in antisocial orientations or complete compliance with social order, provided that the latter orientation was representative of the individual's uniqueness. W. W. B.

**justice:** see lex talionis.

**juvenile delinquency:** The consideration of youth as a special province of court procedure in matters of offense is receiving wider attention in our day. Not only the crime but the circumstances which brought it about at early age are now receiving legal consideration and appraisement. The first children's court was established in Chicago in 1881 and is now a widely recognized legal procedure. Legally the chronological age must somewhere be set as to what constitutes "youth" (some hold seventeen to be the dividing line) but the age is no longer considered to be other than artificial.

One school of thought holds that certain children brush against the law because of "criminal tendencies"—heredity and/or early environment being the causes. Such theory dates back at least to the times of Jeremiah and Ezekiel (who protested against it). Lombroso* held that the criminal is born to be a criminal—a species apart. Aside from some exponents of a theory of morally delinquent inheritance, among students of criminology the Lombrosian emphasis is today discounted. Many point out the noticeable parallel between mentally deficiency or subnormality and the conditions of crime. In many noticeable cases too physical defects parallel crime. (In both instances the "solution" in some opinions has been a proposal of controlled breeding or eugenics.*) Home environment is now being stressed as a major cause and to it more attention is being paid by sociologists.

Early environmental factors leading to juvenile delinquency, as pointed out by students of the subject, are many: poverty or the economic situation (the greatest proportion of juvenile offences have been found to affect property infringements); ill treatment by parents, parental dissension, lack of direction to skills and to trades, overcrowding in houses and neighborhoods, use of alcohol and drugs, habits of gambling, wrong ideals fostered by motion pictures, cheap literature, more leisure time (as compared with former long hours in factories), love of adventure and of rebellion. (The latter against rigidities in family life.)

Individual factors are receiving their due. Such include emotional conflicts, undirected impulses, pleasure principle (for Freud:* untamed animal nature) and reality principle (with which pleasure comes into conflict in dealing with codes), repressions in the unconscious which on occasion become explosive, sex, self-esteem, inferiority compensated by self assertion, suggestions of crime from success of those older who have become idolized, neglect or love starvation or the feeling of not being wanted, companionship with the older set which prefers to put greater risks on the younger who are unsuspecting (Dillinger, famous outlaw, came into bad companionship as a youth with older boys—declared Dillinger's father), sibling jealousy (brother and sister relationship which does not function smoothly in competition for parental attention), child-spoiling rearing by an overly affectionate parent (particularly the only child or the youngest), etc. One writer (Cyril Burt, *The Young Delinquent* [1931]) declares that defective discipline is a major factor in as many as sixty-one percent of cases of delinquency. (Too harsh or too soft.)

There are no simple solutions to the problems involved. Such a simple panacea as the establishment of a neighborhood club does not seem to reach the roots. All in all, delinquency causes are found deep in emotional frustrations which express readily in distorted behavior. The latter seems to satisfy or compensate for the former. The language of a delinquent frequently is that of fear, anxiety, guilt, antagonism, over-aggressiveness or over-passivity. Such manifestations of emotional disturbances appear early and usually there is a history of overt misbehavior before there is the kind that comes before the attention of some court of law. One study has found that the average age of the first delinquency is nine years and that some five years of overt misbehaviors antedated court appearances. (E. T. Glueck and S. Glueck *One Thousand Juvenile Delinquents*.) It is suggested that the first signs require treatment for effective therapy. Truancy is an early sign. So also are moodiness, marked inattention, boredom, overactivity (suggested by scars on the body), excitability, excessive lying, poor performance in school work compared to ability. Children with these or any such marked characteristics should receive the attention of psychiatric and child guidance clinics. Childrens' Courts may offer counsel even before it need assume guardianship. See child training; social maturation; teen-agers.

*Bibl.* J. Arthur Hoyles, *The Treatment of the Young Delinquent* (1952). Offers excellent bibliography. Article "Juvenile Delinquency" by William Leavitt, M.D., in *Encyclopedia of Aberrations* (1953), edited by Edward Podolsky, M.D.

# K

**Kant, Immanuel:** see psychical research and parapsychology.
**kidney function:** see aging process; hypertension.
**kinaesthetic senses:** see sensation; taste.
**knee jerk:** see patellar reflex.
**knowledge:** see intuition; psychology of religion (J. C. Flower); reasoning; thinking.
**Koffka, K.:** see psychology, schools of.
**Köhler, W.:** see psychology, schools of.

# L

**labor:** see atmospheric conditions and work capacity; child training; work; work and rest; work inhibitions.

**laissez faire:** see children and religious beliefs.

**laliphobia:** see phobias.

**Lamprecht, S. P.:** see ministry, the, and counseling.

**language:** see dreams; emotive language; figurative language; juvenile delinquency; self.

**lapsus linguae:** see slips of the tongue.

**laughter:** see child training; emotion; emotional tensions, release of; sleep.

**law of parsimony:** Sometimes referred to as "Occam's razor" (formulated by William of Occam [d. 1349?]). The Latin form is *entia non sunt multiplicanda praeter necessitatem*, which in translation is: entities must not be mulitplied beyond necessity.

It is a rule of good thinking to simplify. A sign of confusion is verbosity and the multiplication of concepts (where simple concepts may explain). See instinct; Morgan's canon.

**law of reversed effort:** see autosuggestion.

**law, the:** see criminal types.

**laziness:** see myxedema; success.

**leadership:** see group psychotherapy; sociometry.

**learning:** All human behavior involves the process of learning: of change, modification, adjustment, growth. This may come about deliberately or, in the case of a forced situation, without desire. It may involve a change of ideas, of motor responses, of emotional reactions or a combination of them.

All organisms begin with two sets of receptors: the external (eye, ear, skin, etc.) and the internal (drives, such as hunger). The former pass on external stimuli through a system of connectors which, in turn, passes them on to muscular responses, speech, etc. In the early stages of the life of humans these responses are indiscriminate and diffuse. The organism, however, internally sets up physical and biochemical energies which become physical movements or psychical modifications of patterns. An inner condition may modify the health of the physical organism, even as the external may modify the mental health of the subject. Every stimulus leads to some reaction, internal or external. Learning is the name for those changes of more or less permanence in the interchange of stimuli and responses.

Learning involves, thus, the making of connections between receptors and effectors involving continuous modification. A circuit pattern once established tends to persist although modifications or alterations are possible.

As the organism continues to develop, it responds increasingly to more complex clusters of stimuli, responding similarly in more complex patterns of response. In critical situations the reversion to simpler responses often takes place.

A very young organism is more subject to the crude stimuli of the environment than is an older organism which has acquired specific response patterns. The internal responses with older age come to have increasing effects on the organism as experiences pile up on experiences. Experiences are registered in the form of neural patterns of response. However, at a very old age, with an increase of inflexibility, the organism becomes increasingly subject to the cruder stimuli of the environment— thus passing into the period of second childhood. During its whole career the organism is in a delicate state of balance— eager for modification, on the one hand, and setting itself against change, on the other.

In the complicated processes of learning (modification) certain factors are noticeable. 1) An organism learns in so far as it is ready. This is to say that it is interested, eager or possesses drive. In the drive of hunger it may by trial and error accomplish satisfaction; but it is the drive that induces the learning of how to get food. A drive of some kind is basic to learning. The will to succeed is, like hunger, a drive that initiates the possibilities of modification or learning. The drive may be pleasant or unpleasant, positive or negative. 2) An organism learns by exercise or practice. Sometimes this becomes simple; other times it is a long and persistent type of procedure. Certain skills which are related reduce the time necessary to practice to learn. Others, more remote in relation, require their own formula of exercise. 3) An organism learns in terms of the effects achieved. Successful acts have a tendency to become fixed in the nervous system; and success (satisfaction), being a pleasure principle, is a strong impulse to learning.

Thinking itself is a process of learning, a trial and error performance in which concepts are "manipulated" to project solutions to problems.

What has been called the ideo-motor theory raises the question of the significance of imitation as a basis of learning. The theory holds that motor activity tends to follow immediately after the idea of action. This theory as it relates to imitation in learning is being discounted by psychologists who, following Thorndike,* hold that imitation itself does not stand alone in learning. Imitation follows upon the same principles of readiness,* exercise and effect and without these factors imitation would not occur. A word will lead to motor action only where previous experience will favor it. "Be good, my boy" cannot lead to motor action unless the child already has some organization within himself to be good in the sense of the directive. "Don't be nervous" is a shallow command to one who has no history by long learning of poise and calm. Words themselves are unproductive of action. To know from the experts how to drive a car may be but verbal learning; but verbal learning is far from learning in performance. Many experts are experts in performance and not in translating the performance into the "know-how" of words. There is no necessary relationship between words and performance in learning. Previous learning and experience are the raw material in the fabric of new learning.

The problem of learning has raised the question of discipline and of transference of learning to other areas or fields of activity. Any expertness requires a long period of learning and the formation of many patterns and connections. Obviously, to transfer these long-time acquired patterns to other fields in itself requires a long period of discipline and learning. Only too often is this simple fact overlooked, e.g., when some person eminent in one field is made out to be an authority in some other (sometimes even by himself). An eminent scientist may be very naive in theology and religious expertness and yet his name may be used as an authority in fields unrelated to his expertness. (See occupational fallacy.) That one may transfer habits of careful thinking from one field to another is certainly a possible easy transition; but there still remain many new patterns of chain reactions to be acquired by long discipline to attain the stature of expertness.

Learning—to summarize—involves three fundamental factors: desire or intent, practice or exercise and results or effects which promote sufficient satisfaction to promote and deepen the patterns acquired. See apperceptive mass; child training; deceit (and character); emotion; memorizing; memory; old age; reading performance; relearning; sentiments; social perception; talents.

**left handedness:** see sinistrality.

**Lehman, H .C.:** see creative thinking.

**leisure:** see juvenile delinquency.

**Leonard, Mrs. O.:** see psychical research and parapsychology.

**Lesbianism:** A female homosexual. Sappho, ancient Greek poetess, is said to have founded the cult of Lesbian love (Lesbos, an Aegean island). Sappho hated men and loved those of her own sex. Lesbianism, sometimes known as Sapphism, is widespread, according to anthropologists. Causes are both organic and psychogenic*; some factors are dissatisfaction with the role of women, sexual protest, endocrine defects, etc. See homosexuality.

**Leuba, James H.:** (1868-1946) A pioneer in the field of psychology of religion,* Leuba is perhaps best known for his study of the beliefs of American scientists relating to the existence of God and immortality. In 1914 and 1933 he conducted questionnaire surveys. In the earlier survey, one thousand scientists listed in *American Men of Science* were contacted. He divided them into greater and less eminent groups. He found, in general, a greater percentage of disbelievers among the eminent class, whether physicists or biologists, the biologists producing a much smaller number of believers in God and in immortality than the physicists. Psychologists rated lowest in the percentage scale for positive beliefs.

Professor J. P. Pratt* interpreted this to mean that at the time scientists held such reverence for the scientific method as to preclude professional or even personal interest in such less precise fields as metaphysics and religion. Biologists and psychologists who came closer to the area of human interests were low, he said, because of their resolute habit of regarding man as a part of the animal world rather than as a spiritual being. The principle of reality feeling* was invoked by Pratt to explain the results of Leuba's investigations and has been regarded as perhaps the bare psychological account for such disbeliefs. There are, of course, other considerations, such as, natural negative reactions to conservative theology, dubious ideas of God and vagueness in conceptual images of what immortality may imply, etc.

Professor Leuba (a Clark University doctor of philosophy) taught psychology at Bryn Mawr College from 1889 to 1933. His best known publications were: *A Psychological Study of Religion* (1912); *The Belief in God and Immortality* (1921); *The Psychology of Religious Mysticism* (1925); *God or Man* (1933). For an autobiographical account see *Religion in Transition* (1937), edited by Vergilius Ferm.

**lex talionis:** The principle of an "eye for an eye" or "the unwritten law" of primitive justice without regard for circumstances. Courts of law in modern times make distinctions between motives.* Legal philosophy has progressed in so far as it recognizes more discriminately the motives to action, ranging from accident to deliberate intent with many factors in between.

**liberalism:** see motives; repetition compulsion; sancta of religion.

**libertine:** see displacement.

**libido:** Freud's* term for psychic energy. When this energy is directed inward toward the self, the result is called "narcissism." When it flows in the direction of a real object the result is called "object love." When the flow of energy is back to childhood, the result is termed "regression." This flow of psychic energy, or libido, coupled with the energy of self-preservation, Freud called eros or life. See fixation; Jung, Carl; psychology, schools of (psychoanalysis). W. W. B.

**library:** see minister, the, and his books; minister, the, and money.

**lie:** see lying.

**lie detection:** see deception.

**Liebman, J. L.:** see psychology of religion.

**lie detectors:** see deception; Marston, W. M.

**life:** see change of life; changed life, fruits of.

**life after death:** see belief in God; Leuba, James H.; psychical research and parapsychology.

**life expectancy:** see adult, the; old age; success.

**life situations:** see sermons, preparation of.

**likes and dislikes:** see fatigue; symbols; talents.

**liking a subject:** see sentiments.

**line of life:** see palmistry and pedomancy.

**Link, H. C.:** see psychology of religion.

**listening:** see confession; visitation; visiting the sick.

**literature, great:** see minister, the, and his books.

**loafing:** see boredom.

**logos:** The Greek word for word, reason, knowledge, study. Words ending in "ology" (from *logos*) (e.g., psychology*) suggest: inquiry into, study of. See psyche.

**Lombroso, Cesare:** (1836-1909) A student of criminology, a physician. His theory of genius as due to instability and degeneration is well known. See genius; juvenile delinquency.

**longer life:** see success.

**longevity:** see adult, the; old age.

**love:** see emotion; marriage, disharmony in; pastoral counseling and case studies; sex differences, psychological.

**love and hate:** see ambivalence.

**love starvation:** see juvenile delinquency.

**loyalty:** see peace and war.

**Lund, F. H.:** see emotion.

**lying:** see child training; deceit (and character); deception; juvenile delinquency.

**lysis type:** see divided self.

# M

**maladjustment in marriage:** see marriage, disharmony in.
**malaise, feeling of:** see coenesthesis; organic sensations.
**male and female responses:** see marriage, disharmony in.
**male climacterium:** see climacterium virile; menopause.
**male menopause:** see male climacterium.
**Mann, Thomas:** see psychical research and parapsychology.
**mannerisms:** see defense mechanisms.
**manners:** see child training; eonism; teen-agers.
**manual labor vs. mental labor:** see atmospheric conditions and work capacity; work and rest.
**manuscript, use of:** see sermons, preparation of.
**marriage, disharmony in:** Floyd H. Allport in his *Social Psychology* (1924) sums up the causes of marital disharmony as follows: Any agency which acts as an impediment to the normal sexual attraction and function of marriage partners tends to destroy the family relationship. Home-breaking and desertion are the result, most frequently, of difficulties involving sex. These difficulties in turn are set up by a variety of causes: a neurotic personality in one of the partners, unfortunate attitudes toward sex established in childhood or youth, false religious teachings relating to sex and ignorance of differences in male and female responses. Circumventions or "secondary love interests" are often substituted where adjustments are not normally achieved: such as, lavish attention to animal pets, religious and philanthropic activities energetically engaged in, excessive doting upon children. Psychologically they are

symptoms of marital maladjustment though religiously or altruistically the behavior seems commendable.

Many other factors (besides sex) bring about disharmony in marriage. Among those listed (by Allport) are: unwise methods of control by either or both partners (dominance is ofttimes a compensation for insufficiency felt under circumstances outside the home); an excessive demand for sympathetic attention, particularly by wives from husbands with less natural responses in little matters of consideration; the failure to spur love responses by carelessness in deportment and appearance; martyrdom techniques which increase resentment; defense mechanisms* (in abnormal cases) where escapes are evolved by such devices as feigned (or real) illness, fatigue, parental loyalties, placing of household responsibilities on others, or social engagements (clubs, etc.). Such symptoms are not signs of malicious deception but a protest of the unconscious mind* against the environment. Understanding of the cause of such circumventions is the necessary first step toward any possible harmony. In some cases marital harmony may be impossible since the causes preclude it. The establishment of a life upon an entirely new basis may be the only solution.

Chronic jealousy is a grave indication (according to Allport) of sexual maladjustment. Fear of loss of attractiveness may bring on delusions of a husband's infidelity; similar delusions occur on the part of men who have suffered some physical misfortune. Resort to tears or reproaches as controls only serves to repress discontents and conceal true feelings. Thus hostile attitudes are gradually built up which widen the breach.

The romantic element (continues Allport) tends to diminish in marriage. Courtship is left behind, with all the devices aimed at mutual attractiveness. Periods of separation are aids to the restoration of romance, if the fires have not been put out by a deluge of built-up hostility.

To the above account, a minister will likely wish to have added other possible causes of breaks in the marriage relationship, such as age differences, cultural differences and even conflicts in religious loyalties or the lack of any religious interests. There are, undoubtedly, many possible factors such as these which will prevent the ship of matrimony from moving on a relatively even keel. But, all said and done, any marital relationship cannot persist harmoniously without deep mutual attraction of one partner toward the other in what is usually and appropriately called "love." And though time will deepen this relationship in a kind of spiritual sharing, there is nothing gained and much lost in not acknowledging the factor of a kind of deep-seated physical attraction which people single out in others although they can not give reasons which wholly justify such attractions. (On the same basis people are repelled from each other—for reasons deep within their physiological being rather than from any spur of the higher brain centers.) To nourish this attraction is the sensible and normal way to avert disharmony in a society committed with justification to the relationship of monogamy. Or, to put it more bluntly: one wise minister advised the husband of a couple whose marriage had gone completely stale to revive a former good habit of frequent use of soap. See pastoral counseling and case studies; sex differences, psychological.

**marriage counselor:** see in-laws; pastoral counseling and case studies; pastoral counseling: case studies; pastoral psychology: its governing limitations and qualifications.

**Marston, W. M.:** (1893-    ) American psychologist whose work in the psychological field, in criminology and related areas, has attained the stature of eminence. He is the inventor of the so-called lie detector, a test involving systolic blood pressure variations. See deception.

**Martin, Lillien, J.:** see old age.

**masks of self:** see personality; self.

**masochism:** A term formed by Freud* from the name of an Austrian novelist, von Sacher-Masoch, who wrote about the erotic gratification in suffering pain. The term may have reference to actual pain or symbolic suffering.

**Massachusetts General Hospital:** see Cabot, R. C.; hospital chaplain, the.

**materialism:** The view that all Nature (or the Universe) is matter or some form of physical energy. Materialism should not be confused with naturalism.*

**Mathews, S.:** see psychology of religion.

**maturation:** see social maturation.

**maturity:** see adult, the; emotion; psychology of religion.

**maturity, emotional:** see peace and war.

**May, Mark A.:** (1891-    ) He is best known for his character studies (with Hugh Hartshorne\*). Professor at Yale (educational psychology and a director of the Institute of Human Relations), some of his other books are: *Education in the World of Fear* (1941); *A Social Psychology of War and Peace* (1943); etc. See deceit (and character).

**McDougall, William:** (1871-1938) His well-known work is entitled *Social Psychology* (1908) and his position is that of a defender of vitalism in psychology. More particularly stated, his view is called "hormic" psychology in which the concept of purpose (teleology) is stressed. See emotion; instinct; psychical research and parapsychology; psychology, schools of.

**meaning responses:** see apperception; memorizing; memory; reading performance.

**mediate senses:** see symbols.

**medical science:** see aging process; geriatrics; pastoral psychology: its governing limitations and qualifications; psychosomatics.

**medicine and religion:** see hospital chaplain, the; physicians; psychology of religion; psychosomatics.

**mediocrity:** see success; talents.

**mediums:** see psychical research and parapsychology.

**medulla oblongata:** see brain.

**meetings for therapy:** see group psychotherapy.

**melancholy:** see anxiety, anxiety neurosis; climacterium; climacterium virile; depression, mental; menopause; pastoral counseling: case studies; sthenic; temperament.

**memorizing:** Memorizing by rote has been the traditional educational procedure down through the centuries. In church circles, learning the catechism by heart by constant repetition is a well-known method still fresh in the memory of many.

In the 1880's Ebbinghaus\* made some experimental studies—notably his nonsense syllables arranged in series and memorized to the point of retention and reproduction. The results, after checking and controlling, were set up by him as general rules and formulae. The rate of acquiring the material and of forgetting is dependent to a certain degree upon: difference in length and kind of the material, continued practice and the relations of the parts of the subject matter. Relearning material was checked against the time required for original rate of retention thus revealing "the savings method." Forgetting takes place very rapidly after learning.

Continued studies in memorization have established the view that economy in memorization is effected by spacing the practice with time intervals (instead of trying to memorize all at once). Cramming does not make for permanent retention. However, in the memorization of material that calls for active thinking, continued study, once under way and once set in motion by interest, calls for a longer span of time of concentration for economy.

Memorization of meaningful material, already involving associations, has the advantage over rote memorizing. For many people memorization is greatly enhanced by rhythmic vocalization (varying with people).

Time is also saved by learning material as a whole rather than by splitting it into separate parts to be separately memorized.

An active rather than a passive approach has the advantage in the acquisition of material. So also reciting it from time to time.

Differences in age are involved in memory abilities. This is so because of the plasticity of a child in comparison with frozen habit patterns (prejudices) of much older people. Improvement of memory can only mean improvement of methods or ways of learning, of studying.

Many people are aware of the value of association in recall. New faces, names, terms, may be fastened in the mind with the aid of the strangest associations which foster recall when attached to the new material. Darwin's *Origin of Species* is remembered by this writer as published in 1859 by the quirk association that this year preceded the founding of alma mater in 1860, a date somehow easily remembered (perhaps by some campus sign). See memory.

**memory:** Memory has been called the "keystone" of most, if not all, the higher mental processes. Memory varies with modifications in thinking, imagination and learning.\*

Marked decline in memory appears at about 45. At 55 the median level has dropped to the average 13-year old level. (Studies published in 1928 by Jones, Conrad and Horn.)

At every age level there are individual differences both for learning and memory. Persons with superior intelligence and education maintain their abilities of memory and learning longer than others.

Learning and memory are part of a common process. Learning precedes memory. Apperceptive mass* is important in both.

Memory, according to Woodworth,* may be analyzed into: learning, retaining and recalling.

Memory by rote is the reproduction of learned material without meaning. See amnesia; memorizing.

**memory, social:** see sancta of religion.

**men:** see adult, the; age; aging process; climacterium virile; husbands and wives; menopause; sex differences, psychological.

**Mendel, Gregor:** see human genetics.

**Mendel's laws:** see human genetics.

**menopause:** "change of life": The term given to that period in the life of the human female when the previously normally functioning gonadal tissue (ovary) begins to undergo senescent changes and the production of female hormones* and mature ova by this tissue diminishes and then ceases. This usually occurs during the fifth decade of life. The change may take several years and is accompanied by varying degrees of physiological and psychical reactions, including the so-called "hot flashes," headaches, vertigo, "nervousness," insomnia, acute depression, etc. The organism gradually adapts to the withdrawal of the hormones and becomes readjusted to life without them. Substitution therapy by the injection of hormones sometimes alleviates the acute phases. Artificial menopause may be induced by the surgical removal of the ovaries or by the irradiation of these tissues with x-rays. In recent years, it has been recognized that a counterpart of this reaction probably occurs in males—the "male menopause." The senescent effects are not as striking anatomically in the male as in the female for the testicular tissue continues to produce viable spermatozoa until very late in life. The psychical reactions in the male menopause (dependent on the physiological changes, in part) may be very striking, as in the female, but, again as in the female, the organism usually adapts to these changes in time. See climacterium; climacterium virile. V. H. F.

**menstruation:** see endocrine gland; menopause.

**mental ability:** see ability; mental age; phrenology.

**mental age:** Devised initially to determine the mental ability of the mentally deficient, scales to determine normal level of intelligence by answers to questions of varying difficulty have seen set up. The most commonly used scale is the Stanford revision of the Binet-Simon test.

One's mental age is 1) one's ability to acquire knowledge like others of the same age; 2) one's mental development measured by comparisons with average persons at various levels of chronological development.

Alfred Binet (1856-1911), a French psychologist, conducted experiments on higher mental functions and set up a scale of measurement in 1905, revised in 1908 and 1911. Simon collaborated with him.

The Stanford revision of the Binet-Simon tests is an individual test of intelligence developed in 1916 by Lewis M. Terman (1877-    ), an American psychologist, and his associates based on the Binet-Simon scales. In 1937 a new revision was set up, yielding "mental age" and "I.Q."* scores. See adult, the; aging process; genius; juvenile delinquency; mental deficiency; social maturation.

**mental catharsis:** The release of the tensions caused by the selective agency of the censor.* See analysis; free association; psychology, schools of (psychoanalysis).

**mental conflicts:** see conflicts, inner; emotional conflicts.

**mental deficiency:** A person who is mentally deficient is handicapped by subnormal development. This may show itself at a very early age according to the type and degree of the deficiency. It is evident at maturity. It is of constitutional origin, perhaps of cerebral dysfunction or condition.

Feeble-mindedness and mental deficiency are generally used as interchangeable terms. Feeble-mindedness is a state of arrested development (mental and social) and is not the same as insanity. Feeble-mindedness is a subnormal state; while insanity is an abnormal condition. Both are found very seldom in the same individual. Insanity is infrequent in youth while feeble-mindedness appears prior to mental maturity (14-15 years) and then persists.

Degrees of feeble-mindedness are given certain terms.

1) Idiots are the most severe degree of mental deficients (below three years in mental and social ages).

2) Imbeciles are the middle group (three to seven years

mentally, and three to nine years socially).

3) Morons are the highest grade of deficients (Binet mental ages from eight to eleven or twelve years, approximately, and from ten to twenty years socially).

These grades are sometimes expressed in terms of I.Q. and S.Q. (social quotients). Within each grade it is the practice to speak of "low," "middle," and "high." See juvenile delinquency; mental age; social maturation.

>Bibl. Edgar A. Doll, "Mental Deficiency" in *Encyclopedia of Criminology* (1949), edited by V. C. Branham and S. B. Kutash.

**mental depression:** see depression, mental; old age; psychoneuroses.

**mental disorders:** see catatonia; dementia praecox; diagnosis; Esquirol, Jean Étienne Dominique; euphoria; glands; menopause; monomania; old age; paranoia; paranoid; phantasy; polylogia; psychogenic disorders; psychopathology; psychoneuroses; psychosis; psychotherapy; resolution, the doctrine of; schizophrenia; sex and the counselee.

**mental efficiency:** see atmospheric conditions and work capacity; efficiency; work and rest.

**mental fatigue:** see fatigue; work and rest.

**mental health:** see health, mental.

**mental health and religion:** see confession; psychology of religion; religion and mental health; role playing, success.

**mental hospitals:** see hospital chaplain, the.

**mental hygiene:** In 1907 there appeared a remarkable book by Clifford W. Beers (1876-1943) entitled *A Mind That Found Itself*. This frank autobiography of a patient in a mental hospital became the stimulus to the founding of a mental hygiene movement representing the dedication and efforts of psychiatrists to apply their insights to the work of prevention of mental disorders. The National Committee for Mental Hygiene was organized in 1908 by Beers. *Mental Hygiene* is the title of the quarterly magazine published by the National Association for Mental Health, Inc. The term, however, is now a general designation of interest in mental health.\* See adult; religion and mental health.

**mental illness:** see analysis; Council of Clinical Training of Theological Students; illness; mental disorders; pastoral counseling and case studies; psychoanalysis; psychotherapy; self; trauma.

**mental outlook:** see prayer and autosuggestion.

**mental traits:** see traits of personality; traits, racial; traits of success.

**mental work:** see atmospheric conditions and work capacity.

**mesmerism:** see psychical research and parapsychology.

**metaphor:** see figurative language.

**metaphysics:** The literal meaning is: beyond nature. The term dates back to Andronicus (40 B.C.) who in his collection of the works of Aristotle placed those dealing with topics of ultimate nature *after* the topics of nature (*physis*). Metaphysics came to mean such questions in philosophy* as: the nature of reality (ontology*), body-mind relationship problem, God, ultimate causes and purposes, nature of the soul or spirit, freedom, destiny, cosmic good and evil, and the like. Positivism* in philosophy declares these metaphysical questions void in interest and significance.

**methodological naturalism:** see naturalism.

**Meyers, F. W. H.:** see psychical research and parapsychology.

**middle years, the:** see old age; visiting the sick.

**mind:** see thinking.

**mind, teleological character of:** see teleological character of mind.

**mind, unconscious:** see unconscious mind.

**mind-body relations:** see psychical research and parapsychology; pineal gland; psychogenic disorders; psychosomatics; somatogenic disorders.

**Mind-cure movements:** see healthy-mindedness.

**minister and psychiatrist:** see displacement; religion and mental health.

**minister as a person:** Any professional man is tempted to conceal his real person under the character of his profession. This is particularly evident in the profession of the minister. Perhaps the traditional marked disassociation of the priesthood as a special sacramental order as over against the layman has engendered this phenomenon. The wearing of the clerical garb accentuates the division, particularly when worn from day to day on the streets. It would seem that a distinction of quality rather than a badge of apparel would be quite sufficient to designate the office, at least in the ordinary relationships of life. All this helps to create the illusion that the wearer of the garb is no ordinary human being and thus induces an artificial response on the part of both the wearer and those upon whom the effect is intended.

Add to this the questionable theory that life is to be dichotomized into the sacred and the secular, the minister the exponent or representative of the former—and there is again accentuated a class distinction not altogether as wholesome as intended. Protestant ministers may well be reminded of Luther's insistence that all life is sacred, including the honorable vocations of men.

To set himself off from his fellowmen may have certain benefits but the opposite effects tend to outweigh the intended virtues.

Not even the founder of Christianity, it may be conjectured, concealed his real person in his work. The impression of the records, at least, suggests that he did not seem professional: that he lived normally, ate and drank with his friends, worked at menial tasks, dined with special friends and proudly acknowledged them. At least mores and codes never stood in the way of a natural human expression—within the decorum of his religious commitment.

The other extreme in minister-behavior is the "good Joe," who becomes all things to all men and in being one of the boys has seemed to forfeit any genuine claim to his profession.

A minister's temptation is thus toward both extremes. In the one case, he acts unnaturally and proudly affirms he has no special friends or shows any special favors. In the other case, he also acts unnaturally by a forced jovial benevolence and has the kind of friends who take advantage of his calling and sooner or later cause situations of embarrassment.

A minister, to remain normal, should have his own circle of friends and sufficient relaxation to keep himself normal and strong. He may never distinguish between people when he offers his services; but there should be ample opportunity for the expression of himself—his predilections towards satisfying intimate friendships, relaxation and refreshment.

His integrity must be inviolate: in promises given and executed, in paying his obligations when due (certainly not to expect special privileges); answering his correspondence promptly, conserving his physical well-being and protecting the rights of intimacy of his own family. He does himself the greatest harm when he tries to be other than himself,—in imitation of someone he can never be like, in false piety, in assuming a prosaic demeanor when a sense of humor is in order —in short acting unnaturally and not genuinely.

His psychological appeal will greatly increase if he is seen to be himself, a man of mistakes like all men, but ready to acknowledge and correct them, as a person who is not acting a role but is a human being upon whom some divine cause has descended not as a decorative halo but as a possession on the inside. He may mingle with anyone on such basis and even enjoy the company of sinners without fear of criticism that he has joined their ranks.

He should have a family life and should insist upon a reasonable slice of time—from his ecclesiastical week—to share in the joys of an evening at home. By properly delegating his work he may conserve many necessary values of normal life. His voice must never succumb to pretension either in pitch or timbre. His clothes should be in fashion—and so the cut of his hair. There is no virtue in black attire to suggest some drab profession which certainly his is not. His dignity should become him but it should not remove him from the family of men. He should be masculine as intended without being ruggedly "Western." And he will be his age—proud if he is old since this is the badge of maturity and humble if he is young since this becomes the inexperienced. The high calling should square with his person, his genuine person and not the person to square with a calling which would make him other than he is—except in the commitment. And as should become him, he will look upon others in the same profession not as competitors but as fellow workers working with their own capacities in a special vineyard suitable to them. He will recall with tonic effect that in a religion such as his there are no real distinctions other than opportunities for special service. See emotional tensions, release of; ministry; pastor; preacher; role playing.

**minister, the, and his books:** The modern minister is haunted and pressed by so many tasks and interests that he has little time, it would seem, to be in his study with his books. These distractions are, of course, in many cases inevitable; but, at the same time, they are deplorable since they rob him of the opportunity to refresh his mind. And yet, the minister is called upon for more speeches, sermons,* and public addresses than any other single profession. He is expected to be informed in the widest areas of subjects and to be a leader and inspirer of thinking on the most profound themes of human experience. How can it be possible to keep pouring from a vessel without pouring something into it?

There can be only one answer: he must, at all costs, discipline himself and budget his time so that there will be periods each week for serious reading and reflection. On any other terms, he will run dry. Or, in desperation, he will turn to others to give him the artificial respiration represented by "inspirational" sermons. Such substitutions will be readily discerned as material conveyed and not possessed. People will tire and only "the saints" will persevere from Sabbath to Sabbath.

Even a busy man—if he wills—can find the time for his health—if it is necessary. Continued reading is the absolute requirement of a spiritually healthy minister. There is no substitute—not even the best sermons of others. There is no excuse for laxity—although it is easy to find reasons. Books are the tools of the trade—but they are more: they are companions along the way without which the journey is lonely and a life impoverished. No single experience of a single life can be enough to interpret life with all its complexities. Companionship of great minds is indispensable in such heavy responsibilities as attempting to find the way to life's ultimate meaning and to lead others to it.

It may be assumed here—without a further word—that the Scriptures of one's high religion are a primary source of a minister's reading. (To this may be added: so also the Scriptures of other great faiths, since this world is now rapidly shrinking into international relationships of an increasingly intimate nature.)

But, what of other books?

Surely, no one list can be set down for the variety of temperaments, experiences and backgrounds of the men "who wear the cloth." Good reading, like listening to good music, requires disciplined taste—developed through the years—a taste that should have been acquired in college and seminary days and deepened through the years of maturity.

Books fall into classes: those which give fullness to the mind; those which inspire and suggest; those which affect style of language and expression; those which interpret life; and those which offer the companionship of spirit.

Those which give fullness to the mind are the kind that fill the bottom of the glass with enough depth and strength to cause the overflow at the top. They are not sermonic; rather, they are the kind that touch the depths of experience. Here belong books on history, biography, psychology, the sciences, and philosophy. History gives the perspective of time and the long look; biography shows forth the sense of mission which certain people feel for life and the story of their journey to achievement; psychology provides an understanding of the ways of people with all their complexities; the sciences demand exactness and precision of concepts so necessary to good thinking; and philosophy unifies ideas into patterns of thought and marks out the big issues and viewpoints, enlarging the vista of the mind.

Sermons are the result either of hunting material or of being haunted by material. The latter kind of sermon tends to be profound and self-possessed and emerges only gradually out of the fullness of reading and imagination. Wide reading provides a solid base for stature and stature implies rising above the commonplace.

Every devout reader will, in due course, point back to "watershed" books—the kind that represent a turn in direction and insight. Such reading sometimes is set by circumstance of time and, it may be, by chance. This writer has had a number of such "watershed" books which represent wholly new chapters in thought. (One such book was J. A. Thomson's *Introduction to Science* which revealed how high, indeed, are the morals of the scientist who devotes himself unselfishly to the pursuit of truth and courageously resists the crushing opposition of traditional mores and challenges the entrenchments of tradition.) Some books are reread over the years. (William James'* *The Varieties of Religious Experience* is such a book for this writer. Each time something new and fresh springs forth from those pages as a wider experience sees more in them.) Dr. Gaius Glenn Atkins, a top preacher of the last generation, has said that he re-read Dante once each year! The greatest writers do not preach. They simply interpret. And generally what they say most profoundly is really what is left unsaid.

Those books which affect style are the ones which affect us unconsciously and subtly. Some books are like friends whom we greet gladly and stop to chat with; others are like those we meet on Main Street and merely greet in passing by. The test of great literature is its way of persistence in spite of the changing climates of generations.

A minister should have close acquaintance with the history of ideas. Such acquaintance gives poise when the winds of doctrine beat about and toss others to and fro to this or that extreme. If he is philosophically minded he will reveal it by the probing spirit of his mind, sorting the essentials from the circumstantial and possessing a sure compass when others lose their way in lesser matters. Philosophy nourishes analysis and critical insight—indispensable assets to creative thinking.*

Poets and essayists stimulate by suggestion, breaking the ice of frozen thought patterns and rendering the mind fluid to the new while making more out of the everyday plane of living. Such literature helps one also to dream; and a minister should never move far from the possibility of dreams. For dreams are hopes, visions and the abodes of ideals as real and living things.

Biographies may well be the revelation of Spirit as it works through lives touching them, with the breath of Reality and a revealing sense of Destiny in tasks undertaken.

A minister cannot hope to be a scholar (despite exceptions). But he should know where the scholars are, what they are doing and how to discriminate the truth-seekers from the propagandizers. The latter he will spend little time with—for there is too little time to toss around. A minister is a craftsman and a good craftsman insists upon good tools in his hands.

Reading must be motivated like any other pursuit. Can there by any greater motive for a minister than the high privilege of presiding in a pulpit as a wise teacher of life? Can there be any public service greater than to interpret soundly those fundamentals by which the journey of men takes on meaning;

to point out *the* better way and to know the directions to the higher reaches of this world?

No one understands life by himself. It is a cooperative venture—and books are the accumulated testimonies of this common sharing of experiences—many of which may well offer the very transfiguration that is needed when life becomes drab and commonplace and the routine dulls its shine and lustre and zest. See minister, the, and money.

**minister, the, and money:** We live in a realistic world in which money is the medium of exchange for goods and services. A minister must eat, clothe himself, provide for sickness and retirement, help his children to their start in life, as well as meet the reasonable demands of his wife for a life of self-respect in appearance and social obligations and privileges—all of which moves in and out of the area of money.

Money, therefore, is a reasonable concern and there need be no diffidence about it. A minister, along with members of his parish, must stand in line at the A&P and pay cash before his groceries are carried out of the store. Living in this kind of civilization, he should honorably seek to provide for a reasonable livelihood and be frank with his congregation about the necessity of providing him with a respectable status in the community.

He should ever be mindful that others in the same profession live in the same kind of world, and he should be sensitive that their services for him or his parish should be paid for when rendered.

He should remember that a manse (and its repairs), provided for him, represents a definite income (for which, otherwise, he himself would have the responsibility to pay were he in another vocation). To meet his financial obligations promptly as contracted for is an absolute essential for integrity and responsible moral leadership. This, as in all cases, requires a budget which should be respected as one respects the law of gravity.

A budget is a simple procedure. Insurance premiums are known in advance (and a married minister should provide insurance for himself) and, divided by twelve, will decrease his cash each month. This he sets down in his business journal as an item no longer in his possession for indiscriminate use. Groceries are, on the law of averages, divisible into a monthly allotment and can be marked as such, with the corresponding percentage available each week. And so on for clothing, dues, utilities, car payments, running expenses (stamps, tobacco, gasoline for pleasure, occasional magazines, etc.). There is no excuse—other than illness or unforeseen tragedy—to upset any budget with its assurance of prompt payment of obligations. Special funds for education, vacations and the like should be a part of the monthly deductions from earned income. Beyond the limits of his budget, no one can live respectably—no matter how large or how small it may be. It should be respected as a command from Mt. Sinai. A cooperative wife will know the limitations and be governed by the sheer mathematics involved.

Each minister must have tools, like any carpenter, mason, inn keeper or tradesman. Books and professional magazines are the tools of the trade. Since these tools are in the service of the profession it is a legitimate request if a minister asks of his church a reasonable annual budget allowance (over and above salary) for this purpose. Not less than one hundred dollars per year is the minimum requirement for books. Not to have these tools and not to have their continued use is an invitation to professional senility which will come inevitably within but a few years. A public or university library may be counted on for large works (encyclopedias and the like). But current books are legitimate possessions of the trade. Such books should be in the minister's own library as symbols of his earnings—and not collections to be placed in a church library.

A minister will budget his benevolences like any other person, remembering that even tithing is not confined to a specific church but represents the whole area of sharing (Red Cross, Community Chest and the like).

No consecrated minister will seek monetary wealth for himself and his family. But it is his moral obligation to see to it that the standards of living set for him by his congregation are met honorably. He should, without shame, make plain his sum-total needs to his congregation, not surreptitiously or cowardly but openly and manfully. Honorable people will respond understandingly. He should make it clear that as a servant in the community he is called upon to share in more projects than the average person limited to average demands (business men excepted!).

When he invites someone to substitute for him, he should make it clear at the very moment of invitation that the service will be paid for at an agreed sum or that the service is expected to be gratuitous. If the latter, there should be the expressed willingness for similar reciprocation. Whether paid or gratuitous, the invitation should be clear and above board. Expectations, then, will be according to realistic procedure and the transaction is honorable. Such payments should, if agreed upon, be rendered promptly (to give no occasion for doubt of integrity).

A minister should never accept payment for rendering service for the sick and the needy, or for the performance of sacramental privileges. No one ever should pay for baptism or participation of the sacrament of the altar. If there is any insistence upon the part of an appreciative beneficiary, such payment should be directed to the church or some worthy cause—but not to the person performing it. The exceptions here are weddings and funerals.

A minister may honorably accept a fee for a wedding, since marriage primarily is a civil and legal function (as attested by the requirement of a license). Church weddings often require a considerable portion of a minister's time (rehearsals, etc.) and should be paid for as a professional service. Funerals are more variable in this respect. Members of a church who call upon their minister for such services need not concern themselves over payment since it would seem most inappropriate. But calls for such service on the part of those who have made no effort to show interest in the church may well be considered by the minister as occasions appropriate to the acceptance of payment, especially when elaborate provisions are made involving other services (florist, undertaker, etc.). In case of any doubt, a minister may accept such payments in behalf of his church and render an account thereof. In most cases, however, it would seem honorable to accept such payment for honorable service.

The polite word of "honorarium" may well be banished from the vocabulary of professional service transactions. A payment (like a rose) is no less sweet or honorable called by any other name.

A minister should shun handling any church funds. If an occasional necessity forces such a situation the minister should render and record accounts by the usual business procedure of receipts. Never shall there be cause for even a breath of suspicion of mistrust in any financial transaction on the part of a minister. All church expenditures are organizational matters and must be properly approved and appropriately transacted by proper functionaries of the church.

All in all, the handling of money is a psychological and moral affair, psychological for personal peace of mind and self integrity and moral in establishing honorable dealings with others in the daily transactions of living. See minister, the, and his books.

**minister's children:** see morality and psychology.

**ministry:** see analysis; confession; counseling; cure of souls; emotional tensions, release of; fees; funerals; hospital chaplain, the; minister as a person; minister, the, and his books; minister, the, and money; ministry, the, and counseling; occupational prejudice; pastor; pastoral counseling: case studies; pastoral psychology; pastoral psychology: its governing limitations and qualifications; preacher, the; preaching; problem complex; professional reference; psychological frames of reference; psychology of religion; psychotherapy; religion and mental health; sacrifice, a psychological concept; sancta of religion; sermon; sermons, preparation of; sociometry; sublimation; talents; visitation; visiting the sick.

**ministry, the, and counseling:** The minister is one frequently sought out for assistance in solving problems which produce anxiety and conflict. In addition to his availability to the members of his church community and his general knowledge of personality structures the minister can approach the counseling situation uniquely from a theological context. It has often been the case that a minister has attempted to counsel a troubled person by pointing to stated moralistic passages from the scriptures. This method of approach ignores the basic contribution which theological structures can offer as an avenue of clarification to personality difficulties. Not by looking at the scriptures but rather by looking at the experiential bases of the theological structure can the minister-qua-minister be counselor. Theology is the statement of the means of a healthy relationship between man and God, and man and his brother.

Theology as a statement of relationships did not precede relationships and experiences as such but is fundamentally descriptive statements about relating and relationships.

Let us look briefly at several theological terms common to most of the eleven world religions. With some exceptions these theologies speak of man as sinner enjoying grace, searching for salvation through prayer and love. These terms in their minimal descriptive meanings are statements, writ large, of the human personality. The experiential phenomena which primitive man labelled grace, sin, salvation, and prayer were personality labels rather than theological dogma. That experience which man distinguished from all other experiences and labelled grace, for example, distinguished itself to the experiencer in terms of its special meaning in his life. Without attempting to develop the philosophical and psychological bases for descriptive definitions of these terms let us attempt to define them in relation to the personality structure.

Let us say minimally that grace is the expression of receiving that which is in actuality not deserved, that sin is the personality's failure to utilize its potential abilities, that salvation is the personality's acceptance of an honest dependence upon sources of power in areas where it is incapable of satisfying its own needs and at the same time an acceptance of the responsibility for independence in areas where the personality has powers for its own fulfillment, and that prayer is simply a description of the needs and abilities of the personality. (We may note that God, for theological purposes, represents the source of power not present in the personality upon which the personality is dependent.) We may say that grace, sin, salvation, and prayer are at least these things and without attempting to compare one personality's salvation qualitatively with that of another personality we may see that the minister is dealing in each case with a personality conflict similar to a theological structure.

In this regard we may only add enthusiastic endorsement to the statement of Professor Sterling P. Lamprecht in an essay entitled "Naturalism and Religion" in Yervant Krikorian's volume *Naturalism and the Human Spirit* (1944) when he said "But at least we do not need less theology; rather we need better theology. Perhaps in a narrow sense of the term 'theology,' a better theology would cease altogether to be theology . . . If religion be a way of life, theology would, then, be the theory that explains and seeks to justify that way." The minister then has a point of departure for his approach to the troubled personality. In this approach he is prepared to help the counselee find himself, and thereby recognize his needs and abilities and also learn acceptance of a necessary dependence upon values outside himself. He will see that guilt* is the result of sin (where sin is not utilizing what is potential in the personality) rather than a moral transgression. He will see prayer as the continued effort upon the part of the personality to state its dependence and its independence. Inasmuch as the minister is often expected to see the troubled personality in the light of his profession we can say with assurance that the minister who understands the human personality in its many daily experiences will see in those experiences the outline of the very theology he expresses. (Note: We must hasten to add that the kind of theology will play an important role in the degree of solution to the personality problem. For example, a theology which denies man any worth whatsoever and sees salvation as absolute dependence on an ultimate power may serve to create personality problems rather than solve them. An analyst in a classroom of one of our large universities was heard to say that the theology of the Roman Catholic church often prevented any degree of solution to personality problems in a reputable psychoanalysis.* The fact that the aforementioned theology has decreed against psychoanalysis, save its own variety indicates an unwillingness on the part of that theology to set the human creature free insofar as he is free. In fairness, Protestant hell, fire, and brimstone probably did little to serve as therapy in its day. Any theology, Christian or otherwise, which preaches the degeneration of freedom of all parts of the human soul is psychologically an enemy to the healthy expression and reasonable adjustment to life of the personality which is a manifestation of that soul.) See hospital chaplain, the; pastoral counseling and case studies; pastoral counseling: case studies; pastoral psychology. W. W. B.

**miracle:** see pastoral psychology: its governing limitations and qualifications.

**misanthropy:** A term for aversion to people as a result of unsatisfactory experiences in social relations.

**misfits:** see success.

**money:** see child training; fees; in-laws; minister, the, and money; pastoral counseling and case studies.

**monism:** see belief in God.

**monomania:** see paranoia.

**monotheism:** see belief in God.

**monotony:** see fatigue; routine.

**mood:** see creative thinking; emotion; projective techniques; temperament.

**moodiness:** see juvenile delinquency; teen-agers.

**moral conduct and teaching:** see deceit (and character).

**moral consciousness:** see conscience.

**moral disease:** see psychology of religion; psychoneuroses.

**moral equivalent of war:** see peace and war.

**moral neurasthenia:** see psychoneuroses.

**Moral Re Armament:** see group psychotherapy.

**morale:** Morale may be defined as an attitude or disposition of an individual or the response of the "group mind" to be ready to react appropriately to a situation that is challenging. Morale is judged by the degree of appropriateness of response to a given situation; by the degree to which an individual has identified himself with a cause, a leader, a group; by the degree of self-esteem that motivates his response. The morale of a group comes from the united strength of individuals composing it, from the bond of common tradition, purpose and vigor.

When morale is on a decline in an individual he may become anxious. He is conscious of his inability to live up to expectations. If it continues he will lose his identification with his group or accustomed situation.

Mental and emotional discipline helps to sustain morale. When any situation moves on smoothly morale does not come into play. It is only when that situation is challenged, by some crisis of threat, that morale comes to the fore. See adult, the; success.

**morality and psychology:** From the psychological point of view the term "moral" (involving some standard of conduct or ideal) involves a conflict between a person's will to pursue some ideal end and his impulse, or between two impulses. Moral disorders are such conflicts where the resolution is problematic or unattained.

Every age, to some extent, has a distinct set of moral standards. From the viewpoint of the Olympic state religion Socrates was immoral in stirring the youth of Athens to ask questions. From Socrates' viewpoint and by the standards of critical inquiry it would have been immoral not to have stirred inquiry. What is moral for one country, one age, would not necessarily be moral for another. What is right for one age level is not necessarily right for another—in certain degrees and matters. A boy may express pugnacity and be smiled upon; but a grown-up man would be condemned for carrying on a physical fight. A boy may, at his age, be forgiven for not "telling on" his big brother—an age of hero loyalty; but an elder would be expected to maintain integrity even at the expense of his friends. If the former were pressed beyond the code of his circle of comrades to act without regard for that circle he would possibly be encouraged to act as a betrayer which, at a later age, might become a vice under other circumstances. The point is that each age level has its distinctive psychological slants and it would be bad ethics to impose standards which do not take into consideration the implications of the particular age. It would be folly to expect a minister's son to behave like his father, to be "an example" to the parish. Such ethical standards may—since they fail to consider age and circumstance—conceivably bring about disorders affecting the young personality. Young people need not behave like adults and follow the adults' closed circle of standards; and neither should the old behave like the young. There has long been a tendency to impose unnatural moral standards upon those unfitted to bear them either by age or circumstance.

The question may well be raised: psychologically, can there then never be a universal standard of morality? To this query a positive answer may be given in this manner: that that standard of morality is psychologically universal when it is seen as a moral *principle*, viz., that morality is always a relationship proper to every age and promotes the fullest expression of the psychological functioning characteristic of the age and in the context of human possibilities. In other words: Goodness (psychologically) is a moral *principle*, if considered in terms of how the good may be expressed, say, by a twelve year old boy in the specific environment of the Eskimos, or in terms of an adult of eighty in an environment totally different. That the good will be expressed differently (reflecting the specific age and circumstance) is itself a universal principle.

It must be understood that the above characterization of morality is *psychological* rather than theological or philosophical. There is here not the question of an absolute morality. Rather, morality is viewed as a psychological situation which involves processes of human development, functioning and specific conditions of life. See belief in God; child training; children and religious beliefs; conscience; motives; original sin; peace and war; saintliness; teen-agers.

**morality, unconscious:** see psychology, schools of (psychoanalysis).

**morbid fears:** see defense mechanisms; phobias.

**morbidity:** see autosuggestion; introversion; psychoneuroses.

**Moreno, J. L.:** see sociometry.

**Morgan, C.:** see projective techniques.

**Morgan's canon:** So-called from the axiom of C. Lloyd Morgan to the effect that the simplest explanation of fact is the best theory. This is a restatement of the law of parsimony.\*

**morons:** see mental deficiency.

**morphology, human:** see physiognomy.

**mother complex:** see complexes.

**mothers-in-law:** see in-laws.

**mothers:** see parents; teen-agers.

**motivations:** see atmospheric conditions and work capacity; children and religious beliefs; Freud; genius; motives; psychology of religion; religion and mental health; talents; tobacco smoking and psychological efficiency.

**motives:** The primary motives of men are related to human drives\* (discussed elsewhere).

Many motives are linked to the developed sentiments.\* The prejudices that make up so much of life are just such sentiments (complexes\* when these sentiments operate pathologically). Emotional reactions become, by habit,\* attached to specific stimuli that bring them about and have "the right of way" once aroused. These constitute motives to behavior and response. Routine habits nurture the direction of our drives and constitute motives of action. We act by the motivation* of habit, resisting any interruption of the usual pattern. Taboo is a term denoting such departure from custom. We tend to regard as right that which accords with habit and as wrong (the taboo) which interferes with it.

Motives which are social are those modes of responding which men find it profitable and even necessary to express in order to gain social approval and thus make for easier adaptation. The conservative thus is on the side of the angels psychologically. His is the eaiser method—there is less to jar his tranquil adaptation.

Conflicts between motives are common. This makes for drama: comedy and tragedy. Young people face those conflicts as they weigh and make decisions for a career. When one motive becomes victorious over another most commonly the conflict is resolved and harmony restored. The ability to tolerate conflicts varies with individuals. In the case where resolution is difficult and the emotional experience intolerable we have the "neurotic," the "psychopathic," "nervously unstable." Some people seem naturally inclined to tolerate a difficulty and to meet conflicts.

Compensation* often is the resolving factor of such conflicts. A desperado may be a desperado to overcome timidity or inferiority. Rationalization often is another resolving factor of such conflicts. A student cheating in an examination may resolve his behavior with his moral ideal by assuring himself that the practice is common procedure in his college. Sublimation* often is another resolving factor of such conflicts. An unrequited lover may resolve the frustration by a dedicated love to God in full service (becoming a missionary, a nun, a monk or engaging in some high calling). There are other ways of resolution. See emotional tensions, release of; instinct; lex talionis; peace and war; projective techniques.

**motives, primary:** see drives.

**motor activity:** see alcohol and efficiency; ideo-motor theory; sleep.

**motor arc, sensori-:** see sensori-motor arc.

**motor nerve:** see afferent-efferent fibers.

**mountain of Venus, the:** see palmistry and pedomancy.
**movie mania:** see boredom.
**multiple sclerosis:** see sclerosis.
**Murray, H. A.:** see projective techniques.
**music:** see hymns; talents.
**mutations:** see human genetics.
**myophobia:** see phobias.
**mysophobia:** see phobias.
**mysticism:** see intuition; psychology of religion; symbols; visions and hallucinations.
**myxedema:** see thyroid gland.

# N

**Nancy School, the New:** see autosuggestion.
**narcissism:** see Freud; libido.
**Nascher, I.:** see old age.
**nationalism:** see peace and war.
**native intelligence:** see adult, the; I.Q.; mental age.
**native reactions:** see drives.
**natural selection:** see human genetics.
**naturalism:** Naturalism as a philosophical point of view is the view that Reality is of one weave: there is no super or "beyond" this Reality. Nature is Reality. But Nature is not necessarily all matter (materialism*). Nature may be fundamentally akin to spirit (spiritualistic naturalism). Many authors wrongly equate naturalism with materialism. (*Some* naturalists are materialists.)

There is what is called "methodological naturalism": the way of the sciences, viz., that all explanations are looked for within the framework of nature.

Supernaturalism is the long theological and philosophical tradition in the West. It affirms a world here and one beyond (super). Some naturalists believe that God is within Nature, transcending it as mind does body but nevertheless immanent throughout (even in the vicissitudes of nature). Such naturalists hold that supernaturalism rests upon an outmoded cosmology* (two-storied world), at the same time asserting that all the real values of supernaturalism are within the framework of unity.

**nature of the religious response:** see religious response, the, nature and origin.

**negro question, the:** see peace and war.

**neighborhood clubs:** see juvenile delinquency.

**Neo Freudianism:** see psychology of religion; psychotherapy.

**neo-orthodoxy:** see psychology of religion.

**nerve cell:** see neuron.

**nerve-fibers:** see afferent-efferent fibers.

**nervous disorders:** see complexes; deception; glands; menopause; motives; psychoneuroses; sthenic; success.

**neurasthenia:** see psychoneuroses.

**neurology:** see human genetics.

**neuron:** The nerve cell. The archineuron responds to a stimulus. The teleneuron transmits an impulse to an effector (gland or muscle). See synapses.

**neurosis:** A term for functional disorder(s) which brings maladjustment. In psychoanalysis\* the term is synonymous with psychoneurosis. See Adler, Alfred; Adlerian approach to therapy; emotion; Freudian approach to analysis; genius; Jung, Carl; Jungian approach to therapy; motives; psychology, schools of (psychoanalysis); psychoneuroses; religion and mental health.

**neurosis:** This is the term applied to relatively fixed patterns of maladaptive response. Dr. Norman Cameron in his volume entitled *The Psychology of the Behavior Disorders* (1947) stresses that the distinction between neuroses and psychoses is more of a legal and practical distinction rather than a psychological or mental one. A neurosis is a milder form of nonadjustive behavior for which institutional care is not required. A more extreme type of consistently non-adjustive behavior which may require institutional care is for all practical purposes a psychosis.\* A word of comment seems warranted on the use of the word neurotic. Any of us who persist in some form of non-adjustive behavior regardless of its gravity or its minor implications can be termed "neurotic." This classification applies to all human beings save those perfect souls of whom there is every reason to suspect that there are none. In this sense it seems wise for the minister or counselor to bear in mind that the use of this term is descriptive of most of the human race and is not a qualitative term. The fact that we en-

counter "neurotic personalities" should not concern one. The thing to be appraised is the degree of severity of non-adjustive behavior and its avenue of solution. See psychoneuroses. *Bibl.* L. F. Shaffer, *The Psychology of Adjustment* (1936); Karen Horney, *The Neurotic Personality of Our Times* (1937).
W. W. B.

**neurosis, actual:** A term referring to an actual physiological anxiety disorder of the nervous system as contrasted to *psychoneurosis* which refers to an anxiety disorder which is psychological in origin. W. W. B.

**neurotic, the:** see criminal types; sex and the counselee.
**neurotic personality:** see neurosis; psychoanalysis.
**neutral words:** see emotive language.
**New Dynamic School of British psychologists:** see psychology of religion; psychology, schools of (psychoanalysis).
**New Nancy School, the:** see autosuggestion.
**New Psychology, the:** see psychology of religion; psychology, schools of.
**New Thought:** see healthy-mindedness.
**New York Psychoanalytic Society:** see Freud, Sigmund.
**nickel therapy, the:** see Alcoholic Anonymous.
**night and day, and efficiency:** see efficiency and time of day.
**nociceptor:** see sensations.
**noise disturbances:** Noises are regarded as unfavorable to efficient work. In many cities to remedy this situation anti-noise campaigns have been set up and codes effected.

It is found, however, that workmen subjected to almost deafening noises in a shipyard rapidly adapt themselves and make no complaint. All of us make adaptations to noises to such a degree that they may become unnoticed.

Studies of this subject show that continued loud noises do affect adversely the efficiency of a small proportion of manual workers and the efficiency of a larger proportion of office workers. Surprising and irregular noises are disturbing to all workers. In general, noises do demand increased expenditures of energy by persons—even those seemingly well adapted to them—and bring an earlier fatigue.* There is indication that people must make extra effort to compensate for the disturbance of noise.

It is thus suggested to those given to study (students, ministers, teachers) that even TV (on its audible side), radio, music and any other possible distraction, may be adapted to but nevertheless such an adaptation drains off energy which otherwise might have been directed to the tasks at hand. See autosuggestion; sleep.

**nonsense syllables:** see memorizing.
**non-philosophical criteria of truth:** see truth.
**normalcy, flight into:** see flight into health.
**nosophobia:** see phobias.
**nurse, the:** see hospital chaplain, the.
**nyctophobia:** see phobias.

# O

**obedience:** see child training.
**object love:** see libido.
**objective worship:** see worship.
**obsessions:** see psychasthenia.
**Occam's razor:** see law of parsimony.
**occult, the:** see psychical research and parapsychology.
**occupational fallacy:** A very common psychological fallacy is the appeal to someone's position—his profession, the prestige of his job—as a qualification for a wide area of authority. The bigger the job, the larger and brighter the halo of authority. As these lines are written, a well known New York radio minister quotes a newly appointed university president "as saying" so-and-so about religion and education—to undergird the soundness of the preacher's idea. Evidently if the man quoted were not in that high administrative position he, even if known to the speaker and uttering the same thoughts, would not be quoted. It is the high position of the man that renders him quotable. Of course, the gesture is psychological, not logical. A university president may have come by his job as a money-raiser, a capable administrator of a complex organization who also has personable qualities, and know much less about the complicated field of philosophy of religion and education than the professor in that field on his faculty. But the professor does not occupy a position of glamor and thus makes poor psychological appeal. It is assumed that an administrative head of an educational institution is Plato's philosopher-king and

thus his words are golden. The fallacy is common in conversation and among public speakers: don't you see I am right because so-and-so of such high position says what bears me out? See fallacy of rationalization; learning.

**occupational prejudice:** A person's pattern of ideas tends to be set by the particular job he holds. He may not be willing to admit this and thus engages in the fallacy of rationalization\* but it is a part of the psychological principle of reality feeling.\*

A Methodist bishop (to use only a random example) will reflect a pattern of religious and theological ideas suitable to his position. His election to his high office may have come from many factors; but once in office he tends to reflect the religious pattern of his office. A college teacher or an officer in a denominational college will have a pattern consonant with his type of college (liberal, conservative, fundamentalist). An independent business man will reflect in his political thinking the type of government justifying and promoting his investments. The "haves" will reflect one phase of a political party; the "have nots" another. A young minister from a seminary will reflect the theology there current—it was his job to be acceptable to his church seminary and to his theological alma mater.

Ideas, thus, are more determined by occupations and institutions than would perhaps be admitted. A priest reflects his institution; a prophet much less so.

**ochlophobia:** see phobias.

**odors:** see smell.

**Oedipus complex:** This phrase indicates an unconscious erotic attachment by a child for the parent of the opposite sex. The term itself is derived from the famous Oedipus myth of the Greek drama. (When this attachment is that of a female child for the male parent, it is often called "the Electra complex." The term *Oedipus complex* covers both the implications of the attachment, male or female.) This term has been used so widely, and misused so widely, that it has become a cliché-explanation for all psychological problems. It will be well to remember that each and every human being is touched by this dynamism in the course of his or her lifetime. It takes on therapeutic significance only when this attachment is unresolved and prevents the individual from loving others of the same sex and others of the opposite sex. At such a point, expert therapeutical aid is necessary. Such complexes are seldom "cured" by merely pointing to the structure of the relationship. W. W. B.

**old age:** The average length of life among us has increased in the past fifty years by some sixteen years for men and eighteen for women. More people live today to the ages of sixty, seventy and eighty, although there seems to be no increase in the number of centenarians.

"Geriatrics" is a term for that branch of medicine which has to do with the diagnosis and treatment of old age diseases. The term was coined by Dr. Ignatz Nascher of New York City in 1909.

"Gerontology" is a term for the study of the aging process in general, including all organisms.

"Senility" which means "old age" is a less fortunate term since it has become associated with the idea of mental disorder or degeneracy.

Mental abnormalities of old people are not necessarily the result of age. Many such difficulties are of long standing. The realization of old age and adaptation to it constitute one of the most difficult periods in which to maintain mental stability. Those who have shown poor adjustability to other circumstances of life will probably have the greatest difficulties in making healthy adjustments to the period of old age.

Actual psychoses* of old age are not all caused by blood-vessel and brain-cell deteriorations. Psychoses may simulate the degenerating physiological processes. It is now realized that organic brain changes may even be precipitated by social influences. Mental disorders which began in the period of youth may continue into old age, causing a confusion in diagnosis and treatment if the whole picture is not known. A depressive psychosis at 80 may be but a re-occurrence of much earlier attacks and thus is not a characteristic of old age.

Some mental difficulties of old age, such as depressions, may be caused by intoxications from drugs, by deficiencies of nutrition, by cardiac trouble, by illnesses and by overpowering misfortunes. Shock therapy* may help in some cases of depressed states; so also, in some cases, proper diet, inclusion of vitamins and the elimination of drugs. Appropriate treatment often is rewarded by a complete recovery. The actual destruction of brain tissue, on the other hand, continues to find no cure.

The slogan "a healthy mind in a healthy body" is as true in the period of old age as it is in the period of youth.

People grow old at different rates. Some are very old at fifty; others young at seventy. Age is not a matter merely of years but a matter of functional capacity. Society and custom have too long regarded the number of birthdays—for example, in the matter of compulsory retirement—as indicative of functional capacity.

Physicians now are coming to the conviction that many mental difficulties in old age are preventable. A changed social environment frequently is the beginning of the cure, such as a better understanding on the part of relatives and associates to overcome the feelings of rejection, isolation and loneliness.

Changes, such as the gradual slowing up of the sensory processes, of memory, attention, and the like, appear at different rates in different individuals. They are generally more partial than total. An old person may learn "new tricks" if he really wants to, although he may find it more difficult to change habit patterns. In general, an older person resists changes: of ideas, scenes, forced pressures—often leading to anxieties, depressions, moroseness and even stubbornness.

Tensions of old age are often brought on by the disillusionment of independence. Many feel the bitterness of actual dependency on others even after having prepared for independence and security (e.g., the factors of prolonged illness or financial depressions with diminished values of savings) and, in the case of some, the loss of privacy. There is a feeling of loss not to be a part of the work-a-day world—particularly among older men.

It is becoming more evident among those professionally concerned about old age problems that serious anticipation of old age should be made in the middle years of life. The Standard Oil Company of New Jersey has effected a pre-retirement counseling plan to point out the value of serious preparation. Adult education is, in general, such a provision. The cultivation of new interests, handicrafts, hobbies, reading habits is something that should begin well before the age of retirement from any occupation. Even the area of sex has come in for consideration by those who plan such counseling since, as the medical profession points out, there is the mistaken and widely prevalent opinion that this area of interest recedes when "old age" sets in.

Dr. Alvin Johnson, formerly the director of the New School for Social Research (New York), has organized retired college professors to utilize their mature wisdom for further service in the educational field.

Many agencies have contributed to the care of the aged: notably the hospitals, specific homes, home-care programs, case workers (the first counseling center for the aged was established in San Francisco in 1929 by the psychologist, Dr. Lillien J. Martin). Newest of the ideas for help to those ripe in years but still in reasonably good health is that of a recreation center (e.g., the Hodson Memorial Center for the Aged in New York). Such centers are multiplying since they are functioning enormously well toward the happiness and contentment of both old men and women. The church, too, is an agency of great help—the minister often being the healing physician and the harmonizer in the tensions often found in families of great differences of age.

In 1950 The First National Conference on Aging was held in Washington. This group included physicians, nurses, social workers, biochemists, economists, psychologists, sociologists, anthropologists, labor-union representatives, clergymen, educators, and others. This conference reflected the principle of "community interest," acknowledging the mutual and common problems of old age in geographical areas rather than as concerns only for families or small groups (lodges, churches, etc.). See adult, the; aging process; climacterium virile; learning; menopause; pastoral counseling: case studies; social maturation; visiting the sick.

*Bibl.* E. Stieglitz, ed., *Geriatric Medicine: The Care of the Aging and the Aged* (2nd. ed., 1949); E. Clague, *Employment Problems of Older Workers* (1950); Thomas Desmond, *Never Too Old* (Legislative Document, No. 32, Albany, N. Y., 1949); Kathleen Newton, *Geriatric Nursing* (1950); Homer Kemper, *Education for a Long and Useful Life* (Bulletin, No. 6, Office of Education, Federal Security Agency, 1950); Paul B. Maves and J. L. Cedarleaf, *Older People and the Church* (1949); *Planning for Health*

*Services—A Guide for States and Communities* (Public Health Service of the Federal Security Agency); *Community Action for the Aging* (New York State Association of Councils of Social Agencies, New York City); F. D. Zeman, M.D., "Constructive Programs For The Mental Health of the Elderly" in *Mental Hygiene* (April, 1951).

**old psychology:** see psychology, schools of.

**olfactory sense:** see sensations; smell.

**once-born, the:** see healthy-mindedness.

**ontogeny:** The developmental history of an organism and its relationship within its specific major animal or vegetable group.

V. H. F.

**ontology:** An inquiry into the fundamental nature (character) of the world. It is a basic question in philosophy.* See metaphysics.

**ophidiophobia:** see phobias.

**opinion:** see autosuggestion; psychological frames of reference; truth.

**optimism:** see belief in God; euphoria; healthy-mindedness; pastoral psychology: its governing limitations and qualifications; temperament.

**organic sensations:** A broad term referring to those sensations* which arise from receptors* within the body (e.g., muscles, tendons,* viscera,* etc.). Hunger refers to the mass of uneasy muscular sensations from the viscera, particularly from "hunger contractions" in the stomach. Thirst arises from the mucous lining at the back of the throat and is stimulated when that membrane becomes dry. In both hunger and thirst there appears to be no mode of stimulation or receptor type other than those of other senses.

The so-called viscera are the smooth-muscle* organs encased in the abdominal cavity and stimulated by the autonomic nervous system.* The diffuse pattern of sensation associated with the viscera is known as coenesthesis* which contributes to feelings of malaise, well-being, energy, sloth, etc.

**origin of the religious response:** see religious response, the, nature and origin.

**original drives:** see drives.

**original sin:** No reputable psychologist would hold the ancient theological and anthropological theory that sin is passed on from generation to generation. The term "sin" is now reserved for conscious and deliberate acts of a person against accepted norms or mores of his society and the ideals associated with a moral God. Sin is thus a *responsible* misdemeanor. Original sin has, however, an element of psychological validity, viz., the fact that weaknesses of personality ingredients have a history beyond the pale of conscious responsibility.

Our inherited drives,* for example, are our equipment. As such they are a-moral. They function for biological purposes. When in conflict with standards of conduct they make for trouble and become easy predispositions to (deliberate) sin. Add to this the disorders provoked by early environment*—beyond the will of the individual—and there is the picture of a handicap on the kind of social adjustment called "moral."

If it is true that all of us have genetically come out of the forest primeval with a long standing equipment to employ in the hard struggle for survival in a world not too easy (temperature changes, wild animals, floods, disease germs, etc.) and in the course of social development have attained a kind of set of interpersonal social relationships which call for softer dealings with others, then it is easy to see how difficult it is to adjust elemental drives useful for one kind of hardfisted world to another which demands their curbing. Biologically, elemental drives have a way of persisting in spite of an environment calling for their softening. "Original sin" is an unhappy term for the elemental failings of man to live as he ought to live in a social order where virtues of altruism are supposed to eliminate selfishness. But there is this truth in "original sin," viz., that man's long history has not been erased in spite of ideals emphasized in developing society. So long as there is this disparity (for which the individual person is not responsible) there is more than a myth in the doctrine that we are not easily made into saints. See psychology of religion.

**over activity:** see juvenile delinquency.

**over affection:** see juvenile delinquency.

**over aggressiveness:** see juvenile delinquency.

**over compensation:** see psychology, schools of (psychoanalysis).

**over eagerness:** see in-laws.

**over passivity:** see juvenile delinquency.

**over pleasing:** see ambivalence.
**over sexed:** see sex and the counselee.
**over simplification:** see fallacy of over simplification.
**Oxford group movement:** see group psychotherapy.

# P

**pacifism:** see peace and war.

**pain:** see anxiety states; autosuggestion; complexes; masochism; pastoral counseling: case studies; sadism.

**pain sensation:** see sensations.

**palm readers:** see palmistry and pedomancy.

**palmistry and pedomancy:** Palmistry, also known as chiromancy, is the "science" of looking into a person's future from indicative lines of the palm of the hand or the shape of the hand. Pedomancy is the similar "science" of reading from the soles of the feet. Of course, there are many interpretations of lines (skin creases)—a practice of ancient standing. Many palm readers agree, however, on some major line interpretations. For example, at the base of the thumb where ends the muscular swelling is the "line of life." The length of this line, its terminations, its interruptions are taken to be indices of life. The muscular swelling itself (at the base of the thumb) is called the "mountain of Venus" and is taken to indicate the degree and kind of love (charitableness, lust, etc.). The many other lines and their crossings also are indicative of one thing or another; so also the shape of the hand; moisture or dryness, hardness, softness are also held to be personality trait indicators. Lines on the sole of the feet also have their significance as read by those engaged in pedomancy. It is, of course, evident that hand or foot lines are the result of muscular swellings and skin thickness due to formation and use. Although an attempt to develop palmistry into a discipline of respectability has been sought (e.g. C. Wolff *The Human Hand* [1943]) the "science" is regarded sceptically by most academic psychologists who prefer to classify it as pseudopsychology.*

**panphobia:** see phobias.

**parables and fables:** see children and religious beliefs.

**paranoia:** This term usually means the type of mental disorder* characterized by persistent delusions, frequently with hallucinations,* but without serious impairment of other mental functions. A persecution delusion, for example, is called monomania (a mental disorder involving one set of ideas or predominating motives).

**paranoid:** A form of schizophrenia* with a mental disorder* distinguished by a more or less systematized formation of delusions.

**parapsychology:** see psychical research and parapsychology.

**parathyroid glands:** These are small endocrine glands located near the thyroid.* Ataxia (muscular incoordination caused by lesions in the nervous system) is an immediate effect when these glands are removed from a dog. Muscular spasms and death in about ten days follow. Hypoparathyroidism is believed to be a cause of convulsions in children. See endocrine gland.

**pardon:** see confession.

**parent fixation:** see fixation; Oedipus complex.

**parents:** see adult, the; children and religious beliefs; child training; fears, conditioned; juvenile delinquency; pastoral counseling and case studies; personality; readiness, principle of; role playing; sentiments; sex differences, psychological; speech pathology; success; talents; teen-agers.

**parents and in-laws:** see fixation; in-laws.

**parish visitation:** see visitation.

**Parker, Theodore:** see healthy-mindedness.

**parsimony, law of:** see law of parsimony.

**parthenogenesis:** literally "maiden beginning." The mature female germ cells (ova) of animals are distinguished from their male counterpart (spermatazoa) by their relatively massive size (large quantity of yolk or deutoplasm), the presence of a different type of sex-determining chromosome, and the apparent presence of embryonic differentiators and organizers.

**passivity**

Natural fertilization requires a complete union of both the male and female germ cells to form a normal fertile offspring. However, in some lower invertebrate forms (*e.g.*, some insects and crustaceans) certain eggs of the female normally develop into mature adults without the union of the male germ cell. This phenomenon is known as parthenogenesis. In bees, such adults are known as "drones" and are all male and sterile. In some higher forms of animals, especially the amphibians, development without fertilization by the male germ cell has been artificially induced by mechanical means (immersing the eggs in strong saline solutions, pricking the eggs with needles, etc.). It is important to emphasize that parthenogenesis with development into a free-living form is not a known natural occurrence in higher animals, including man. V. H. F.

**passivity**: see over passivity.

**pastor**: The term is from the Latin word *pastor* meaning shepherd. A minister is called pastor when he is regarded respectfully and even affectionately as a spiritual counselor in his community. The pastoral ministry is distinguished from that of a manager or director of a church organization or a minister in the role of a preacher. See counseling; hospital chaplain, the; minister as a person; ministry; pastoral counseling; visitation; visiting the sick.

**pastoral conversation**: see hospital chaplain, the.

**pastoral counseling and case studies**: Pastoral counseling must be understood in the light of the problems in which people become involved. Let us begin by looking broadly at the world to understand something of the nature of the problems.

That it is a complex world, no one will deny. The nature of its complexity is not always fully appreciated. More is involved than the social disruptions resulting from two World Wars and an economic depression. Perhaps the factor which contributes most to the present complexity is what is generally termed the "technological revolution." Technological changes have led to a constant shifting of population and changing of occupation. In 1800, approximately 96% of the people lived on farms or in communities of 2,500 or less. Today more than 85% of the people live in cities of 25,000 or larger. The population of our country has increased at the rate of more than a million a year for the past fifty years. The rate of increase is greater today than at any time in the past.

Several factors should be especially noted: In shifting from an agricultural to an industrial economy, people have left the soil, with all the security the good earth gives a man and his family, and have become involved in factory or shop work which may be seasonal. Instead of a cellar well stocked for the winter months, the average man uses a semi-monthly pay check to buy food supplies at the super-market grocery. His employment is uncertain. In the crowded urban areas, he may or may not know his neighbors. The specter of ill health haunts him constantly. Through installment buying, he has mortgaged his future. He saves little. The radio and television have brought into his living room strange ideas, morals and mores. The urban industrial worker lives in the same dwelling an average of eight months. Young men and women court each other on the run, and marry after brief acquaintance.

These are some of the factors which contribute to the complexity of our times. Out of the conditions created by these factors arise many "pastoral problems." People are frequently in need of moral support, a sustaining faith, good counsel, and skilled assistance.

The pastor who tries to shepherd his flock hears the constant bleating of the many who are lost, confused, frightened, hurt, displaced, maladjusted, frustrated and desperate. Their problems are diverse and complex, but not beyond general classification. There is the problem of becoming oriented, adjusted, and accepted in community life. Other problems revolve around occupations, getting along with those with whom and for whom they work; family and domestic difficulties; sex,* gambling, drink and financial difficulties. Theological difficulties, or matters concerning religious faith as such are not common. Rarely does such a "problem" appear by itself. Usually a problem is a complex of factors having a long history, in no instance easy of solution. In most cases, there is a spiritual aspect which requires skilled handling and direction. Basic philosophies and religious convictions are at the root of every disorder.

To illustrate how these cases are handled by the writer, several actual case studies and records will be given, with comments and explanations.

There is a constant and endless routine of pastoral work and counseling that is part of every day's work. The pastor must "build up his congregation" by trying to interest newcomers to the community in the church. At his earliest convenience, after receiving a newcomer's name, he makes a call. During the visit he tries to learn something of the background of the family, the occupation of the husband, the number, names and ages of the children, also any special interests or talents the various members of the family might have. He then offers his services in trying to orient the family to the community, and advises them concerning the various organizations in which they might find a special interest. He tries to discover any particular problem they may have, such as a backward or handicapped child, occupational insecurity, or ill health. He will try to advise them where they might find friends having a common interest. He will invite them to the church and then ask some of the officers or women of the church to call on the new people and extend an invitation to them to attend church, or to attend some of the organized activities of the church, to invite and even offer to bring the children to Sunday school.

A nationally known rabbi said recently to the writer that in the early days of his ministry he felt his most important function was to indoctrinate the people with the final word of truth, but that in his more mature ministry he believed the greatest work the church or synagogue did was to offer friendship and a spiritual home to the strangers and wayfarers as they came into a new community. For such a home gives people a feeling of security and an opportunity to become identified with the more constructive and healthy elements in a community.

When calamity befalls a family, as it does sooner or later, the pastor tries to reach the family without delay. If it is a case of accident or serious illness, he goes first to a nurse or member of the family to ascertain the facts in the situation. Then he goes directly to the patient and from that point on uses his best judgment. If the patient is desperate he will offer a prayer, but if the patient is disposed to be hysterical and the situation does not lend itself to prayer, the pastor will stay but for a moment, speak a word of encouragement, tell the sufferer he will keep him in his thoughts. The following day he returns, and offers his services if there be special need for anything from taxi service to running errands. He will offer to bring reading matter, read the Bible, pray or perform any other service which may seem welcome. In any event, the pastor does not remain in a sick room very long—never more than a few minutes, unless the patient wishes to confer with him alone and at length about some matter—which is frequently the case.

Recently a twelve-year-old girl was struck by a car. She was taken to the hospital in an unconscious condition, from which she never recovered. The pastor went immediately to the hospital, found the parents in the corridor, talked with them, sat with them, found out what was being done and who was doing it, entered the room where the girl was in an oxygen tent and, although she was unconscious, he offered a prayer. He then departed, leaving word that he would appreciate being called at any hour of the night if it seemed advisable for him to return.

A five-year-old son was fatally struck by a car, taken immediately to the hospital where a pulmotor was used in an attempt to revive the child. The anxious parents and pastor had been sitting in the waiting room for an hour when the doctor called the pastor out of the room to say the child was past help. It was then the pastor's duty to inform the young parents. They were told every effort had been made but the doctors now believed the boy was past help. The news was imparted in a manner designed to avoid any unnecessary shock or crudeness that might add to the bitterness of the situation. Accompanying them to their home, he saw to it that friends were called in so that the couple would not be alone. Relatives were called and, as far as possible, all domestic matters were looked after.

In the writer's church, there is a Women's Organization, made up of eight groups, of which every woman of the congregation is automatically a member. Whenever death occurs in the congregation, the group with which the family may be connected is called. Members of that group then go to the home prepared to offer sympathy and to look after all domestic duties, such as preparing the meals, or taking on any housekeeping duties that may be necessary for the arrival of relatives and friends.

Not long ago a man in his fifties, a good churchman and

citizen, suffered a heart attack and died while returning by car after a day's work from a neighboring city. His employer was with him. When they arrived in our city, the employer came immediately to the pastor insisting that he break the news to the stricken man's wife. The pastor agreed on the condition that the employer accompany him. They found the wife in the kitchen singing cheerily, preparing the evening meal for her husband. In her greeting she remarked she was expecting her husband momentarily. The pastor then said he had very bad news for her and told her what had happened. After the first shock, he called the family doctor, and neighbors were called in to look after things. The doctor arrived shortly, gave the wife a strong sedative, and put her to bed. In such cases, everything must be done to prevent severe shock so as to forestall serious consequences.

One day a young woman in her early thirties came to the pastor's study apparently deeply upset. The family were members of the congregation. Her husband seemed like a very fine chap; they had two lovely children about five and seven years of age. Having visited them in their home the pastor had the impression they were happily married. The young wife slumped into a chair, buried her face in her hands and wept for a full five minutes. Finally, when able to speak with some measure of control, she announced, without explanation, that she was going to leave her husband. The pastor began asking her the usual questions: was there another woman in the case? No, she said, there was none, of that she seemed reasonably certain. When asked if there was another man she seemed startled at the very question. She insisted she really loved her husband and the children and the conversation led to several things relative to what makes a good and happy marriage. The reason she was leaving her husband was that he got on her nerves to such an extent that she could not stand having him around. It seems he was a salesman, a nervous, wiry, high-strung type. He worked hard, always came home tired, and never left his worries or his work behind him. The evening conversation invariably was a recital of his difficulties with his customers, most of whom he seemed to feel were stupid, dishonest scoundrels. His continual dismal song seemed to send her spirits tobogganing. The two children were at a most demanding age

—healthy and full of vim and vigor, they wore her down to such an extent that when night came, she was tired out. Apparently her's was a simple condition of nervous exhaustion,—but she could not tell her husband how she felt. She could not even tell him of her plan to leave him.

She seemed honest enough, and during the pastor's exploratory questioning, he found no clues which might lead him to suspect she was hiding anything. So he told her he thought he might be able to help, and asked her to have her husband call the pastor at his earliest convenience.

The following Saturday afternoon the husband sauntered into the church whistling cheerily. After making the customary polite remarks, the pastor, wasting no time, delved into the immediate problem. He told the unsuspecting husband that his wife had called previously, that she was much upset, and had said she was planning to leave him and take the children with her. He jumped to his feet in amazement wanting to know who the other man was. The pastor assured him there was no other man and went on to tell him the gist of the conversation and of her complaints, which was, that he and the children "got her down" so deeply she felt she could not endure him any longer. His expression became most pitiful. He said he had no intimation his wife felt that way,—he had talked about his work because he thought she would be interested in his day's activities and, "maybe he wanted to impress her with the fact that his work was difficult—he was trying to make himself look good in his wife's eyes." The pastor began by giving him a few suggestions about what a wife really wants—love and affection mostly, and an appreciation of what she goes through day after day trying to rear a couple of children. He listened attentively and then asked, "What shall I do?"

The pastor asked how long it had been since his wife had had a vacation from him and the family. He said,—"She wouldn't want to leave us,—she's never been away from us." It was then suggested he go home and tell her he was going to send her to Florida—even if he had to borrow the money—Florida, for three weeks.

Surprisingly enough, he did just that, and did it immediately. He packed her off the next week. Her mother came to take care of the home and children. Three weeks later the young wife returned, as happy as could be, and joy had returned to that household.

Thereafter, for a number of years, on their wedding anniversary, they remembered the pastor with a greeting card, sometimes with a gift.

A seminary professor used to say that when life appeared dark and unbearable, what a person usually needed was eight hours' sleep* and three good leisurely meals. Few cases, however, are as simple as that of the young wife. Usually domestic difficulties are complex, the result of months and years of incompatibility.

Typical of many cases is that of Family "K." Mrs. "K," married twenty-four years, with two children, a son twenty-three and a daughter twenty, came asking help. It seems her husband earned good money. He was self-employed, with an income of more than $10,000 annually. But he gambled recklessly, and drank quietly alone—both bad signs. Not only were they always without funds, they were deeply involved in debt. The two children and the mother were arrayed against the father. The wife said they had had no home life for ten years, that they were bickering and wrangling all the time, and that he was secretive about his finances. He, on the other hand, accused her of being extravagant and without judgment in the use of money. The wife felt terribly insecure, and feared she would be held accountable for her husband's obligations for which she was not responsible.

With her consent a conference was held with her husband and a course of action was suggested—that he go to work for some employer, hire a lawyer to administer his salary each month on a budgetary basis, and that he give up gambling and drinking. He was advised to seek new outlets as a means of restoring his own self-respect. He would thus recover the confidence of his creditors and work himself out of the unhappy situation into which he had fallen in the course of some twenty years. But he was not much interested in the suggestions. He began immediately to accuse his wife and children of grave shortcomings.

There was a sex angle to this situationt—the wife accused her husband of weird and offensive sex practices which she could not stand, and which disgusted her and led her to despise him.

The whole affair became so involved that the pastor felt he could do very little, inasmuch as the husband refused to cooperate, and the wife refused to face her own shortcomings. She did have a desire for more money than was at her disposal, and money, complicated with sex, make a bad combination. The advice in such cases is that the couple seek the expert counsel of an established Family Relations Center, or consult a good psychiatrist.

A distinguished businessman and community leader,—a Mr. "H"—had had a difficult time during the depression. In fact, his wife earned the family living and he was on relief. But with better times his earning capacity increased. His salary was approximately $15,000 a year. His wife bore him three children, and they had built a home. He became involved in an affair with his secretary, who did not discourage him although she was engaged to a man then in the service in the Pacific. Mr. "H" told his wife he wanted a divorce,—that she had grounds for it and he wanted it. He insisted she give it to him, for he intended to leave her anyway. The wife came to the pastor and related the story. He checked with a few friends and found the facts to be as the wife had reported. She was then counseled not to give her husband a divorce under any circumstances—regardless of what he did or threatened. With her consent, the pastor wrote a letter to Mr. "H's" secretary, telling her to leave town within 24 hours, or a wire would be sent to her fiancé giving him all the facts. Also the letter indicated that Mrs. "H." would prosecute her at law, that she would stand no chance of marriage with Mr. "H" for at least seven years, and then went on to describe to her what a "heel" Mr. "H" was,—or any man would be who would treat a wife as he was treating his. Then she was asked if she imagined for a moment Mr. "H" would treat her any differently after a few months, than he was now treating his wife.

The letter was mailed to the secretary, and the pastor personally took a copy of it to Mr. "H" asking him to read it. He read it slowly, and looked out of the window a long time. Finally he turned and said, "Maybe you are right about it." This was his only comment. The next day the secretary left town, apparently thoroughly frightened. She was not heard from again. Later Mrs. "H" called to say she thought the matter was going to work out, and what would the pastor suggest that her husband do? It was suggested he consult a psychiatrist. The psychiatrist advised him to seek new outlets for his energy, such as sports or aviation, and find new community and social interests, such as the church. Mr. "H" took an interest in both aviation and the church. Seven years later the family were still together, respected in the community and apparently happy in their life together.

Mental cases are the most difficult. Early in our ministry there came to the community a very able and gifted musician —he had sung in light opera in New York, and was the soloist in three of the leading Fifth Avenue churches. His brother had been night editor of the *Wall Street Journal*, and his mother was the president of a large mattress factory. Mr. "J" was in his forties, and was suffering from an acute persecution complex—twice he had nearly succeeded in committing suicide by cutting his throat and wrists. His brother had lived with a girl in "common law" marriage; they had a child. The brother died, and so did the girl with whom he lived. The brother bequeathed the musician the care of their child,—but left no money or means of any kind to provide for the child's care. Mr. "J" was a sensitive artist. He could not cope with the circumstances which had enveloped him and he came to the small town to "recuperate." Fortunately he chose an able man as his doctor. Both the doctor and the pastor, separately, took Mr. "J" on long walks through the countryside. Periodically he would call, in great agitation, perspiring profusely and insisting "they were after him." He could never identify "they," but he might have read an ad in the *Saturday Evening Post* and imagined it was directed specifically at him. He was a tormented soul. One day, in the early hours of the morning, he came saying, "They were after him again." After a long carefully guarded conversation designed to assure him he was imagining things, he calmed down, and finally said, "Well, you know they do talk about me." Trying to be agreeable and understanding, the pastor replied, "Of course, they talk about anyone who is a public figure." He jumped to his feet and shouted, "There, you admit they talk about me. I knew it!" and off he went to his home and tried to commit suicide again.

## pastoral counseling and case studies

That afternoon the doctor came to see the pastor and really gave him a tongue lashing—he was a profane man and expressed himself freely, saying, "You ought to know how such cases work—you know you've got to lie in such cases,—lie like the devil."

Well, the pastor learned something. A pastor must establish himself as a man of integrity and honor. But he must also have good sense, and realize that when he is dealing with an abnormal mental case, he must use abnormal methods to suit the case. Later the artist was advised to take up Christian Science, which he did with amazingly happy results.

The pastor and the doctor had a mutual friend, a lawyer and judge. The three worked together on many cases as a team. When a problem case would come to one, and he thought one of the other two might handle the case more effectively, the person seeking help would be so directed. A phone call describing the case and an opinion regarding it would be made immediately to prepare the way for a right disposition of it. When the pastor was asked to perform a marriage which he preferred not to consummate, he would invariably send the couple to the judge, and when he was approached by people on the fanatical fringe, he would refer them to the doctor. Often the judge would send couples to the pastor who needed some marriage counseling more than they needed a divorce, and often the doctor would send patients to the pastor when he felt they needed spiritual healing more than they needed pills.

One quiet November morning the study phone rang. A downtown lawyer was speaking. He said a young woman was being held in custody in his office on a serious embezzlement charge. She had refused to talk to anyone,—except the pastor. The lawyer gave the woman's name over the phone, but the name did not register. In the lawyer's office the story unfolded. It seems the young woman had grown up in the local community. Her parents never "got along." In fact, the evening she was to be graduated from high school, her father came home drunk, "beat-up" her mother and was so violent the girl called the police and had to wait until her father had been taken off to jail before she could leave home for the commencement exercises. During her high school days she had worked

## pastoral counseling and case studies 188

as a waitress to earn enough to buy her clothes. She had worked for nearly two years as a bookkeeper in a small shop, and had, during sixteen months, embezzled a large amount of money—her employer said it totalled more than $20,000, while she insisted the amount was not over $4,000.

It seems she had married twice. The lawyer said it was important that she tell her story to someone, for the offense was serious and since she had two children the case had complications. As it developed, the lawyer greatly under-estimated the "complications."

After conferring with the lawyer, the pastor entered another room where he found the young woman looking out of the window. Her face seemed remotely familiar. It developed that some ten years previous she had married a G. I. on short acquaintance and the pastor had officiated at the service. It was a war marriage that lasted less than three months. The G. I. disappeared and she had never heard of him again. Subsequently she married another soldier who was a fairly decent fellow. Two children were born to this union, but when the husband left for the wars, estrangement followed which resulted in a final separation. In the meantime, the young woman had kept the two children. She was an excellent mother and had an affection for her children which seemed to reveal a hopeful side to her nature. Her one comment was that if "they" took the children away from her she would commit suicide. The lawyer and the pastor believed she meant it. Other than this, she was non-commital for an hour.

Finally the pastor asked her this question: "If you could write your own ticket in this case, what would you ask?" "If you could be placed on probation, with the understanding you could keep your children, and would secure honorable employment and repay a certain reasonable amount each month to your former employer, would you cooperate?" Her reply was, "That sounds fair enough to me."

The employer and lawyer were agreeable, so the young woman was placed under voluntary probation to the pastor. He helped her secure employment as a waitress in a nearby city, and for a month or more things worked out very well. Then, one day she arrived in town, went to the hospital and was delivered of a child. The lawyer called the minister.

Neither had known she was pregnant, inasmuch as she had concealed her condition by wearing a loose winter coat each time they had met with her.

Since the child was born out-of-wedlock, the law was ready to step in and ask whether or not the mother was fit to keep the child. In such cases the County Court can assume custody and responsibility for children. It developed that a local gigolo was involved. He was called in, said he was a Catholic and could not marry the girl because she had been divorced and so could not be married in the church, and it would be a great sin not to be married in the church. As the story unfolded, it seems the young woman had given some of the embezzled money to the young man. He had lived in luxury, was driving a good car, played the races, and had all the comforts of a home without any domestic responsibility.

He, therefore, became accessory to the crime. He turned out to be "no good" and the young woman refused to turn Catholic or have anything more to do with the gigolo. However, to save himself from court action, he promised to pay back some of the money he had received, and also to contribute to the support of his child. Her second husband was contributing to the support of her first two children, which were his.

Without going to court, it was agreed that the original "probation agreement" be continued. It worked well enough for two months, when, about Income Tax time, the former employer claimed his losses by embezzlement had been close to $30,000. Apparently, at least, that was the amount he intended to deduct for income tax purposes and in order to make such a deduction hold, he had to have court action. So he forthwith swore out a warrant for the arrest of the young woman. The police drove fifty miles to the restaurant where she was working, arrested her, would not permit her to return home to look after her children or make arrangements for their care, and placed her in the county jail.

The first thing she did was to call the pastor and ask him to look after the children. This the pastor did. On a hard-pressed Saturday afternoon he drove fifty miles, bought an assortment of groceries and baby food and took it to the home where a baby-sitter promised to take care of the children over the weekend.

The pastor then sought out relatives who signed bail to release the young woman from jail. She returned to her children and the pastor interceded with her employer to enable her to continue as a waitress in his restaurant.

Later she was brought to trial, given a severe sentence which was suspended on condition that she pay $2,500.00 in cash to her former employer and $25.00 a month for five years.

Through this entire case, the young woman confided in the pastor alone, and apparently trusted him. His concern was primarily for the three children, secondly to see that justice was done with mercy, and thirdly to try to rehabilitate the young woman. Hours and hours of time were given to this case. Expert advice was sought from many sources. The pastor ran the risk of being slandered by the town gossips for showing an interest in a condemned woman. But after several years, the woman has thus far justified his confidence and faith in her. She is keeping her word to the court, is caring for her children in a meticulous fashion, and is living a straight life as far as is generally known.

Another case may be of interest for its racial angle. During World War II, a Japanese family came to our small city and knocked on the pastor's door. They were Nisei, and had been compelled to leave Los Angeles on two weeks' notice "for security reasons." They came to our town through the suggestion of their pastor in Hollywood. The family consisted of a father, mother, sister and brother. The sister had been a sophomore in UCLA, and the brother was in high school.

They had been sent to another pastor in the town, but he was afraid of public opinion, and quietly sent them to the writer, who was unaware of the whole situation. The pastor found a place for them to live, and a job for the father. Adverse public opinion against the Nisei ran high, and bitter things were said about the pastor for having anything to do with them. His role in this case was not easy. Fortunately, he had the good judgment to keep his session informed of every detail and every step taken in the whole matter, and his session supported him all the way.

The first day George, the son in the family, attended high school, the students, egged on by their parents, threatened violence if "that dirty Jap" was permitted to stay in school.

The principal, a wise and good man, kept George in his office all day to prevent any untoward act. Late in the afternoon he saw from his office window the baseball team practicing on the athletic field. Upon inquiry, he learned that George played ball, that he was a pitcher. The principal took George out to the field and told the coach to put him in as pitcher. George did such a good job pitching that the boys all claimed him as a member of the team, and he was a top man from that hour on. No further word of criticism was heard about having George around.

The family attended church every Sunday. They conferred with the pastor on every detail. A local citizen of means, and of great Christian spirit, provided an apartment for them. Later the father died, and the night before his services were conducted, the mother and daughter and son sat by the casket and read their Bibles for more than an hour. This made an indelible impression on many church people who had been critical of the Nisei.

Still another case of a father who, after twenty-five years of marriage and four children, left his wife and family for another woman. He asked his wife for a divorce, saying she was physically repulsive to him. At the pastor's request he came for an interview. The pastor told him that he was either physically, mentally or morally and spiritually sick, and he ought to find out which it was. At the pastor's suggestion, the man had a physical examination with the report that he was in good physical health. He consulted a psychiatrist who gave him a clean bill of health. The pastor then told him he was spiritually a sick man and ought to seek God's help before it was too late. Apparently it was too late. The pastor, however, spent literally hundreds of hours in conversations, interviews, conferences, letter writing, trying to help the family. When no reconciliation could be effected, he advised a divorce in an attempt to secure a financial settlement for the wife and children.

The pastor goes on the assumption, in any case of spiritual and mental depression or anxiety, that there is a physical basis for the disorder. Health is a matter of major importance, and a prime factor in all religious, social and personal problems.

A man of very great ability, nationally and internationally known for his published books, went through a period of "climacterium virile."* Among women, the menopause* period, often lasting several years, is common. All pastors must understand the physiological and psychological aspects of this change in life, for many cases will come to him which he can help only if he does understand the symptoms, manifestations, causes and characteristics of this "change of life."

This particular man was going through an acute case of "climacterium virile." The pastor himself had experienced the same physiological condition a few years previously. The symptoms are hard to describe, but extreme depression, melancholy, fear of death and fear of permanent disability are part of the condition. The patient becomes nervous, experiences fluttering of the heart, inability to concentrate and often extreme physical weakness. He cannot stand being in a crowd or appearing in public without approaching nervous collapse. Strangely enough, there appear to be no physical symptoms a doctor can find to indicate anything is wrong.

Few doctors seem to understand this condition, which is an extremely serious disorder, and few seem to know how to attend a patient having this trouble. The pastor, having gone through the ordeal over a period of several months, understood something of its nature. He conferred with the man frequently over a number of weeks, tried to restore his confidence, tried to get him to understand his own case well enough to help himself. Understanding and sympathy and unhurried friendships have excellent therapeutic effects.

Often the pastor has had to explain many things relative to this condition to husbands, as well as to wives, and even to their children. It is a period that calls for patience, faith, and an understanding friend who will recognize the seriousness of the condition and give it the consideration it requires.

The writer is called upon to do considerable counseling with college students. In some respects student counseling is in a category of its own. Although students live under the watchful discipline of college authorities, they are making the transition from the sheltered life of a child in the home to that of an independent and free being in an adult world.

Most students who have come to the writer have had problems involving parental relationships, difficulties in self-discipline, or turbulent love affairs. For the most part, students are in themselves their own most perplexing problems. Occasionally a group will come full of social passion demanding an immediate solution to the local racial discrimination in the restaurants and stores. There is an old saying quoted by Carl Sandburg, "When pups bark, old dogs keep right on doing what they were doing." This fact seems to convince young people that their elders are hopeless reactionaries and conservative die-hards.

When a group of ardent idealists come to a pastor expecting leadership in a social crusade, they must not be turned away, or let down. Instead, they must be properly briefed on what has been done, who has been doing it, and what progress has been made. It must be impressed upon them that individually they must hold truly to their ideals, but only as they work collectively will their efforts bear fruit. They must be warned that today "prophets" are given treatment just as severe as they received in Biblical times.

By and large, their real troubles are personal. A young man and a young woman wish to marry. They still have a year or two ahead of them in college. Usually the parents object to undergraduate marriage. The pastor's job is to help this young couple to look at marriage objectively and enable them to see the social and economic aspects involved. Love and grocery bills go together in marriage; and marriage on a college campus radically changes one's social status.

The pastor must try to interpret to young people the thinking of their parents, and maintain in their minds a respect and affection for the parents and an appreciation of parental efforts through the years. At the same time, he must remind the parents of one important fact of life, which is that the sex glands are most active during the late teens and early twenties. He must remind them that when young people make up their minds to be married, parents must learn to relinquish authority over their lives and assume the role of sympathetic counselor. All parties involved must be reminded that there is nothing inherently evil in early marriage, but that the time for young people to marry is when they are mutually in love and can see their way clear economically and socially to enter into the state of holy matrimony. The writer pities most the unmarried, and next the childless. Other things being equal, marriage is to be encouraged, not discouraged.

One young man came, wildly in love, but frantic in mind and spirit. He had dated a girl steadily for a year. She did not repulse him, nor did she throw herself at him as he wished she would. She received and even sought his tokens of affection. In fact, according to his story, she repeatedly insisted on full sex satisfaction. On the other hand, she refused to accept an engagement ring from him or even to discuss marriage. She seemed to delight in tormenting him through pseudo-quarrels, taunted him constantly with the statement that she was pregnant and would commit suicide before she would either have a child or marry him.

He repeatedly insisted that, to him, sex was not a moral issue, but a biological fact which he accepted as he did his other appetites. He did not like what he called "the damned sex angle" of his predicament. What worried him was that his girl friend, whom he declared he loved and wanted to marry, would accept sex so casually but not accept his love. It was not sex he wanted, he said, but her true love.

The pastor must admit that this was a new angle to an old story, but he tried to conceal his thoughts and reactions. He knew it was no time to preach, moralize or lecture. He listened thoughtfully and finally advised the young man to "keep his head" and tried to assure him the girl, at heart, really loved him. She had come from a good home and had a strong religious background. Her part in the whole affair might have several explanations. The boy was advised to be patient, keep himself under control and await developments.

Interestingly enough, the young man returned two weeks later to discuss a matter involving the validity of traditional religion, but began his conversation with the casual remark that he and the girl friend were planning a summer wedding—he was a Sophomore and the girl was a Junior. He gives the pastor credit for being a very wise man, whereas the latter still cannot fully understand all the factors involved in the case.

When students come seeking counsel regarding college courses, the first step is to search out their true interests. On general principles, students are advised to take all the history, philosophy and English possible and to take these subjects from the very best teachers on the campus. They are advised not to fall into a single religious pattern, but to attend as many different churches as possible, and to hold fast to the basic religious truths they find in their searching. Conformity in religion in the student years can be deadly. A healthy interest in religion generally is a sign of life.

The pastor is in a strategic position to introduce students to leaders in business, industry, and the professions. He should go out of his way to do this, for it is a service appreciated by all parties concerned.

From these case studies, it is evident that the problems which come to the pastor cover the whole range of human interest, activity and error. Actually, few people come to the pastor inquiring the way to the Kingdom of God, or asking for knowledge of God, of immortality or for soul salvation. They come instead, asking help in trying to disentangle themselves from a disagreeable love affair or marital situation, for help in seeking a job or in holding one, for assistance for a husband, a wife, a son, a daughter or aged parents. They come as students seeking quick and final answers to profound questions for which there are no final answers. They come as socially, economically and religiously displaced persons, seeking ways and means of finding an anchor. They come in joy and in sorrow, in sickness and in health.

Obviously, the pastor, whose professional training has been largely in the field of theoretical religion, and most of whose working hours are spent trying to keep the multiple organizations within a church functioning harmoniously, and whose hours in the stillness of the night are spent trying to write sermons or speeches, is not qualified as an expert in the whole range of human experience. Nevertheless, he must develop certain basic skills in the area of human relations, and he must qualify as a better than average amateur in the field of medicine, law, economics, psychology and the social sciences. During any given working day he may be called on to counsel a person involved in legal entanglements, to suggest ways of establishing peace in a quarreling family, to advise and comfort a person who is physically and mentally ill, to see a teacher on behalf of a student and an employer on behalf of an employee, to give aid and comfort to the bereaved, counsel with a young couple entering marriage, fix a leak in a furnace pipe, tell an electrician what to do about a faulty public address system, administer healing to one who is spiritually sick, confer with Sunday School teachers concerning teaching methods and curriculum materials, write several personal recommendations and sit in on a number of committee meetings of church boards, community councils, and planning committees.

He must have a wide knowledge of many things. He must know whom to call for information he himself does not have. He must know his limitations, and at the same time act with assurance and courage when the situation calls for these qualities.

He will come to the end of many a day wondering where the time went. For time is a most precious item.

Dr. Frank Crane, in one of his syndicated columns, made a suggestion which would save hours of a pastor's time. It is that before seeing the pastor, people be required to write their problems down on paper, stating as definitely as possible just what sort of help they seek and what their own thoughts may be toward a solution for their case. If the pastor has such a statement beforehand, it will save hours of preliminary conversation. Furthermore, when people write down on paper their own story, they may find it is not as important as it was at first thought, and they may find the solution to it themselves.

The average pastor today has very little time for social visiting among his flock. He must be available when his services are needed, but he must guard his time carefully. Counseling takes time—much time. The medical doctor may be able to read a thermometer, make a quick diagnosis, leave a few penicillin tablets, advise the patient to stay in bed, and gracefully depart, all within ten minutes. The pastor's approach is more difficult. He has no disciplinary authority over his patients and no quick drug cures. He must sit and listen by the hour and show an interest in the person talking. He must confer with others, often a score of others, to make certain the facts in a given case are as they are represented. He must weigh carefully every suggestion he offers, lest it be misunderstood.

Many people are pathetic victims of situations beyond their control; they are trapped in tragic circumstances they cannot handle. Many come seeking help but try to hide their real problem. (Frequently they come seeking help for another.) In these cases the pastor must develop a skill in diagnosing human ills of the mind and spirit—and this skill cannot be acquired through books; it is acquired mainly through experience.

The pastor must avoid inhabiting an ivory tower; he must learn to live and move and have his being among people. As a student of human nature he must let everything flow through his net and retain the sort of knowledge and experience that might be of value to him in counseling others.

He must beware of the pitfall of flattery, and be mature lest in a moment of naiveté he fall into the snare of a designing woman, a financial sharpie or a professional do-gooder who "uses" everyone in sight but serves no one in particular.

To do his work well, the pastor must keep himself in mental and spiritual health. Toward this end, there is nothing more valuable than proper rest and diversion. He will develop the moral courage to face situations honestly, fearlessly and without evasion or delay. Above all, he must never lose sight of his mission. In the final analysis, all human problems boil down to a theological and philosophical residue. If he has a sound philosophy of life, and a valid, constructive, vital theology, his work will reflect it into the smallest act and word. See counseling; hospital chaplain, the; marriage, disharmony in; ministry, the, and counseling; pastoral psychology; professional reference. J. R. W.

**pastoral counseling: case studies:**

### I.

A mother came to me in great distress of spirit regarding her second daughter, whom the clergyman had known for years as a student in his religious school, as a young bride at whose wedding he had officiated, and as a young mother, whose first and second child he had welcomed and named at Sabbath services. Soon after the birth of her second child, the young woman had grown melancholy and had spoken frequently of taking her life. She betrayed obvious evidences of a "breakdown." The mother, a person of considerable piety, expressed to the clergyman the hope that he could speak a "magic word" which would quickly restore her daughter to health. The clergyman inquired into the circumstances, learned that the young matron was under psychiatric care, and counseled the mother and the married sister, that they should rely upon the guidance of the psychiatrist. They should expect no rapid cure, but should cooperate in every respect with the psychiatrist and the physician. They should not do anything contrary to their advice, and should maintain their own composure during the emotional illness of their daughter and sister. The clergyman consulted with the physician son-in-law regarding the circumstances and informed him that the best assistance he, as a clergyman could offer, lay in the confidence that in time the young matron would be restored to health, unless her condition was too deeply rooted, and that her family could gain spiritual sustenance by a knowledge of cures in similar cases, by attendance at religious services, and by faith in the medical and psychiatric care being given their loved one.

## II.

A young father and mother came to the clergyman in great grief over the "breakdown" of their son, well-known to the clergyman from his infancy, in his boyhood days as a pupil in the religious school, and as an active worker in the youth groups. In his early college years it had become necessary to place the lad under psychiatric care, and the parents were beside themselves with anguish. The mother mentioned to the clergyman that she feared her son had been tormented in his adolescent years by the fear that he would go the way of an older child who had developed psychological difficulties and was confined to an institution. The clergyman assured the parents that no two cases were the same; that he was certain their son would respond to psychiatric care; that they should be patient and confident, and eventually they would be rewarded by their son's return to health. The mother professed to be of non-religious tendencies, but she accepted as valid the assurance given by the clergyman, based, as it was, upon wide experience. The boy made an excellent recovery after a period of prolonged rest and treatment, and has resumed his studies. His case was representative of a number of similar cases of young people from fine families who, in their adolescent years, have required psychiatric care. The clergman has conceived his role to be the recommendation, if necessary, of a suitable psychiatrist, and the persuasion of the parents that they give the psychiatrist their thorough-going cooperation.

### III.

A husband and wife, with two married children and a number of grandchildren, had separated following a severe quarrel. The clergyman had been called upon to minister to them several years before under similar circumstances, and had placed them under the guidance of an eminent psychiatrist now deceased. In the second major conflict and separation, the clergyman to whom both the husband and wife came for conversation and suggestion, finally convinced them that they should go to a wise psychiatrist whose word they would be willing to heed. The clergyman was informed of the basic factors in the whole situation, and took it upon himself to remind the husband of the ancient dictum: "Forsake not the wife of your youth." He also sought to demonstrate to the wife the importance of understanding and dealing discreetly and with forbearance with her somewhat ebullient husband. But he aided in establishing a situation whereby both the husband and wife, at first independently, and then in joint meeting with the psychiatrist, faced each other at last, gradually overcame their hostility, and finally reached a *modus vivendi*. They now are living under the same roof; their children are, of course, happy at their reunion; certain mistakes have been rectified (the exact arrangements being outside the clergyman's knowledge or desire to know), and the social prestige of both husband and wife, in the eyes of their family and friends, has been recovered.

### IV.

The mother of a young industrialist at whose marriage the clergyman had officiated, was in her late seventies and eager to be released from the pain she was suffering. She was beyond medical help, but she believed that perhaps the religious teacher could make her lot easier. The clergyman visited her; sent her literature to read; brought her case to the attention of a religious group which professes to combine "spiritual healing" with medical and psychiatric science. The clergyman, however, felt that the care of such a patient required constant, scientific attention, and that it would be hypocritical and wrong to lead her family or the elderly lady herself to believe she could be "cured" by get-well-quick means. Her mental distress had been diagnosed as the result of the hardening of the arteries, and the clergyman hesitated to make unwarranted pretensions beyond the capacity of medical science to alleviate her difficulties. Even at the risk of an anti-medical healing cult taking hold of the case for its own benefit, the clergyman would do no more than pastoral attentiveness could offer.

## V.

A father and mother came to the clergyman for counsel with respect to their son who had changed his religious allegiance and become an adherent of a denomination both foreign and obscurantist in their eyes. In a few months they informed the clerygman that their son had married a young woman of this group under ecclesiastical auspices repugnant to them. The clergyman learned that the son had been in the armed services and had seemed to be a changed person on his return to civilian life. He had sought unsuccessfully to gain admittance to a medical school, and had then turned to scientific research. He had been jilted by a young woman of his own faith and community, and for days remained in a state of shock, making himself incommunicado. The father showed the clergyman the boy's letters telling of his conversion to the alien faith, and of his inability to persuade his son to return to his family religion. The clergyman did not advise the father to visit the son before his marriage outside his own group, but the father did so, without result. The clergyman did his best to console the stricken parents, who recognized their son's emotional condition, and quoted to them the words of tradition: "If your son seem to you to transgress, love him more than ever." The clergyman told the parents that they should not drive their son and his wife from them; they should always welcome them at their home, and let them go their own way in matters of religion, if to do so meant the preservation of the boy's psychic health.

Again and again the clerygman has found it necessary to give this advice: namely, that even though children may do eccentric things, the consideration of their health takes precedence above all else. The children of religious liberals may become orthodox, but if reliance upon orthodoxy stabilizes them, the parents should not interfere.

## VI.

A father and a mother asked the advice of the clergyman to locate their adolescent son who had run away from home. The clergyman knew the lad as a former pupil in his religious school. He was shown the letter which the runaway had left when he suddenly took his departure, and learned other facts regarding the boy's personality and behavior. The mother was the owner and manager of a mercantile establishment, and the father was a reasonably successful business man. The boy was an introvert, but had a fair rating at the private school he attended. The clerygman suggested that the parents consult an eminent psychiatrist, whom he recommends only on rare occasions, in view of the fact that the psychiatrist has more cases before him than he has time to handle. The psychiatrist gave the parents advice as to steps they should take in helping to locate the whereabouts of their son. The boy after a few weeks made his appearance and returned to his home. He visited the psychiatrist once or twice, but then declined, apparently at the suggestion of his parents, to return for psychotherapy. (In this connection, it may be said that the psychiatrist had great difficulty in receiving appropriate remuneration for the many hours he had given both the parents and the boy.) The clergyman has not been informed of the present state of the young man's health, the parents belonging to the large group of persons who will come to a religious institution or a religious leader only when they need a specific benefit they believe at the moment it can confer.

## VII.

A mother wrote from a distant city to the clergyman telling of the involvement of her daughter with a young man. The clergyman found himself traveling long distances in order to settle the matter: the marriage took place; the child was born in wedlock, and the clergyman receives at the new year each year a remembrance card from the girl's mother. See counseling; ministry, the, and counseling; pastoral psychology: its governing limitations and qualifications. L. I. N.

**pastoral problems:** see ministry; pastoral counseling and case studies.

**pastoral psychology:** A relatively recent term which has

come to designate that area of a minister's work as pastor* involving human relationships with particular attention to the psychological factors involved.

Psychology* has to do with the behavior of man, the life of mind and its intimate relationship to the body. Medical men are now speaking of psychosomatic* medicine indicating the close correlation of mind and body.

A minister who deals continually with people rather than things will naturally be a student of human behavior. He is a practical psychologist, for better or for worse. Pastoral psychology is the disciplined application of whatever information the studies of human psychology may offer to the understanding of the pastor's professional relationship to people. As a representative of high religion he will want to act wisely; and wisdom is the insight into disciplined knowledge and the practical application of it together with the accumulated experiences of life situations.

Some of the most successful in this field are those whose wisdom has come through critical common sense in the maturing experiences of years in the field of personal counseling. Not all ministers (or even educators) who study psychology are persons of wisdom in this field. The field of psychology offers the grist for the mill of understanding. But more is required in the practical application of this information.

A minister as counselor will naturally have a liking for people and in the passion to help them will have a good measure of critical common sense and what may be called a flair of understanding human nature. He will never be consciously professional or academic. More like the geniuses of practical religion, such as Christ, he will understand the raw stuff that goes into the making of people. He will speak their language and idiom, understand their work-a-day world, their spontaneous and natural impulses and responses, the emotions* common to all, the factor of temperament* and organic drives,* the colossal forces of predisposition and habit,* the possibilities and difficulties involved in the change of habit patterns of both thought and action, signs of aberrations from the normal patterns of response, the motives* of men, the human age* levels and their characteristic responses, the behavior of crowds* and all known factors of human psychology. And he will want to know what theories are taught by the "schools" (in psychology)* so as better to understand what is natural and human.

The religious approach, if it is of the highest type, will not flout the laws of human psychology (wherever these are in evidence). A pious approach without respect for human characteristics will not promote the highest ends.

It is necessary to remember that when people are religious they are also human—including the minister himself. There is no special religious psychology. Rather psychology is itself a basic discipline which has many ramifications. Such ramifications are designated in some areas as religious, in other areas as political, social, artistic, etc., but the human characteristics remain the same. The minister, as pastoral psychologist, will not approach psychology from the angle of religion; rather, he will come to appreciate religious behavior from the point of view of basic human psychology. Ideals (religious—ethical) may be theoretically valid; but ideals unattached to human responses are no subject-matter for pastoral psychology. So unattached they belong purely to philosophical speculation (which, of course, has its place and value).

The field of pastoral psychology includes the whole province of human relationships, people interacting with people, the minister interacting with people, the minister's own behavior as a member of the same genus as his fellowmen. It includes directing, counseling,* educating and setting the sights for whatever possibilities of fuller living that are within the range of human responses. See Cabot, R. C.; old age; pastoral counseling: case studies; psychology of religion.

*Bibl.* Rollo May, *The Art of Counseling* (1939).

**Pastoral Psychology:** see psychology of religion.

**pastoral psychology: its governing limitations and qualifications:** Pastoral psychology is a term with which to conjure in the modern ministry. From time immemorial, however, clergymen have given attention, in psychic and spiritual terms, to the needs of their flock. One is reminded of the surprise of Molière's *Bourgeois Gentilhomme* who was delighted to learn that all his life he had been speaking prose. Many are surprised today to discover that the ministrations of the priest, the pastor and the rabbi have a sound scientific foundation, and the renowned psychiatrist, Karl Menninger, writing on "The Religion of a Psychiatrist," declares that the relationship of a clergyman to his congregation is a subject deserving of close and appreciative study. Articles and books are written on pastoral psychology, and some of the more effectively written volumes remain for a long time on the non-fiction best-seller lists.

It is necessary, however, to approach the domain of pastoral psychology with common sense and restraint. Excessive expectations are unhealthy, and the confidence that the religious ministrant has an especial magic in his technique is regrettable. Religio-therapy is a recognized field of treatment today, but it has its distinct limitations. A short-cut to physical and psychic health is just as dangerous in the 20th century as in all previous eras. The *Shulhan Arukh,* the Code of traditional Jewish Law and Practice, compiled in the 16th century has the following statement:

> The Torah has granted the doctor the privilege of healing, as it is said: 'And he shall cause him to be thoroughly healed.' (Exodus 21:19) Therefore the sick person should not rely upon a miracle, but he is in duty bound to act according to the custom of the world and call in a doctor to heal him, and many of the world's pious men have been cured by physicians. He who avoids calling in the doctor is guilty of two evils: in the first instance of transgressing the rule forbidding one who is in danger to rely upon a miracle; the other evil is that he manifests presumption and pride in depending upon his righteousness to cause him to be healed in a miraculous manner. One should call on a competent doctor, and with all this his heart should hope for the help of Heaven and he should plead for the mercy of the Faithful Healer, Blessed be His Name, and his heart should trust in God only. *Kitzur Shulhan Arukh,* cxcii, 3 (New York, 1927).

Thus a classic religion, Judaism, even in its orthodox form, seeks to combine a reliance upon medical science with religious faith. But today many so-called healing cults condemn the resort to the care of the physician and surgeon; moreover, they look askance upon the psychiatrist, and refuse to subject themselves to the methods of psychoanalysis, psychiatry or psychotherapy. They believe they have a secret beyond the knowledge of those who are trained in the practice of medicine and its allied sciences. They assert that the Divine Mind can furnish healing, even in the case of organic ailments. With respect to healing cults, such as "Jewish Science," its leaders, at the same time that they turn to the physician and the psychiatrist, nevertheless strive to develop their own religio-therapeutics, conducted by their own practitioners.

As for religion in general, and liberal religion in particular, no attempt is made to put forward claims to an authority and effectiveness unmerited by the realities. It is understood that the entire system or organized religion is in and of itself a means for the healing of the healthy as well as the spiritually and psychically ill. For example, the sermon of the minister as preacher, has a definite ameliorative value. Congregants "feel better" as a consequence of worship, combined with ethical instruction from the pulpit. They are encouraged to accept a mood of optimism; they are taught that God is good and the Universe benevolent, despite the obvious contradictions and tragedies of circumstance and experience. The sermon is delivered in an endeavor to sharpen the judgment of the listeners concerning the problems of life, relating to the individual and the community alike. It strives to bring persons of varied outlooks into contact with the actualities of living, so that they may not unduly escape from its impacts. The sermon can also have an inspirational quality enkindling the listener's heart and spirit; it can give him or her a vision or a larger and fuller personal life; it can furnish the impulse to enlist in movements of altruism and enterprises of charity. Merely by virtue of the emanations of the clergyman's personality, particularly if the influence of the sermon is reinforced by closer associations in church or synagogue auxiliary groups, the congregant can gain a form of "healing," the effect of which is hard to put into words.

The inspirational books, like worthwhile sermons, can also function as manuals or guidebooks for happier living. The book-stalls have had a surfeit of such volumes, but there is always room for another which phrases the classic truths vigorously and originally. Every piece of writing is in the nature of a "confession" by the author, and no unworthy spirit can pen a genuinely worthy book. But it is not enough for the liberal religionist to rely upon the printed page to mould the character and personality of the reader, nor should extravagant pretensions be advanced in any book which inevitably are unmasked. There is no substitute for the gruelling lessons of experience, in accordance with the individual's particular equipment of physique and psyche, and the writer sins against the unwitting if he deludes them into believing they can be lifted out of and beyond themselves.

Every clergyman, at the grass-roots of pastoral service, is a shepherd to his charges. He advises young people and adults in critical hours of decision; he counsels them in the art of perfecting amiable human relations; he jubilates with them in their hours of rejoicing; he condoles with them at the time of their bereavement. In Hasidic Jewish literature there is the story of the disciple who gave this account of the Great Maggid: "When we journeyed to him, most of our desires were stilled upon entering town. Whoever had a particularly keen desire was soothed upon entering the Maggid's house. But if there was one among us whose soul was rocking like a boat, when he beheld the Maggid's face, he came to rest." If this pacifying effect is deepened by the pastoral call in the home, or a conference by a distressed person in the clergyman's study, the therapeutic value is immeasurable. Moreover, the religious institution, organized today as a seven-day, seven-night a week social, cultural, religious, welfare and recreational center, enables masses of persons to assemble under favorable auspices, and thus to know "how good and how pleasing it is for brethren to dwell together in unity." The personality of the clergyman should permeate the entire institution, and he can never expect to be helpful by "absentee leadership" or by "remote control." Children are instructed in the fundamentals of the particular faith; their parents, in the parent-teachers' organizations, the sisterhoods and brotherhoods, gradually become seasoned, adult and mature persons. The young people in their social groups make friendships which oftentimes lead to marriage, and, in any event, preserve them from loneliness and social resentments. The middle-aged find an outlet for their energies in the good works of upbuilding the religious institution and its complete program, thereby appreciating the pristine message that "man does not live by bread alone." The aged are made to feel at home, in consonance with the words of a contemporary sage who said: "When a man gets old, he sits in the park and goes to church or synagogue."

Needless to say, the pastor also stands at the side of those who are ill or in the presence of the Angel of Death. Physicians and psychiatrists often rely upon the clergyman to ease the departure of a stricken patient. In a discussion as to whether the fatally ill patient should be "told the truth," Dr. E. M. Bluestone remarks: "If we are to tell the patient, how shall we do it? How shall we soften the blow? Certainly it is inhumane to tell it outright without the softening words which the minister of God is trained to use." Even the humanist clergyman or those ministers who profess not to believe in a Universal Personality, or in the blending of the individual intelligence with the Eternal Intelligence, have their own formulas of solace wherewith they minister to those *in extremis*. Thus it is clear that both directly and indirectly, religion as a system of belief and practice and its representatives, the clergymen and their lay co-workers, play a decisive role in the domain of pastoral psychology.

There are congregants, however, whose ailments are not those to which ordinary, reasonable well-adjusted mortals, are heir. These persons stand on the border-line between the emotionally healthy and the emotionally ill. When dealing with such individuals, the clergyman is called upon to decide whether the person seeking his guidance is in the throes of a breakdown or is approaching it. For this reason, it is well for clergymen to secure formal training in pastoral psychology, to the degree that it has become a science today. Only a few clergymen have taken a medical degree or been licensed as psychiatrists. Nor is it sufficient to be known as a "marriage counselor" or the like. Attendance at a series of lectures on "Pastoral Psychiatry" does not give a clergyman the requisite qualifications for ascribing to himself special faculties and powers. Nor does the reading of the most authoritative textbooks or popular studies endow him with the necessary wisdom.

Moreover, the many-sided aspects of the clergyman's calling make it impossible for him to furnish to individuals of neurotic tendencies the care and treatment they require. He must be sufficiently skilled to discern those who are psychotic or near-psychotic, and he must likewise be able to determine, among those who are not specifically ill, those persons who can respond to the necessary treatment. It is his duty not to try to enact the role of the psychiatrist, but as quickly as possible, he must refer the sick person to the professional man. Oftentimes he must secure the judgment of the psychiatrist regarding the symptoms which a petitioner displays. Moreover, the clergyman, in such instances, must place himself under the direction of the psychiatrist, in the event that the latter believes his assistance as a religionist is helpful. Psychotherapy and religio-therapy demand consistent, patient treatment, over long periods of time, and the clergyman rarely finds the hours to furnish this. Therefore he must have a specialist as a member of the staff of his church or synagogue, to whom he can refer cases. Or if such a professional is not a member of the institution's staff, he may be a friend and advisor of the clergyman when required. All this entails the expenditure of time and money, and it must not be forgotten that while the clergyman is willing to give his time freely, the professional psychiatrist must make his hours count in monetary terms. Too often distressed persons come to the clergyman when they have been unsuccessful in their consultations with the psychiatrist, but it is an astute pastor who immediately turns them back to their psychiatrist.

Frequently the clergyman and the psychiatrist can work hand in hand, especially in the case of parishioners who, at one time, will accept guidance from the clergyman, and, at another moment, from the psychiatrist. Husbands and wives have been brought together as a consequence of this technique. Sometimes the psychiatrist will recommend to the clergyman that he accept a convalescent youth as a member of the religious institution's young people's organization, in the hope that social opportunities will accelerate the cure. Sometimes the psychiatrist will appreciate the value of attendance at divine worship, the reading of religious literature, and the performance of traditional rites and ceremonies. In every such instance, the psychiatrist must be the mentor and the director of the treatment.

A clergyman who seeks to establish himself as a psychological consultant will soon find himself overwhelmed with appeals for help. He will be besieged by telephone and in person by the distracted, the psychically upset and specifically ill. He must then choose whether he wishes this type of service to dominate his ministerial activity. If so, other ministers must fulfill his responsibilities as preacher, executive, organizer, representative of the church or synagogue in the community, and pastor. His work will become chiefly that of a clinician in the field of religio-therapy, and though he may write books as the harvest of such service, he ceases to enact the role of the modern clergyman in all its varied departments.

Therefore, let us understand the problem humanely and discreetly. If we wish to do a superficial piece of work, we can solicit a reputation in pastoral psychology, by underscoring this enterprise above all others in our ministry. But if we wish to be fair and upright in our conception of the tasks of the contemporary pastor, we must be satisfied with the religio-therapeutic effect of the traditional activities of the minister —through the medium of the sermon, the lesson, the pastoral call, the ministration in time of joy or sorrow, and the multitudinous other agencies of personal influence long identified with the calling of the clergymen. We must avoid building up false hopes among our congregants and the community, by accepting as valid the report that we are akin to medicine-men and magicians in the art of healing. We must not offer panaceas in the form of slogans, get-rich-quick or get-well-quick catch-phrases, which may make us for the moment the cynosure of a myriad eyes, but in the end prove hollow and deceptive. We must not anticipate too little of ourselves as ministrants to the souls of our people, but, in the name of our lofty calling, we must not lead them to anticipate too much of us, who are frail mortals like themselves. See pastoral counseling: case studies.

> Bibl. The following volumes are mentioned here without indicating in any way whatsoever an opinion regarding their contents or the merit of their viewpoint. Leslie D. Weatherhead, *Psychology, Religion and Healing*. A survey of the methods of healing through psychology and religion (1951).

A. A. Brill, *Basic Principles of Psychoanalysis* (1949).
———, *Lectures on Psychoanalytic Psychiatry* (1946).
James H. Vanderveldt and Robert P. Odenwald, *Psychiatry and Catholicism* (1952).
Carl Gustav Jung, *Psychology and Religion* (1938).
Erich Fromm, *Psychoanalysis and Religion* (1950).
Sandor Lorand, *Psychoanalysis Today* (1944). See essay on "The Psychology of Religion" by Ernest Jones, pp. 315 ff.
S. Z. Orgel, *Psychiatry Today and Tomorrow* (1946).
Joshua Loth Liebman, *Psychiatry and Religion*, by 15 American authorities (1948). Also J. L. Liebman, *Peace of Mind* (1946).
Carl J. Schindler, *The Pastor as a Personal Counselor* (1942).
Morris Lichtenstein, *Peace of Mind* (1927); also *Jewish Science and Health* (1925); also *Cures for Minds in Distress* (1936).
Numerous other essays and books on the relationship of organized religion to healing are available, and will be mentioned in my forthcoming volume on *The Healing of Modern Man*.　　　　　　　　　　　　　　　　　　　　L. I. N.

**patellar reflex:** The forward jerk of the foot (with the leg relaxed and bent at the knee) known as the knee jerk. This reflex\* is produced by a blow just below the patella or kneecap.

**pathetic fallacy:** see anthropopathism.

**pathophobia:** see phobias.

**Paul:** see divided self.

**Pavlov, Ivan Petrovitch:** (1849-1936) A Russian physiologist who experimentally (with dogs) showed the fact and significance of the conditioned reflex. The latter is the principle of the initiation of a response by a substitute stimulus (the original stimulus being taken over by association with a secondary stimulus). Pavlov's example: a dog will salivate at the sound of a bell (sounded before the presentation of food) after (by repetition) the food itself is removed. The importance of this response at the human level is obvious. See experimental extinction.

**payment of a fee:** see fees; sacrifice, a psychological concept.

**peace and war:** Strife was once thought to be but the expression of the "pugnacious instinct." Freudians speak of it as the "death instinct."

Both leaders and followers are involved in war. To wage a war leaders must, by some means, secure support of the majority of followers. To achieve this end there must be a feeling of loyalty to the leadership, a sense of exaltation, a mind-set against the enemy, a release of energy ready to serve the end of war, a feeling of frustration against some potential or actual menace (a cause) and a focus upon some situation that will give a sense of urgency.

What may be called "social prejudice" is an important factor in engaging in the conflict of war. For example, a hatred for the British red-coats of Revolutionary times, painted as overlords in conventional histories of America of a generation ago, has made it difficult for many Americans to look upon England as an ally. So the Jewish question, the Negro question (particularly in the south) and now Russians. A child may easily develop a natural hatred against or feeling of superiority over a whole nation, not one member of which has ever harmed him or even is known to him, by the sheer social pressure of prejudice. Wars are fanned by such social suggestion. So, likewise, the cause of international peace.

What is called "projection"\* also plays into this process. Seeing oneself in others is the phenomenon of projection. A cheater may easily believe that everyone cheats. The imputation of motives\* to others reflecting our own is common. This becomes effective in social propaganda, particularly in a war psychology. There is a common frailty, also, of balancing virtues and vices, with the favorable balance of virtues "on our side" of the fence. It is common to commit the fallacy of "absolute-contrast" in which all good traits are on one side and all bad on the other.

Nationalism as a passion acquires the idea of national virtue in contrast to vice which is identified in the enemy nation. Aggressiveness in war is discounted as an ingredient to motive even on the part of an aggressor. The defensive motive is psychologically and morally a greater inducement.

Glorification of war virtues is also a part of the psychological picture. There are those of heroism, fame, strength, bravery, courage, commitment, loyalty, sacrifice and the symbolism of a great cause. During peace time men tend towards pacifism. Psychological studies have found that those groups which are passionately nationalistic in political and economic thinking rate higher in approval of war. Organized veteran groups are in this class—and understandably so. A relatively low nationalistic feeling, similarly, rates low on war approval.

The fortunes of a war knit nationalistic feelings. If unfavorable, the enemy becomes more brutal and the defense mechanisms of hate increase.

Social psychologists are pointing out that a peace program must consider 1) methods to decrease frustration which will weaken any tendency toward aggression; and 2) a type of education to reveal the causes of tensions and dangers of irrational hostility propaganda. Channeling ideas on the level of a common humanity rather than on the more or less fixed boundaries of inherited divisions offers the better chance of a peace economy. Exposing the common psychological features in judgment (such as projection, above mentioned) would be integral to the psychology of peace. If a person better understands himself psychologically (and others) he has a better chance of being saved from premature and unwarranted ideas of others. Emotional maturity is a must in any sound educational program. Democracy, at its weakest point, as Plato long ago pointed out, is inherently beset by the danger of a majority vote on an immature emotional level. To further the democratic way is to raise the emotional tone which is appreciative of the universal rights of others who belong to the same bundle of humanity. Isolationism is the inherited barrier to the goal of universal peace. With nations as well as with men maturity involves the discipline of understanding, tact, patience and even generosity. Where villains are involved self protection and inherent dignity may force peace-aspiring peoples to methods of brutal persuasion much as a police force acts to preserve social values against inhumane acts of self assertiveness.

Strife is not something that is overcome. But strife itself may, as William James once suggested, be redirected into channels which are perchance the "moral equivalent[s] of war." All life is a struggle and particularly the making of a moral character. The biggest area of conflict is in ourselves where there is excitement and cause enough to make life interesting and significant—and so, also, in the society in which we live. There are social struggles sufficient without the necessity for gun powder or atomic weapons. Each level of conquest raises newer issues which, in turn, must be met by the greater insights into their nature and still more emotional maturity—but nevertheless in a total framework of peace-without-war.

*Bibl.* E. F. M. Durbin and J. Bowlby, *Personal Aggressiveness and War* (1939); P. Hopkins, *Psychology of Social Movements* (1938); Mark A. May, *Social Psychology of War and Peace* (1943); Ross Stagner, "Opinions of Psychologists on Peace Planning," *Journal of Psychology* (1945); Q. Wright, *A Study of War* (2. vols., 1942); Ross Stagner, "War and Peace" in *Encyclopedia of Psychology*, ed. by P. L. Harriman (1946).

**peace of mind:** see confession; psychoneuroses.
**peak of tension:** see deception.
**pedomancy:** see palmistry and pedomancy.
**penitence:** see confession.
**perception:** The awareness side of a sensation* is called the perception. See apperception; Wertheimer, Max.
**perception, extra-sensory:** see extra-sensory perception.
**perception, social:** see social perception.
**performance:** see learning.
**periods of counseling:** see counseling periods.
**persistence:** see deliberate effort; success; talents.
**person:** see personality.
**personal counseling:** see counseling.
**personalistic psychology:** see psychology, schools of.
**personality:** The original use of the word *persona* is the mask which an actor put on to reveal the character he wished to portray. This mask became transferred to the individual himself: his total self and character. A personality is the continuing character of the individual in the circumstance of change. The person as a metaphysical entity came to be thought of also as an empirical entity; the metaphysical person being the underlying substance which "has" thoughts, feelings, volitions; the empirical person being the individual's total experience,

**personality** 214

that which is of interest to psychologists. The latter have given to the concept meanings in accordance with basic psychological presuppositions (see psychological frames of reference). Some psychologists take the whole empirical personality as their base (personalists); others take the overt action of organic responses (behaviorists) while still others some deeper phase of operation as base (depth psychology*).

There is a horrible confusion of terms among psychologists even as there has traditionally been among theologians and philosophers in the use of such terms as "individual," "self," "person,"—although the psychologists have almost unanimously dropped the traditional terms (of theology and philosophy) of "spirit" and "soul" (suggesting a metaphysics rather than a psychology). Many distinguish the individual self from personality by suggesting the latter term for social reference. We speak of an individual as a personality when we mean his total impact upon us, in his relation to others. Personality in this sense is an achievement in relationship to others. It is an acquirement. J. F. Dashiell defines personality as "a sum total of behavior trends manifested in [the individual's] . . . social adjustments."

The early environment* of a child is now believed to carry the determinants of personality traits. Much of this influence is indirect, by unconscious imitation through social suggestion. Perhaps most of these early experiences are beyond recall; nevertheless they continue to count heavily. An individual showing an inferiority trait may trace it back to a family situation. So also traits of selfishness, domineering, cruelty, sympathy—no two children having identical experiences even though belonging to the same family circle. It even makes a difference in the order in which one is born into a family; and especially if there is no such order through being an only child. Baby-sitters, now so common, even professionally increase the problem of early determinants.

In the matter of personality ratings the two usual procedures are 1) rating by others and 2) by self. Both methods present handicaps of prejudice. Questionnaires have been rather widely employed. The Bell Adjustment Inventory and The Johnson Personal History Record are of this type. The Bernreuter Personal Inventory attempts to measure six traits, especially to ferret out symptoms of maladjustment. See character; child training; projective techniques; psychology of religion; role playing; self; social perception; sociometry.

    *Bibl.* D. G. Patterson, G. G. Schneidler and E. G. Williamson, *Student Guidance Techniques* (1938); J. F. Dashiell, *Fundamentals of Objective Psychology* (1928); Murphy and Jensen, *Approaches to Personality* (1932)

**personality, complexity of:** see problem complex.

**personality, criminal:** see criminal types.

**personality, dual:** see divided self; psychoneuroses.

**personality, introvert and extravert:** see Jungian approach to therapy.

**personality disorders:** see conflicts, inner; emotional conflicts; mental disorders.

**personality of God:** see belief in God; theism.

**personality ratings:** see personality.

**personality traits:** see traits of personality.

**personality weakness:** see weakness in personality.

**personal survival:** see belief in God; Leuba, James H.; psychical research and parapsychology.

**perspective:** see creative thinking.

**perversion:** see exhibitionism; neurosis; phobias.

**phantasy:** An imagined image of our own creation. Phantasies may be of all types and kinds and both of conscious intention and unconscious wish. In the conscious phase they are "fancies" or "day dreams." * In the unconscious mind (as employed by psychoanalysis*) they are simply phantasies. Generally, in the latter cases, they are exaggerations. They often become accepted. We tend to express phantasies as our true character* (e.g., we may unconsciously imagine ourselves to be pious and "become pious" even by believing it—though we really are not!) Two opposing phantasies tend to bring on a mental disorder (a neurosis). The demands of phantasies may be so great that, failing to perform in accordance with them, they may bring about a nervous and moral breakdown.

**phenomenalism:** see psychology of religion; psychology, schools of.

**philanthropy:** see sublimation.

**philosophical criteria of truth:** see truth.

**philosophy:** Philosophy is the attempt to systematize general knowledge (both undisciplined and disciplined) towards wisdom with reference to the understanding of life and the world. See belief in God; dogmatism; metaphysics; ontology; minister, the, and his books; sermons, preparation of.

**philosophy and psychology:** see pastoral psychology.

**phi-phenomenon:** see Wertheimer, Max.

**phlegmatic temperament:** see temperament.

**phobias:** Phobias are fears attached to objects which are not *per se* dangerous. Hence these fears are called "morbid." They are often the *projected* fears of a person: fears of himself, of "unconscious desires" or some inner impulse.

Normal fears are biologically efficient; abnormal fears (phobias) bring on inefficiency.

Phobias are distinguished by Freud* as 1) exaggerations of emotional experiences (solitude, doom, death, etc.)—all common to normal people; and 2) peculiarities of individual fears toward definite experiences and objects (claustrophobia, agoraphobia, etc.).

Terms are given to specific phobias, such as:

**acrophobia:** fear of height.

**aelurophobia:** dread of cats.

**agoraphobia:** fear of open spaces which offer no shelter.

**aichmophobia:** fear of pointed objects (scissors, knives).

**amathophobia:** fear of dust.

**amaxophobia:** fear of being in a vehicle, especially if it is in motion.

**apeirphobia:** dread of infinity.

**astraphobia:** fear of storms.

**bathophobia:** dread of depths, or falling from a height. Fear of impulse to jump.

**carcinophobia:** fear of the infliction of cancer.

**catagelphobia:** dread of being ridiculed.

**cenophobia:** fear of large halls, enclosures with high ceilings.

**chronophobia:** dread of time, often, in extreme cases, resulting in elimination or destruction of clocks.

**claustrophobia:** fear of being locked up or enclosed

**hamartophobia:** fears associated with a morbid awareness of sin (some writers associate this with adolescence and conversion).

**laliphobia**: dread of the necessity of speaking by a person with a speech defect.
**myophobia**: fear of mice.
**mysophobia**: fear of dirt or contamination often accompanied by incessant hand washing.
**nosophobia**: dread of illness.
**nyctophobia**: dread of the dark.
**ochlophobia**: fear of crowds.
**ophidiophobia**: fear of snakes.
**panphobia**: fear of everything.
**pathophobia**: fear of disease germs or contracting disease.
**phobophobia**: dread of fear itself.
**pyrophobia**: fear of causing fire.
**taphephobia**: fear of being buried alive.
**teniophobia**: fear of tapeworms.
**thanatophobia**: fear of death.
**tontriphobia**: fear of thunder.
**toxiphobia**: fear of being poisoned by someone.
**triakaidekaphobia**: fear of "13."
**xenophobia**: fear of strangers.
**zelophobia**: fear of jealousy.

See defense mechanisms; emotion; psychology of religion; psychoneuroses.

**phobophobia**: see phobias.

**phrenology**: The "science" of determining mental abilities* and traits by the protrusions and recessions of the human skull. It is a phase of physiognomy.* In popular language, the "bumps" of the head are supposed to reveal what you are. Francis J. Gall (1758-1828) developed this "science." Phrenologists have developed a chart to locate some thirty-six mental faculties.

Phrenology has rightly pointed to the brain as the physical correlate of the mind. But it rests on an antiquated psychology (e.g., theory of special faculties, their location on a part of the brain surface, the size determining the faculty, and the surface of the skull indicating the degree of mental power).

It has been shown that localizations in brain areas are much different from the picture set up by traditional phrenologists. Vision, for example, is at the base of the brain at the rear (where Gall believed was located the faculty of "love of children"). Moreover, psychologists now view the brain as operating in wide areas of neural energy in the thinking process thus excluding a major thesis of Gall. The size of the brain is no longer held to be an indication of mental development. Some people with large heads are feeble minded (perhaps an over-supply of cerebro-spinal fluid).

Phrenology is popular among the credulous and is discounted by professional students as an expression of pseudopsychology.*

**phylogeny:** The developmental history, the physical characteristics, and the general interrelationships of a major animal or vegetable group. V. H. F.

**physical characterizations:** see faces, reading of; glands; physiognomy; pseudopsychology.

**physical defects:** see juvenile delinquency.

**physical deterioration:** see adult, the; aging process; sclerosis.

**physical exercise:** see aging process; creative thinking; drives; emotional tensions, release of; fatigue.

**physical fatigue:** see fatigue.

**physical health:** see health; psychosomatics; success.

**physical symptoms of deception:** see deception.

**physicians:** see hospital chaplain, the; medical science; medicine and religion; pastoral counseling and case studies; pastoral psychology: its governing limitations and qualifications; psychosomatics.

**physiognomy:** A "science" which purports to interpret mental characteristics from the morphology of the face and other physical characteristics. A prominent chin is taken to indicate the dominance of will power; a bulldog appearance suggests stubbornness of character; coarseness of skin suggests coarseness of nature, etc. Blonds are taken to be dynamic and fickle, etc.

What is probably of genuine significance psychologically in the claims of physiognomy is the fact that "expressive movement" (facial changes, gait, gesture) does give signs of inward feelings or feeling tone. A gloomy person by setting up a frown may with time develop facial wrinkles to betray his disposition.

The charlatan has entered this field with interpretations that are superficial and given to the unbridled use of analogy.

However there have recently been some serious study of body types (e.g., W. H. Sheldon *The Varieties of Human Physique* [1940]) and corresponding types of temperament to show some correlation. See faces, reading of; phrenology; pseudopsychology.

For a fuller treatment see the article by D. H. Yates "Pseudopsychology" in *Encyclopedia of Psychology* (1946), ed. by P. L. Harriman.

**physiological changes:** see glands; menopause. Also see under physical.

**piety:** see phantasy; saintliness.

**pineal gland:** A small glandular body which, in early childhood, may have an endocrine* function, is situated in the midbrain (projecting backwards above the corpora quadrigemina). René Descartes held that it was at this place that soul and body interacted.

**pipe smoking:** see tobacco smoking and psychological efficiency.

**Piper, Mrs. L. E.:** see psychical research and parapsychology.

**pitch, sense of:** see talents.

**pituitary gland (hypophysis):** The master gland attached to the base of the brain* (see hypothalamus). This gland secretes "trophic" hormones* which directly stimulate and guide the other endocrine glands* in turn, to secrete their own hormones.* A deficiency state of the pituitary (hypopituitarism) thus produces marked clinical effects in man and laboratory animals. Pituitary dysfunction (anterior lobe) is associated with dwarfism* and gigantism.* See aging process; hyperpituitarism; hypopituitarism. V. H. F.

**pity:** see emotion.

**PK:** see psychical research and parapsychology.

**Plato on democracy:** see peace and war.

**play boys:** see boredom.

**playing of roles:** see role playing.

**playmates:** see child training.

**pleasing, over:** see ambivalence.

**pleasure:** see aesthetic experience; belief in God; happiness; sadism.

**pleasure principle:** see juvenile delinquency; learning; psychology, schools of (psychoanalysis).

**pluralism:** see belief in God.
**poetry:** see minister, the, and his books; visiting the sick.
**poise:** see learning; religion and mental health; sermon.
**politeness:** see role playing.
**polylogia:** A stream of incoherent talk by a subject in an excited stage of mental disorder.*
**polytheism:** see belief in God.
**popular applied psychology:** Not all popular applied psychology is spurious. But there is a large area representing pseudopsychology.*

During the third decade of the twentieth century a wave of popular psychology which was highly unscientific though extremely popular spread over wide areas, particularly in systems of applied psychology, lectureships and mail order courses. This wave is described in a book called *Psychological Racketeers* (1932) by D. H. Yates. Course fees were charged by itinerant "psychologists." Demonstrations and "professional" diagnoses added to popular attraction and consumption. These "professionals" had no knowledge of disciplined psychology and betrayed it. Ideas offered were mixtures of Yoga philosophy, success formulae, Christian Science in its spurious form—offering happiness, health and success. In more recent years the field of popularity is astrology with present-day abundance of magazines on horoscopes—the stars said to determine human destiny (as said the ancient Chaldeans).

**population, shift of:** see pastoral counseling and case studies.
**positivism:** This is the view that metaphysics* (as the word suggests) dealing with speculations beyond nature is not or should not be, of concern to philosophers. Positivism is interested only in things within grasp of experience (actual or possible). In religion positivism becomes "religious humanism" (man being the center of attention and interest). John Dewey's* philosophy is essentially positivistic. See instrumentalism.
**possession:** see sex differences, psychological.
**postural response:** A general attitude or adjustment of readiness or expectancy. Every continued activity aroused in an organism tends to persist in the same general direction and, by the same token, is not easily turned to some other activity. That is why it is necessary, in conversation, to engage "in the mood." No salesman is successful who fails to be aware of

the postural response of his potential customer. A minister as a parish visitor knows this full well and adapts his visits accordingly. See social perception; visitation.

**potted thinking:** see fallacy of over simplification.

**practice, persistent:** see deliberate effort; memorizing; reading performance; talents.

**pragmatism:** A philosophy of truth* and a metaphysics.* As the word *pragma* suggests, pragmatism has to do with the practical, the observable, the useful, the functioning of things and ideas.

As a tool or criterion of truth pragmatism is held by everyone when it is said: Let's test this out and see if it works. If it works it is true. If not, it is false.

The concept of workability, however, carries several meanings: works for me (subjective); works in the sense of a laboratory experiment (control, repeatable, verification by others); works in so far as it satisfies purposes, in the long run (William James*); works in the sense of an adjustment to a given situation (John Dewey*).

Such are the *criteria* of pragmatism (essential pragmatism). If truth is taken to be *nothing but* its pragmatic criteria such a view becomes philosophical pragmatism or the view that truth is no more than that which is capable of being tested. In this latter sense pragmatism comes under its greatest criticism. See psychology, schools of; visions and hallucinations.

**Pratt, James B.:** (1875-1944) A well known professor of philosophy in Williams College (since 1905). His long professional career as teacher at Williams gave him opportunity for research and writing and for intermittent travel—reflected in the writing of important books on the subjects of his chief interest: metaphysics, epistemology, psychology of religion and the religions of the Far East. A student under William James he learned about the budding pragmatic theory firsthand. His books were many: *What is Pragmatism?* (1909); *India and its Faiths* (1915); *Matter and Spirit* (1922); *The Pilgrimage of Buddhism* (1928); *Adventures in Philosophy and Religion* (1931); *Personal Realism* (1937); *Naturalism* (1939). His *The Religious Consciousness* (1920) has, over the years, enjoyed the widest use as a text in the field of the psychology of religion—a book unique in its field for a broad and systematic understanding of the whole field. See Leuba, James H.; psychology of religion; reality feeling principle; worship.

**prayer:** see ministry, the, and counseling; psychology of religion; religion and mental health; visiting the sick.

**prayer and autosuggestion:** Prayer as petition is the usual meaning of prayer. (There is, of course, the prayer of obeisance, adulation, mere communication and meditation). Prayer may be vocal or a non-verbal attitude.

Prayer is usually undertaken to come to terms with a higher power and not as a mere exercise in self-effects.

So long as prayer is a human interest and expression it must certainly reveal psychological characteristics. Something happens at the human level—and it is at this point that autosuggestion as a human psychological principle asserts its claim.

There can be no gainsaying that prayer operates as reflective autosuggestion. (See autosuggestion.) Sustained prayer aims to bring desired change in mental outlook. Wherever prayer is undertaken in the kind of faith in its efficacy in which the petitioner is not blocked by a "will" but aided by an inner confidence beyond human endeavor, prayer has the decided advantage in operating effectively as autosuggestion (the latter's effect is in proportion to the decrease of deliberate effort). Surrendering to the Lord is the grand entrance to the effective operation of autosuggestion. Being filled with a Presence of a power greater than oneself invites the atmosphere of the positive which acts as therapy. Prayer of this kind thus perfects the conditions in which autosuggestion performs its function of solution and cure.

Attending a public service in which others are joining in a common attitude of trust and hope and ultimate confidence has a powerful effect in inducing the very conditions of therapeutic autosuggestion. The seeds sown in the unconscious mind may strike root and bear fruit in circumstances quite other than those found in formal worship.

It must be pointed out that from a theological or philosophical point of view prayer and autosuggestion are not incompatibles any more than a theistic view of a teleological world is incompatible with the laws of physics. It may be the better wisdom to hold that answers to prayer come in ways normal and natural through the very processes which are psychological. It is more difficult to believe otherwise. See religion and mental health; worship.

**preacher, the:** see minister, the, and his books; ministry; pastoral psychology: its governing limitations and qualifications; sermon; sermons, preparation of; sublimation.

**preaching:** see minister, the, and his books; projection; sermon; sermons, preparation of; social perception; sublimation.

**precognition:** see psychical research and parapsychology.

**pre-conscious:** see conscious, pre-conscious and unconscious.

**prejudice:** see motives; occupational prejudice; peace and war; racial prejudice; symbols.

**preparation in creative thinking:** see creative thinking.

**pressure sense:** see aphia; sensations.

**prestige:** see success.

**priest:** see ministry; occupational prejudice.

**primitive urges:** see dreams.

**primordial ideas:** see Jung, Carl.

**principle of reality feeling:** see reality feeling principle.

**private confession:** see confession; cure of souls.

**probability and ESP:** see psychical research and parapsychology.

**problem children:** see child training; children and religious beliefs; juvenile delinquency.

**problem complex:** It is seldom that a counselor will encounter a disturbed personality* whose reorientation will require but one solution to one problem. Just as the personality is a complex of experiences and responses to the experiential context, so must the solutions to the problems which disrupt the personality complex be a problem complex. It is often the case that an individual undergoing therapy* or analysis becomes discouraged as he or she solves problems only to discover that there are more than a few problems created in the wake of solution. The successful counselor will realize that this problem complex exists and will seek to communicate to the counselee that no swift logical answer can be offered which will alleviate the discouragement. The counselee will begin to appreciate that all experience is complex and will begin to seek not specific solutions to specific problems but rather, as he develops a sense of self, a problem-solving response to the experiential context. Successful counseling does not remove the problems from the life of a counselee but does hope to assist the counselee in developing a center of response to life and the many problems to be encountered once the counseling situation ends. The counselor must, therefore, have a strong awareness of the nature of the world and its problems as well as a strong insight into the specific problems of the specific counselee. W. W. B.

**problem solving:** see instrumentalism.

**prodigy:** see genius.

**productivity:** see success.

**professional criminal, the:** see criminal types.

**professional fees:** see minister, the, and money; sacrifice, a psychological concept.

**professional reference:** It is particularly important that the counselor such as the minister or teacher know when a counselee needs professional help. Often he will be able to determine this by estimating his own limitations and abilities in terms of the counselee's problem or problems. When the counselor is in doubt as to the necessity of professional reference, it would seem wise for him to suggest an exploratory session or two for the counselee with a competent professional. In this way the counselor may find considerable assistance in dealing with the counselee and if professional help is not warranted, the counselor may feel at ease in having considered the professional need.

In fairness to the counselee, reference to sources of professional assistance should not be postponed or avoided. The counselor should have confidence in his ability to assist the troubled person. An estimation of the counselor's confidence or lack of confidence should indicate readily the advisability of reference.

Many persons who find themselves in the position of counselor may not have ready knowledge of the sources of professional assistance available to them. To determine the place of reference, the counselor should familiarize himself with competent professional sources available to his counselee. The classifieds of the telephone directory is often a poor source of professional listings. While many of the listings are bona fide, a greater number are not. It is essential that the ability of professional help be determined. Practically any state university will be able to suggest the name or names of competent psychological counselors. Many states have psychological associations which have listings of members qualified to give competent help. The medical associations can often suggest names of psychiatrists. Just as not everyone trained in psychology is qualified to give "problem-solving" assistance, so is not every medical practitioner qualified to offer assistance. The medical practitioner should, however, be able to assist in naming reliable sources of professional help.

The counselee can be made to look forward to the outcome of a reference and should not look upon reference as a sign of "serious" necessity. His problems are *his* problems and, whatever they may be, reference can only mean that he will be going to the source of qualified assistance. The lay counselor who suggests the reference can help a great deal by pointing out to the counselee that the limitations of experience warrant that he not waste time and go as soon as possible to the roots of the problems. Professional reference is not a last resort and the counselee must see that it is the honesty of the lay counselor who is capable of making the reference which is in his own best interest.

The counselor who hesitates to utilize professional reference because he may lose stature in the eyes of the person seeking his or her help, will ultimately do more good if he is readily capable of admitting his limitations to the counselee. The counselee will then be able to note that his problems take precedence over the pride of the counselor, who will, in turn, gain stature rather than lose it. Well-meaning do-gooders and uninformed help-givers may do more to destroy the counselee's faith and need for outside help, particularly if such assistance turns out to perpetuate a dependency rather than to bring the problems to some satisfactory solution. Professional reference is the best answer to a counseling situation which shows little sign of movement and where the counselor's ability to deal with the counselee's problems fails to show insight and direction for solution. See problem complex. W. W. B.

**professions:** see success.

**profile:** An arrangement of test scores indicating the relative standing of an individual on various psychological ratings (mechanical ability, linguistic intelligence, educational achievement, etc.).

**prognosis:** A forecast of the course of a disorder. See diagnosis.

**progressive education:** see Dewey, John.

**prohibition, self:** see Alcoholics Anonymous; children and religious beliefs.

**projection:** A term used by Freud* for the process of attributing to others the drives* and complexes* which belong to an individual.

In general psychology projection refers to the localization of sensation at the place of stimulation. For example, visual projection means that place in space of the stimuli in vision which arouse responses.

In Freudian psychology projection is the tendency of attaching repressed complexes (which are refused recognition) to others. We tend to condemn in others what we refuse to admit in ourselves.

Preachers, thus, preaching persistently on a given sin may reveal, unconsciously, their own secret sin. Judgment of others is a confession of our own inner and hidden faults. See analysis; peace and war; phobias.

**projective techniques:** These are psychological methods which, in general, deal with more or less free responses to "unstructured" stimuli and are set up with the view of determining what goes on in the mind of a subject under study.

A subject, for example, is asked to interpret ink blots. Hermann Rorschach (1884-1922), a Swiss psychiatrist, developed a projective technique known as the "Rorschach ink blot test" in 1921 by a study of responses to a standard series of ink blots which, in recent years, has received much attention and usage by psychologists.

The "thematic apperception test" (developed by C. Morgan and H. A. Murray) employed the technique of a subject's telling stories relating to pictures as stimuli to elicit by free responses the subject's mind-pattern.

Earlier, free association* to words as stimuli was employed as projective technique by Jung (1904). Freud* also employed a method of free association. Various media have been employed, such as a lump of modeling clay, toys, drawing, pictures, etc.

All projective techniques aim to uncover by free expression

what goes on in the subject's mind and thus give exposure for analysis. The subject, thus, projects his inner impulses, wishes, anxieties and moods into his interpretation (as the meaning suggests) of ink blots, pictures, etc.

Psychologists regard the prospect of these and other techniques of investigation into the motives and personality of subjects as most promising. See apperception.

> Bibl. C. D. Morgan and H. A. Murray, "A Method for Investigating Fantasies: the Thematic Apperception Test" in *Archives of Neurology and Psychiatry* (1935), 34, 289-306; H. A. Murray, *Explorations in Personality* (1938); H. Rorschach, *Psychodiagnostics* (Eng. tr., 1942).

**proofs:** see belief in God.

**propaganda:** see peace and war.

**property infringements:** see juvenile delinquency.

**prophet:** see occupational prejudice; pastoral counseling and case studies.

**proprioceptor:** see sensations.

**protanopia:** see color blindness.

**pseudopsychology:** Psychology, as in the case of so many human disciplines, has its share of people and viewpoints representing conclusions derived from unscientific methods. Pseudopsychology covers many areas dealing with fancied theories with the support of questionable evidence. Among the popular fields of spurious psychological character—appealing to the credulous—are: the popular lectures in applied psychology; palmistry; physiognomy; phrenology; graphology; and psychological deductions from the pseudo sciences, particularly astrology. Much of pseudopsychology is the result of superstition, pet theories of undisciplined minds and the fertility of its appeal to mass acceptance. Professional pseudopsychologists find here a rewarding field for monetary gain by means of the lecture platform, consultation and in published ventures. See popular applied psychology; graphology; palmistry and pedomancy; phrenology; physiognomy.

**psi:** see psychical research and parapsychology.

**psychasthenia:** see psychoneuroses.

**psyche:** A Greek term which was employed in ancient Greek thought to designate the unique factor of man which is to be distinguished from anything in nature which exerts power. It was held to be indestructible and eternal. Later the psyche was held to be divine and closely identified with mind.

The root word *psyche* became identified with the human soul or human spirit. *Psyche* linked with the Greek word *logos\** (word, study, knowledge or reason) form the term psychology which literally means: knowledge of the human spirit. See psychotherapy: self; soul.

**psychiatrist and minister:** see hospital chaplain, the; pastoral counseling and case studies; pastoral counseling: case studies; professional reference; religion and mental health; visiting the sick.

**psychiatry:** see hospital chaplain, the; pastoral counseling: case studies; pastoral psychology: its governing limitations and qualifications; psychotherapy; religion and mental health; sensorium; therapy.

**psychic energy:** see libido; religion and mental health.

**psychic health:** see health; psychosomatics.

**psychic illness:** see illness; psychosomatics.

**psychical phenomena:** see psychical research and parapsychology.

**psychical research and parapsychology:** Most individuals at one time or another presumably have heard of or have had experiences of a weird nature which seem to foretell coming events or to give information which has not previously been received through the ordinary sensory channels of knowledge. The premonitory dream that turns out to be true; the letters that cross in the mail; the identical sentences that two people speak at the same time; the occasional strange overpowering intuition—these and other similar experiences we tend to reject with some such explanation as 'coincidence' or 'if you investigate long enough, you'll find a physical explanation.' We often assume that the recognized senses are the only ports of knowledge.

But there have been experiences which have occurred for which there is no apparent physical explanation and for which the label 'coincidence' appears too easy—at least without some sort of investigation. In fact, the well-authenticated reports of such unusual occurrences are considerable. Now perhaps all such experiences can be shown not to be what we may call non-physical or psychical. But so far this has not been done. Rather, the evidence has been piling up that perhaps there is more here than meets the eye—that the explanation "it is just chance" really does not explain anything—that here is a field that at least needs to be investigated scientifically. Fortunately we are in good company. For, among those who have investigated so-called psychical phenomena are such well-known names as Michael Faraday, William James,* Bishop Westcott and Professor Hort, F. C. S. Schiller, L. P. Jacks, Henri Bergson, Josiah Royce, and many others.

To give a complete history of the development of psychical research we would have to start a long way back in human history—perhaps all the way back to the beginning; for we all have heard stories of elves, fairies, ghosts, etc.—strange creatures in which people of another age devoutly believed. Alleged psychical phenomena are not of recent origin. In the age of the Hebrew prophets it was "Thus saith the Lord," or the "live coal" at the lips of Isaiah. In classic Athens, it was the "daemon" of Socrates. In medieval times, it was the witch's "Familiar" or the "voices" of Joan of Arc. With the rise of the sciences, however, such creatures and phenomena were for the most part rejected, and only too often the eventual result was that people became crass materialists to the point of denying any realm of the spirit. However, not all persons engulfed in the scientific revolution went to such an extreme. In the middle of the last century there were some reputable scientists who were willing to stem the swelling tide of anti-spiritualism. To back up a bit, Emanuel Swedenborg in the eighteenth century astounded many of his friends by his amazing ability to read the minds of others and to predict future events— things about which he spoke in the same matter-of-fact way that he spoke about his own specialized field of natural science. Immanuel Kant was so impressed by this man's unusual powers that he wrote a book about him called *Dreams of A Spirit Seer*. Kant cautiously concluded regarding Swedenborg's psychical powers: "Philosophy . . . is often much embarrassed when she encounters on her march certain facts she dare not doubt, yet will not believe for fear of ridicule."

A German physician named Mesmer, who lived in the last quarter of the eighteenth century, discovered that one person can influence another person mentally. Mesmer called this type of influence "animal magnetism;" his followers called it "mesmerism;" today we call this phenomenon "hypnotism." Telepathy was the first psychic capacity to be studied, in the main coming out of experiments in hypnotism. A French physician, Dr. E. Azan, found that hypnotized patients could identify a particular sensation of taste while he experienced it. Another experimenter found that pain sensation, too, could be transferred to the hypnotized subject. Dr. Janet of France was able to induce hypnotic trance in his subjects at a distance great enough to rule out any possibility of sensory communication. Professor Charles Richet discovered that the hypnotic state was not necessary or even advantageous for success in thought transference.

Psychical research in the first half of the nineteenth century was, however, the exception rather than the rule. Most of this type of work was laughed at as incredible and ridiculous. When Professor William Barrett, a respected physician from the Royal College at Dublin, read a paper before the British Association for the Advancement of Science in 1876, on his experimental work with hypnotism and telepathy, he was ridiculed, and the Association refused to publish his paper. Sir William Crookes, the inventor of the Crookes tube, and a leading physicist of his day, was almost expelled from the above-mentioned Association for his interest in psychical research. Any research in this unacceptable field had to be done on the "Q.T." Of course, this is to a certain extent understandable. There has always been a great deal of fakery connected with this sort of thing, and many of the alleged psychical occurrences could easily be shown to be fraudulent. And the universities and professional societies, in order to maintain their prestige, could not afford to take a chance on such an erratic and too often superstitious field of experience.

It was in the latter part of the last century that more and more scientists began to feel that these continuing claims to psychic experiences could no longer be completely ignored. Such scientists and philosophers as Michael Faraday, Henry Sidgwick, Barrett and Crookes, F. W. H. Meyers in England; William James in the United States who was the only professional psychologist among the early experimenters; Charles

Richet and Theodore Flournoy on the Continent—these and others began to investigate alleged psychical phenomena in their spare time. They investigated many of the alleged mediums, found many of them to be frauds, but were sufficiently impressed by a few to warrant the continuation of investigations. In the year 1882 a few of these men met to form the Society for Psychical Research, an organization which down through the years has maintained high scientific standards and has had many of the world's leading scientists associated with it. The Society's first Statement of Purpose said that its aim "will be to approach these various problems without prejudice or prepossession of any kind, and in the same spirit of exact and unimpassioned inquiry which has enabled Science to solve many problems once not less obscure nor less hotly debated." The American Society for Psychical Research was founded in 1885, and, although merging with the London Society for a number of years, is still in existence today as a separate organization.

Practically the entire interest of these Societies was focussed on the problem as to whether part of the human personality survives the experience called death. This was the primary question; if survival could be proved, then clairvoyance, telepathy, etc., would seem to be obvious implications. Some amazing results were attained as a result of subsequent research. One of the leading mediums with whom a great deal of investigation was accomplished was a Mrs. L. E. Piper of Boston who was discovered by William James. James himself felt that Mrs. Piper was acquiring knowledge supernormally from an external source, and Dr. Richard Hodgson of Cambridge University concluded that Mrs. Piper's chief "communicators" were personalities who had survived the change we call death. Other mediums were tested, among them Mrs. Minnie Soule of Boston and Mrs. O. Leonard of England; and these new efforts led to new evidence for the support of a belief in life after death. Other methods of testing were devised as, for example, automatism, that is, the ability to write at times without consciously deciding what would be written; and cross correspondences, that is, three or more messages coming to different persons allegedly from the same source, incomprehensible in themselves, but making sense when seen together.

After Thomas Mann spent an evening with a group of scholars observing a medium, he wrote an essay entitled "An Experience in the Occult." The essay contains these words: "It was not possible—but it happened . . . never before had I seen the impossible happening despite its own impossibility . . . you command the impossible, and you are obeyed by a spook, a panic-stricken little monster from beyond the world . . ."

But the results were for many people still inconclusive. Investigations continued, flaws were found, new evidence was unearthed. One discovery that raised doubt over the survival hypothesis was that information allegedly coming from the "spirits" could conceivably be coming from the minds of the living, through mental telepathy. Or the medium could be using clairvoyance, receiving information from physical objects rather than from supernormal controls. There were many such possibilities that had to be explored. Then, too, the phenomena had not yet been subjected to objective statistical methods which could eliminate the subjective element. The investigators tried to meet these criticisms by devising new techniques and new tests. After years of effort they finally concluded that before the survival hypothesis could be proved or disproved, there were other phases that would have to be investigated. Telepathy was one such phase. In most of these experiments the sender concentrated on an object or a drawing of an object as the target, while the receiver, often located in another room, or perhaps at even a greater distance, tried to reproduce it by verbal description or by drawing. One of the most reliable series of such experiments was carried out by Upton Sinclair, reported in his book *Mental Radio*, and even Albert Einstein pleaded for a fair hearing for Sinclair's work. In the 1920's telepathy experiments were conducted in the psychology laboratories of Harvard and the University of Groningen in Holland, both with outstanding success.

The new experiments, it had now been definitely decided, should be performed within the laboratory under rigid scientific precautions. It was at this point that Parapsychology as a science was born. The man largely responsible for this shift of strategy was Dr. William McDougall* who came to Harvard from Oxford University in 1920 to become Head of the Department of Psychology. His interest in psychical research in

England was carried along to his new position where he continued his investigations. It was at Harvard that a graduate student in biology, Joseph B. Rhine, first became interested in the subject of Parapsychology.

* * * * *

In describing Parapsychology, this article will concentrate on the work that has been done at Duke University under the leadership of Dr. Rhine, where since the 1930's the major research has taken place. Before we proceed further, we should define a few terms. Parapsychology is that branch of psychology which is concerned with the 'unconventional' side or "offside" of psychology, differing from psychical research in the strictly experimental methods used. It deals with those psychical effects which appear not to fit into the pattern of what is at present recognized law. By extrasensory perception is meant simply "perception in a way that is non-sensory" or "perceiving beyond the limits of the recognized senses." Telepathy has reference to the perception of the thought or feeling of another person without the aid of the recognized senses. Clairvoyance is the perception of an object without the aid of the known sense organs. Psychokinesis refers to the ability of a mind to influence directly a physical object without the aid of any physical processes. The Greek letter *psi* includes the activities of both ESP (extrasensory perception) and PK (psychokinesis).

The laboratory goal at Duke was to attempt to demonstrate in controlled experiments whether or not there is an extrasensory way of knowing. It is not essential to mention all the developments that have taken place at Duke since the experiments first began. Mistakes have been detected, methods have been corrected; but the overwhelming evidence, as they interpret it at Duke, has pointed to the presence of an extrasensory way of knowing.

A brief statement of how some of the experiments are conducted may be in order. Most of the experiments are built around a pack of cards, called ESP cards, which number twenty-five cards to the pack. The pack consists of five cards each of five symbols. The symbols are a cross, three wavy lines, a star, a square, and a circle. In other respects the ESP pack resembles ordinary playing cards, with uniform backs. The simplest form of clairvoyant testing is for the subject to name the symbol on the top card of the deck which, of course, is face down, although the subject does not even see the back of the card. After the subject names what he believes to be the symbol on the top card, the examiner notes his call, removes the top card, and repeats the procedure with the next card in the deck. This method is followed until the subject has gone through the entire pack of twenty-five cards. Only then does the examiner look to see whether the subject was calling the cards correctly. Another form of testing is to combine telepathy with clairvoyance, with someone looking at the card and trying to convey the symbol telepathically to the subject. A third form of testing is for precognition, that is, knowledge of something before it happens. In this case the subject tries to predict the order of the pack before it is shuffled! Of course, there are many variations of these three forms of testing. Elaborate precautions are taken to prevent fraud. For example, mechanical card shufflers are used to rule out the possibility that the examiner subconsciously might shuffle the cards in a certain way. Different packs of cards are substituted during the testing without the subject's knowledge. Opaque screens are erected between the experimenter and the subject to avoid the possibility of any unconscious physical cues being given. Every precaution known is taken in these experiments to rule out the possibility of sensory perception.

Space cannot be taken here to explain the mathematics involved. In simplest terms, if I put five different cards face down on the table and ask someone to guess the symbol of a designated card, the chance is one in five that he will guess correctly if he has no knowledge of which card is which. The subject can go right through the five cards, and even on the fifth guess he still has the same chance of making a correct guess, provided that he has not been told of the accuracy of his previous guesses. The same principle holds true whether there are five or a thousand cards: the chance is still one in five for a correct guess on each card. Anything above five hits for twenty-five cards is above chance. And if, in extrasensory perception testing, an above-chance score is made for several consecutive tests, this score becomes statistically significant. For example, if the subject goes through the deck thirty-two times and scores an average of 6.5 hits per run, the odds would be 250,000 to 1 against such a score.

During the years of work at the Duke Parapsychology Laboratory a large variety of subjects has been tested. In the first years alone a total of 3,400 runs through the deck, or a call of 85,000 cards, yielded a general average of 7 hits per 25 calls. The mathematical odds against such a score are astronomical. Some individuals have scored far higher than others. One individual once scored 25 hits in a row, and day in and day out for two years this same person averaged 10 hits per 25 cards. Rhine's own estimate is that at least one in five of the persons tested showed ESP capacity. Experiments were carried out to see if distance had any effect in ESP, and in both telepathy and clairvoyance distance apparently meant little or nothing to ESP. In a similar fashion experiments in precognition were conducted, for it seemed reasonable to suspect that, if ESP was space-free, it would also be time-free within our space-time universe of physics. The results, although usually not as high as those of simple clairvoyance and telepathy, were nevertheless statistically significant. Experiments in psychokinesis are common. Here, for example, the subject tries to will dice to land with a specific face or combination or faces uppermost. Here, too, the experiments have been favorable. This would mean, of course, that the mind as a nonphysical entity can produce a physical effect in a non-physical way upon a physical object!

Certainly one cannot come to any final conclusions as a result of this cursory sketch of the Duke experiments. One must be impressed, however, with the extreme caution and care of these specialists who have bent over backwards in their attempts to answer the critics and to establish ESP as an indisputable fact. Rhine and his associates in a book entitled *Extra-Sensory Perception After Sixty Years* have discussed and allegedly refuted thirty-five alternatives to the hypothesis of extra-sensory perception. The reader will find in this book answers to questions which can not be discussed here. On the statistical side, the American Institute of Mathematical Statistics, after a careful study of the methods used at Duke and other places for evaluating the ESP tests, issued a statement in

1937 to the effect that the statistical analysis used is essentially valid. The American Psychological Association held a symposium in 1938 on the experimental methods used in ESP work, and there general agreement was reached that the experiments were sound from a scientific point of view. Since that time there has been very little published criticism of the Duke experiments.

As of 1954, however, Parapsychology has definitely failed to impress the majority of American psychologists. A comparison of similar studies made in 1938 and 1952 to determine the general attitude of psychologists toward the research in Parapsychology shows only a small change of favorable attitude in the intervening fourteen years, despite the fact that the greatest amount of the best controlled work in ESP had been done during that interval. The recent survey indicated that the large majority of the psychologists had had no firsthand acquaintance with the scientific work in ESP and were influenced more by a materialistic frame of reference into which it is difficult if not well nigh impossible to make nonphysical facts fit.

There are also some professional statisticians of probability who continue to question the validity of Rhine's statistics. Since this writer is not sufficiently qualified to discuss the pros and cons of Rhine's use of statistics, he consulted a well-qualified statistician who objected to Rhine's statistical methods and had him set up the conditions under which he might conduct his own experiments in extra-sensory perception. My experiments, of course, were not extensive. I was more interested in following the suggestions of a spokesman for the opposition. My experimental procedure differed in two chief respects from the Duke experiments. First, I did not resort to hand or machine shuffling; rather, I used mathematical tables in which the numbers had already been randomized. This procedure eliminated the shuffling criticism, that it is virtually impossible to shuffle thoroughly by hand or machine a twenty-five card deck consisting of five cards each of five symbols. Secondly, because of this, the conditions were changed from the requirement that each symbol appear equally often in a deck of 25 cards, which was the Duke procedure, to the requirement that each symbol have an equal chance of appearing. Thus, each of the five symbols did not necessarily appear five times in a deck of 25 cards. This new requirement did not change the expectation of the average expected score of 1/5 times the number of trials. For convenience, I tested 30 persons, each person making 250 calls. Following suggestions I established a criterion score of 63 out of 250 for ability and I decided to retest those individuals who made a score higher than or equal to the criterion score (50 out of 250 calls would be the expected number of correct calls). There were three individuals out of the thirty tested who scored the same as or higher than the criterion score of 63. These three scores were 63, 70, and 113. A second and independent experiment was run on these three, and the resulting scores were 48, 44, and 100. The person who scored unusually high in the first experiment also scored unusually high in the second experiment. The *a priori* probability of such a score for the three individuals is about one in fifty thousand. What is even more amazing is that, since two of the three individuals scored below chance on the second testing, we can logically attribute the highly significant score to one individual. My statistician friend concludes that it is his opinion that one individual in the group has real ability. This, of course, was the goal of my experiments, since I was interested not in finding out whether *everybody* possesses extra-sensory perceptive powers, but first whether *anybody* does.

If we were to accept the main conclusions of Parapsychology as facts, what are these main conclusions? First, extra-sensory perception is an actual and demonstrable occurrence. Second, ESP occurs both as clairvoyance and telepathy, and these two apparently are phases of the same function. Third, in ESP there is no experience of localization as there is with the senses. Fourth, ESP is a part of the natural processes of the mind, and is partly under the volitional control of the percipient. Fifth, ESP ability occurs in flashes, and is not found as fully developed or capable of being fully developed in all persons. If these conclusions are true, this would mean that the mind can interact in some direct extra-sensory way with both the minds of other persons and with material objects, and can do so despite any physical barriers set up to exclude all sensory contacts.

All of these conclusions, taken together, hint at the presence of something in the nature of the individual self that is nonphysical or spiritual in the sense of transcending physical properties. The results of Parapsychology, if true, have furnished more scientific evidence than has yet been revealed in favor of the hypothesis of a world of personality transcending the world of matter. My own feelings as of now are similar to those of Dr. S. G. Soal, Senior Lecturer in Pure Mathematics at London University, and a past president of the Society for Psychical Research. He writes:

"The supreme importance, as I see it, of the labors of Dr. Rhine and his fellow-parapsychologists lies in this: that they are providing a slow, painful, but sure demonstration by the methods of science of a truth that the religions of the world have grasped intuitively or that is seen only vaguely through the eyes of faith. I mean the truth that man is more than a physical organism responding to stimuli—that while living in this world he is yet in contact with an extra-sensory order of existence whose relations to time and space transcend those of the world of matter. Of all studies pursued by man, I believe that parapsychology is the most likely to provide an answer to the questions with which human beings ought to be most vitally occupied—the pursuit of happiness and the immortality of the soul . . . extra-sensory perception is a spark now that may one day become a blaze by whose light the darkness of our human destiny may be illumined."

*A Selected Bibliography*

J. B. Rhine, *Extra-Sensory Perception After Sixty Years* (1940).

———, *New Frontiers of The Mind* (1937).

———, *The Reach of The Mind* (1947).

A. J. Smith, *Religion and The New Psychology* (1951).

D.W.F.

**psychoanalysis:** This is a term used to designate a particular method of therapy in the treatment of mental illnesses. It is not confined to psychotic personalities and is in fact most often used with what is called the neurotic personality. There are various psychological schools of thought each with its set of basic concepts governing the method of attacking the problems of patients. In general, however, psychoanalysis, regardless of the school of thought governing its administration, is a definite type of therapeutic technique. The psychoanalytical technique attempts to do three things: 1) to probe into the history of the patient in order to determine the pattern of his responses to life from their origins; 2) to relate these patterns to the contemporary situation; and 3) a re-education process which involves learning to react without conflict and from the central source of an oriented self.

A full-fledged psychoanalysis is a long and expensive process which occupies the patient in hour-long sessions with the analyst as often as five times a week for a period of two and a half to three years. During this period the patient will respond to the analyst in the context of his day-by-day problems, the nature of these responses being fundamentally related to the patient's early childhood responses. The patient will establish the analyst in a position such that the patient transfers his responses to the analyst rather than to the reality-situation. (See transference.) During the early periods of the analysis, the patient's reactions to all things will seem exaggerated. It is this exaggerated response to persons and situations which the analyst and patient use as the grist for the therapeutic mill. Depending on the psychological presuppositions of the analyst's school of approach, he will play a non-verbal role with the patient. Some schools minimize the role of therapist in order to bring about a termination in which the patient has made his realizations under his own steam and with his own insight doing much of the work. In this way the patient may leave the analyst confident that it has been his own insight which has brought healthy adjustment. The cost of analysis plays a factor here, also. The fee for an hour of analysis is often established in order to have the patient make some sacrifice for what is accomplished. Termination is often hastened when a patient becomes aware of the fact that he is spending a great deal of money for his own insights into his problems and can see the value of his insights. Analysts must be well paid also because they cannot work with a great number of patients. Many practicing analysts limit themselves to five or six patients at a time. Psychoanalysis is a professional method of therapy and must be practiced by highly trained men. The practice must be administered by an M.D. (psychiatrist) or a Ph.D. psychologist whose training has been in this field. Not every Doctor of Philosophy in psychology is qualified to be a psychoanalyst. See Adler, Alfred; Adlerian approach to therapy; analysis; censor; conscious, etc.; counseling periods; defense mechanisms; diagnosis; dreams; flight into health; Freud; Freudian approach to analysis; genius; homosexuality; instinct; Jung, Carl; Jungian approach to therapy; ministry, the, and counseling; phantasy; projective techniques; psychology, schools of; psychoneuroses; psychotherapy; religion and mental health; repression; resolution, the doctrine of; sacrifice, a psychological concept.

*Bibl.* Sigmund Freud, *General Introduction to Psychoanalysis* (1920); ———, *New Introductory Lectures in Psychoanalysis* (1933); Healy, Bronner and Bowers, *The Structure and Meaning of Psychoanalysis.* W.W.B.

**psychoanalysis, limitations of:** Like any scientific endeavor which tries to search out each link in a closely knit chain of causes, psychoanalysis suffers the limitations of its method. If there is such a thing as a broken chain—where conscious freedom of choice (by definition) initiates a new beginning apart from what goes before it—psychoanalysis, like all methods, cannot deal with it and thus cannot claim to be a *complete* explanation of human behavior. See Adler, Alfred; Freudian approach to analysis; Jungian approach to therapy; psychology of religion.

**psychoanalytic and general counseling literature:** The psychoanalytical and general counseling terms and concepts which appear in this volume (over the initials of W. W. B.) are indebted, in part, to the following bibliography. Where specific bibliographical references do not accompany the terms as they appear in the text, the following works may serve as a general source list and point of departure for further study and investigation on the part of the interested reader.

*Bibl.* Arthur H. Brayfield, *Readings in Modern Methods of Counseling* (1950); Charles A. Curran, *Personality Factors in Counseling* (1945); J. Mc V. Hunt, *Personality and the Behavior Disorders* (1944); John Levy and Ruth Monroe, *The Happy Family* (1950); Clyde Kluckhohn and Henry Murray, *Personality: in nature, society and culture* (1949); Rollo May, *The Meaning of Anxiety;* C. R. Rogers, *Counseling and Psychotherapy;* Clara Thompson, *Psycho-*

*analysis: Evolution and Development* (1950); Lee Travis and Dorothy Baruch, *Personal Problems in Everyday Life* (1941); Robert White, *The Abnormal Personality* (1948); Helen Witmer, *Psychiatric Interviews with Children* (1946). W. W. B.

**psychoanalytic school of psychology:** see psychoanalysis; psychology of religion; psychology, schools of.

**psycho-galvanic reflex test:** see deception.

**psychogenic disorders:** Disorders which originate in the mind. The opposite is somatogenic.* Cases of psychogenic disorders are paralysis, blindness, deafness, dumbness, headaches, pains, "shell shock" cases which, though physical in their symptoms, originate not in the body but in the mind—disorders due to emotional disturbances. See hypertension; mental disorders; psychosomatics; tic.

**psychoid, the:** see criminal types.

**psychokinesis:** see psychical research and parapsychology.

**psychological frames of reference:** All of us have frames of references by which we accept or reject ideas. In scientific studies the frame of reference is there but may not always be evident to the layman. Psychologists, particularly, approach their research by methods and presuppositions which are limited by the manner in which their methods may successfully be applied and by the initial hypotheses of their approach. So-called "schools of psychology"* are thus distinguished (and limited) by their frames of reference. Objective behavior is emphasized by some, introspection, physiology, the subconscious, by others. Some stress some theoretical and allegedly basic hypothesis (e.g., Freud*), some stress clinical studies of individual cases, others stress the category of the total personality (G. W. Allport). Some, like William James,* approach the subject by a general philosophy. The biological and genetic frame of reference was strong beginning with the wide acceptance of the evolutionary views of the earlier decades of this century (and continuing to the present). Social psychologists have insisted on seeing man in terms of his interrelationships with others.

It is important to be aware of such frames of reference in judging conclusions of scientific pronouncements. Viewpoints will then be seen in their proper perspective and thus under-

**psychological racketeers**                                                    **242**

stood, appreciated and maturely evaluated.

A frame of reference applies to any judgment of anyone. All of our opinions are never to be isolated from the context of our training, approach, culture and the total impact of our own particular past. See reality feeling.

**psychological racketeers:** see popular applied psychology.

**psychological sex differences:** see sex differences, psychological.

**psychology:** The study of mental life and behavior. From the words *psyche* and *logos*. See minister, the, and his books; pastoral psychology; popular applied psychology; pseudopsychology; psyche.

**psychology and morality:** see morality and psychology.

**psychology and race:** see race psychology.

**psychology and religion:** see psychology of religion.

**psychology and worship:** see worship and psychology.

**psychology, schools of:** Schools of psychology are characterized by general points of view rather than by organized effort. The following are the basic patterns of each of the major groups.

1. The old psychology stressed the concept of "soul" as basic and was largely speculative rather than empirical. Scholastic psychology (medieval) belongs to this group.

2. The old psychology which held to the notion of faculties of the mind as explanations is called "faculty psychology." Scholastic psychology and early modern psychology held that there are faculties ("powers") of reason (which explains rational processes), of feeling (which explains emotional responses), etc. This type of psychology is outmoded. Mind is thus too artificially divided.

3. In the development of modern psychology one school stressed the view that mind consists of basic elements, such as simple ideas and simple sensations, which are related in certain ways (their following upon each other, or their similar character). This analytic school developed a theory of association which led to a school called Associationism. In general, the point of view of analysis was an empirical approach rather than scholastic and marked a milestone in the development of a *scientific* psychology. The school was handicapped by a kind of theory of atomism which came under criticism by later

psychologists. Mind may well not be a substance capable of splitting up into minute parts and relations but rather it is a dynamic whole and thus defies spatial categories implied by analysis. Thus said the critics.

4. A school developed by J. H. Herbart (1776-1841), called Herbartianism, stressed the dynamic character of ideas (against associationism) and held to the active assimilation or competitive nature of ideas. New ideas are thus developed and incorporated with those already acquired. We perceive by an existent apperceptive mass and thus inhibit or assimilate as this mass of ideas allows. Herbartianism had its greatest vogue among educational psychologists and did foresee certain characteristics which later psychologists have found valid: e.g., the active character of mind with its accumulated modes of response.

5. The first experimental type of school is credited to Wilhelm Wundt (1832-1920) who in 1879 founded a psychological laboratory in Leipzig. Since that day, psychology has become consciously a scientific discipline, even though the experimental phase has shown itself complex and difficult. Wundtian psychology is introspective. The subject matter is taken to be consciousness and experimentally controlled observation of what transpires there. Consciousness is believed to be analyzable into elemental processes and composed of these in various combinations. Other names for this Wundtian psychology are: Structuralism, Existentialism and Content Psychology.

6. Franz Brentano (1838-1917) formulated a type of psychology known as Act psychology in which the acts of mind (intentions of something) are taken to be as elemental as the mental elements themselves (sensation, images, etc.). This method is empirical rather than experimental, empirical in its observation of the act of awareness. The movement in philosophy known as phenomenalism is close to this viewpoint. (Phenomenalism means the science of phenomena or that which displays itself in pure consciousness—without involving discussion of *that which* the subject refers.)

7. Psychology, in the beginning of the 20th century, particularly American, enthusiastically followed the biological emphasis and in the thought of such leaders as J. R. Angell, John Dewey* and others, developed the functional view. The terms

"adaptation," "adjustment," "the psychophysical organism" came into vogue. The mind is a function of the total organism in relationship to the environment. Psychology is a study of mental life and behavior in this functional way. This school produced some highly fruitful insights into the understanding of human behavior. Instrumentalism* is a part of this school (the mind is a tool or instrument of the organism—J. Dewey). Education, according to functionalism, is an adaptation to environment that promotes success (pragmatism*) and resolves difficulties (thinking as the means).

8. In the second decade of this century the school of behaviorism was in vogue in America under the leadership of John B. Watson. Taking his cue from animal behavior and wishing to make psychology wholly objective, Watson limited the subject to stimulus-response (S-R) activity. Introspection was regarded as wholly outside the purview of *scientific* psychology. Only behavior itself was held to constitute the proper subject matter. In its extreme expressions behaviorism reinterpreted thought processes as objective responses (sub-vocal talking). In his famous experiments at Johns Hopkins, Watson tested alleged specific innate characteristics of children and found that it is the early environmental conditioning that brings on specific reactions of the organism (such as fear* of the dark). Not nature but the situation and the will of the experimenter are determining factors of what have seemed to be inborn characteristics. Behaviorism held high a scientific method but left much of the subject-matter of psychology either distorted by over-simplified explanations or with no explanation at all.

9. The Gestalt school (begun by Max Wertheimer*) under the notable leadership of Köhler and Koffka returned psychology from its emphasis on objective externals to the inner character of mind itself. The mind, it was held, is an organic whole (against atomism) which is further unanalyzable. Experiments with animals showed reactions in terms of flash patterns—much as one sees a triangle all-at-once and not the linear sum of its sides. This school continued to flourish as a natural reaction to the "mind-less" psychology of behaviorism and to analytic psychology in general.

10. What is called hormic psychology—developed by Wm.

McDougall (1871-1938) is the emphasis on the teleological character of mind. McDougall held that human behavior is basically determined by instincts* with which emotions are entwined and psychology must ferret out this dynamic trait of the mind and human behavior.

11. Psychoanalysis* as a school continues to play a dominant role in present-day psychology. Sigmund Freud (1856-1939) developed this into a school of his own from which other schools have emerged. Freud was impressed by the "cures" effected on patients suffering neuroses* by tapping the unconscious forces which underlie the conscious mind, employing developed techniques in the disclosure of the haunting past. Freud taught a psychology based upon a conflict* between the slim conscious ego and the enormous unconscious mind which seethes with elemental urges, mainly sexual. Though the censor* bottles up the expression of the urges it is not altogether successful; for the urges find their substitute fulfilments in circumventions, such as dreams, slips of the tongue, etc. By free association* the censor unguardedly may admit to consciousness some lead to the hidden conflicts. In his more mature works Freud developed a more complex explanation of what turned out to him to be a more complex matter: he introduced the term "Id,"* the basic drives which follow only the pleasure principle; the ego (partly conscious and partly unconscious), the organization of the self to control the Id by the demands of the environment (or reality principle); and the super-ego, the conscience (or the unconscious morality of the person).

C. G. Jung* developed a point of view in psychoanalysis which placed less emphasis upon sex and more upon the concept of a psychological complex. He views a complex as a group of associated ideas or tendencies of response with a common emotional tone and root. He devised a technique for disclosing these complexes. In interpreting symbols (dreams), Jung repudiates the Freudian view that any particular image may have a symbolic meaning the same for different individuals. Rather, symbols must be interpreted in terms of the total symbolic context and the total individual. He holds that the same psychotherapeutic methods do not hold for all individuals. The libido* is for him a universal life force and the individuals are differentiations within it. Jung's version of psychoanalysis is sometimes referred to as Complex Psychology but more widely as Analytical Psychology (particularly in the therapeutic phase).

A. Adler (1870-1937) developed a psychoanalytic theory which traces disturbances of personality to an inferiority feeling (in defeat, in organic defects, in social status). The order of one's rank in the family is a frequent determinant of this inferiority (the oldest having the least). Sex conflicts are secondary outcomes of the feeling of inferiority. Over-compensations often declare the inferiority.

What is known as depth psychology* is a term applied to psychoanalysis because of its emphasis upon the deep and unconscious determinants of human behavior. Depth psychology conducts analytical investigation of the activities of the unconscious.

Another expression of psychoanalysis was that of the so-called New Dynamic School of British psychologists (or "the New Psychology") (*see* psychology of religion) which stressed the principle of fundamental drives as the raw material of human behavior and their play into the maladjustments of life, especially in the moral sphere.

12. There are those in psychology who stress the category of person as a unitary subject, a viewpoint called personalistic psychology. Each person is unique and must be accounted for by seeking out fundamental laws which make for this uniqueness. This school admits the limitations of scientific methods and adopts a philosophy (personalism of one kind or another) as basic to the understanding of human behavior.

The development of psychology has thus proceeded much as the development of other sciences, by positing general principles to cover the whole area of the field: in the case of psychology, the abnormal as well as the normal, the child as well as the adult, the animal as well as the human, the unconscious as well as the conscious. In spite of the various distinct emphases of the several schools there is more agreement than appears on the surface. Contemporary behaviorists now are aware of the problems of motivation and the unconscious (which the Freudians emphasize). Gestalt psychologists and the psychoanalysts have become more aware of the need for more rigorous methods in procedure (the chief contribution of the behavioristic school). Psychoanalyists, too, are becoming more receptive to criticism of their explanations and to hold their approach to be but a part and a method of general psychology. There is a more general awareness in all the schools of an underlying philosophy in all approaches and in the possibilities of a variety of approaches in scientific method. All theories must find some adequate testing even though the method of the tests may assume different forms. See psychological frames of reference; psychology of religion.

*Bibl.* R. S. Woodworth, *Contemporary Schools of Psychology* (1931); E. Heidbreder, *Seven Psychologies* (1933); G. Murphy, *A Historical Introduction to Modern Psychology* (1929, 1932); P. L. Harriman, ed., *Encyclopedia of Psychology* (1946, 1951).

**psychology of religion:** Man's observations of the characteristic human elements in religious ideas and behavior are, of course, as old as critical reflection. Guesses were made as to how religious people operate as they think and behave religiously. Eastern religions developed psychological techniques from practical observation and self-analysis as to how persons might come into intimate terms with the most Real in the Universe and attain bliss. Religious psychology grew up under the guiding and comforting wings of philosophy and theology. Mysticism* was, probably, the most fertile soil for the development of what we would now call the psychology of religion; for mysticism is the expression of intimacy and personal appropriation in religion.

In Western Christian thought and practice, religious psychology became entwined with Biblicism so that, it was thought, there was a special Biblical psychology which would explain the human responses in religious aspirations. As late as the end of the nineteenth century, books were published to point out the lessons which "revealed truth" had to offer to the understanding of religious man and his mental framework.

At the turn of the century, a scientific psychology of religion was being developed which aimed to turn aside from theological and philosophical presuppositions and to set its roots in the soil of psychology itself. The hope was to understand religious man not from the point of view of religion but from the securer vantage point of "secular" psychology. Pioneers in this movement were Edwin D. Starbuck\* (*The Psychology of Religion*, 1899), George A. Coe\* (*The Spiritual Life*, 1900, *The Psychology of Religion*, 1916), James H. Leuba (*A Psychological Study of Religion*, 1912), G. Stanley Hall (*Adolescence*, 2 vols., 1905 and director of graduate studies), William James (*The Varieties of Religious Experience*, 1902), James B. Pratt (*The Psychology of Religious Belief*, 1907, *The Religious Consciousness*, 1920) and others who followed their leadership. It was in America that the scientific psychology of religion had its initial flourish.

When psychology itself—a daughter of philosophy—set up her own house-keeping as a scientific discipline it was natural that a methodology to ascertain facts must be critically scrutinized and followed. The crudest laboratory techniques were set up with only partial success. It was difficult to extricate the subject from a type of psychology predisposed to certain theories of the mind such as that of analytic psychology which viewed mind as an area to be mapped out into relations amenable to analysis and synthesis. The American pioneers of the psychology of religion grasped the question-answer method to establish a technique which they thought sure to give sound scientific conclusions.

Starbuck's pioneer book on *The Psychology of Religion* was a study of a limited area of religion: that of conversion. By the questionnaire method he believed he had applied certain laws of physiological psychology to illuminate religious behavior: that religious decisions followed a definite pattern of the physiological maturing process. Hailed as a revolutionary approach (even William James\* depended upon Starbuck's methods and conclusions in his own monumental work *The Varieties of Religious Experience*) the questionnaire method (employed also by Coe, Leuba,\* Pratt\* and others) soon revealed its limitations. Starbuck's work was clearly channelled to the riverbed of an evangelistic theology which prescribed an adolescent crisis-experience. A definite correlation between physiological maturation and a Methodist revival directed to a certain age-level may well have been a shocking revelation of the human element in religion but it had little bearing on those areas of religion where such crisis-expectancy was not held to be necessary or normative for a wholesome religion. In other words, the early studies of conversion were studies in the psychological reaction to ideological motivations and moved within the framework of group-expectancy as represented by a school of orthodoxy.

There were other methods of promise. William James took to the study of biography and autobiography which offered the directness of testimony. But, as his critics were fond of pointing out, the James study provided a study of striking and even abnormal rather than normal types of religious response. Perhaps the most promising and significant method was that of the study of anthropology because it opened up the wider vistas of religious psychology as opposed to a more parochial study of circumscribed religion and because it emphasized rightly the tremendous role of social psychology operating in religious areas. The anthropological approach produced some classics in the field: E. B. Tylor, *Primitive Culture* (5th ed., 2 vols., 1913), J. G. Frazer, *The Golden Bough* (abd. ed., 1923), M. Jastrow, *The Study of Religion* (1911), E. Durkheim, *The Elementary Forms of the Religious Life* (1915) and the early classic and perennially significant volume by Edward S. Ames, *The Psychology of Religious Experience* (1910).

The anthropological approach developed into what, in more recent years, has become known as the sociology of religion. Stress upon cultural influences—economic, geographic, political, industrial—in setting their stamp upon religious beliefs and practice has, of course, broadened the field of the psychology of religion to be shared by students of sociology. It is considered axiomatic now to view man in his interrelations with others of his particular society. For man is never isolated from a particular group. Religion itself is a cultural phenomenon with powerful group pressures upon the individual to fashion for him his religious thinking and to mold him into the pattern of the social heritage. Institutionalism, a commonplace in any group solidification, from tribal to the most advanced form of community life, continues to transmit the frozen beliefs and the behaviors of the long preceding generations. The church may claim divine sanction for its being, but its *raison d'être* is nourished in the same matrix of group psychology as any other institutional expression (fraternities, nationalistic loyalties, political parties, and the like). Religious psychology includes a folk psychology and thus overflows into the sociological field. Early classics in the social emphasis upon religious beliefs and behavior were W. G. Sumner *Folkways* (1906), Wilhelm Wundt *Elements of Folk Psychology* (Eng. tr., 1916), Max Weber *Gesammelte Aufsätze zur Religionssoziologie* (1920), E. W. Hopkins *The Origin and Evolution of Religion* (1923)—to name but a few. More recent books, typical of the emphasis, are A. E. Haydon *The Quest of the Ages* (1929), H. L. Fries and H. W. Schneider *Religion in Various Cultures* (1932) and, in the field of Christian theology, notably, G. B. Foster *The Function of Religion in Man's Struggle for Existence* (1909), E. Troeltsch *Gesammelte Schrifter* (4 vols., 1912-1925), S. J. Case, *Experience with the Supernatural in Early Christian Times* (1929), Shailer Mathews *The Growth of the Idea of God* (1931) and other of his many pioneer publications.

When psychologists began to take seriously the study of animal psychology under the spell of the functional school (which in turn had its setting in the evolutionary emphasis) much of the wind was taken out of the sails for students of religious psychology. Behavioristic psychology with its magical S-R (Stimulus-Response) bond closed in and took over the field of psychology, thus squeezing out, for a long period of time, any claim to respectability on the part of studies made by any other method. The religious type of response could not easily conform to the limits set by mere animal behavior and to S-R methods even though man is genetically related to lower organic forms.

One very signal attempt to reorient the whole field of the psychology of religion into the pattern of the genetic emphasis in psychology came in the form of a book by J. Cyril Flower, *An Approach to the Psychology of Religion* (1927), a book which did not have the influence it rightly deserved. Its thesis was that all organisms, from the simplest to the most complex, make adjustments to their environment with Nature furnishing the tools. The simpler the tools, the more restricted the environment. Man is Nature's greatest outreach to date: the human mind is capable of awareness of an environment of far-flung areas. Tools to control this wider environment successfully constitute knowledge. Tools of partial control over that in the environment which remains baffling and frustrating are those ideological symbols (faith) which are typically religious and by which religions are nourished. Man becomes religious in so far as he is aware of an environment with which he is unprepared to cope in the day-to-day responses. Religion itself is thus the outgrowth of a genetic development of wider awareness and is not something apart from its natural setting in evolutionary history.

The field of the psychology of religion became barren with the years of the rule of behaviorism in general psychology. Only after the bankruptcy of this orthodox school of psychologists and the rise of the more speculative schools led by Freud* and others could a revival occur. Stimulations which brought about fresh interests came from the struggles and frustrations of war. Scientific psychology seemed remotely encased in laboratories with their experimentations upon animal subjects. Men came home from wars with minds bruised and full of maladjustments. In England a school of religious psychologists grew up with the express purpose of attempting therapeutic aid to the stricken soldiers. Freud's continued probing of the unconscious mind furnished the key for the hopeful understanding of frustrations and phobias* and all other forms of maladjustments. The new Dynamic School of British psychologists poured forth a flood of books dealing with the psychology of religion, scientific in their claim by reason of specific case-studies of shell-shock victims and their return to normal stature by the concrete aid of both religion and psychology.

Prominent among the books issued by this school was J. A. Hadfield's *Psychology and Morals* (1926) and, to a less degree, T. W. Pym's *Psychology and the Christian Life* (1922). Although more or less restricted to an Anglican circle and to more or less conventional Christian concepts this Dynamic School did pioneer work in the therapeutic phase of religious psychology. Many conventional ideas were made reasonable by reinterpretation: such concepts as original sin, moral disease, religious sentiment, faith, regeneration, the God-idea, miracles, conversion, personal salvation, the so-called Christian virtues, and the like.

It was the beginninng of the day when psychologists were fond of such terms as complexes,* repressions,* free association,* instincts,* redirection, integration, and the like. Great stir was created in religious and theological circles by the rediscovered fact of autosuggestion,* the stir of fear lest religion would be thought to be a merely creative expression of the human mind without ontological significance beyond man himself. A flood of theological and philosophical books came to the defense of a realistic theology against the temper of subjectivism which psychoanalysis* had seemed to foster. Both philosophical phenomenalism (in its unique way) and theological existentialism developed to offset the trend.

Religious psychology continued to center upon and to probe the depth of man's fears, frustrations* and inner conflicts. Psychology itself became more human and realistic in dealing with personality problems, many of which became accentuated by recurrent wars, depressions, instability and the conflicts brought on by the swiftly changing modes of living (technological advances in all areas). Neo-Freudianism continued to flourish with modifications of what Freud had regarded as the deepest urge in man (sex), some holding the basic unconscious drive* to be the feeling of inferiority (Adler), while others holding it to be a dominating egocentricity. The present vogue of depth psychology with its flood of books among theologians wishing to defend traditional ideas of sin in the garb of Freudian insights is but an elaboration of Neo-Freudianism. Man as a characteristically sick-soul* rather than as a normally healthy-minded* personality (borrowing James' terms) has captured the interests of many present-day students of religious psychology, particularly among those operating in the circle of neo-orthodoxy in theology. This development is an elaboration of a school rather than a unique contribution to the development of the psychology of religion, although the widespread current interest seems to give the contrary impression.

Popular interest in the whole field of personality adjustment and its relation to religion is evidenced by the widespread acceptance of such books as H. C. Link's *The Return to Religion* (1936), J. L. Liebman's *Peace of Mind* (1946), F. Sheen's *Peace of Soul* (1949) and Leslie D. Weatherhead's *Psychology, Religion and Healing* (1952). Clergymen have become overwhelmingly interested in the psychological field, in "the art of ministering to the sick," in family adjustments, sex education, gerontology* and in the whole area of counseling.* A magazine directed to these interests has appeared under the title *Pastoral Psychology* (in its fourth year, 1953).

What has made the development of the field of the psychology of religion difficult and scientifically disappointing—a field so important to the understanding of both man and his religion—has been the chasm that continues to exist between those who are trained psychologists and those disciplined in the field of religion. Many psychologists are first to admit their incompetence to deal with religion (a highly complex phenomenon) and are cautiously silent, while many theologians who follow the groove of their predecessors seem to develop aspects of a psychological fashion (or school) to support the framework of their conventional religious patterns.

Religion itself is a term which has different meanings to different students. In many cases it is normatively conceived in terms of a particular brand rather than descriptively as a universal phenomenon. Psychology of religion fundamentally deals with the whole area of religion, not with one particular faith. Furthermore, there is no religious psychology *per se*. Men do not take on a nature that is different when they affirm and give loyalty to religious ideas or when they behave in a manner that is characteristically religious. Man is all of one psychological piece whatever the interests may be at the time, whether in art, in community living, in educational enterprise, in a commitment to a destiny (which is religion) or in just the plain business of getting on. It is to the scientific psychologist that religious psychology must turn for its moorings. There is, of course, the deeper difficulty of attempting to develop the field of the psychology of religion in the face of the diffusion into schools which psychology itself has engendered in the growing pains of its own discipline.

A most promising area of inquiry into the field has developed, it must be admitted, in the now commonplace stress of psychosomatic* medicine on the interplay of the body and the mind (in sickness or in health). Personalities are seen to have deep physiological roots of explanation while both organic health and disturbances are equally motivated and nourished by psychic activities. Religion as man's total response to the totality of life or to that which gives ultimate meaning to his own destiny is seen to be of vital significance both to health and illness. There is a present-day ontologic emphasis given to religious ideas, such as God, faith, petitional prayer, which are taken to be of enormous medical significance to personality-balance, an emphasis which was absent among scientifically trained medical specialists decades ago. Both psychology and a religion-with-objective-reference are now seen to be a part of a normal life pattern and not as distinct from each other or both apart from Nature. Certainly, religion is not viewed as something alien or superimposed upon normal living. Ideas, such as the soul, may need revision but the realism to which such religious terms point still registers on the sensitive plate that life presents.

The psychology of religion is hampered by provincial tendencies to regard all religious behavior after the pattern of one faith. The coming *rapprochement* of Western and Eastern religions will correct in time this deficiency. Easterners have given the philosophical rather than the psychological emphasis to religious studies, this because of a long tradition; while Westerners have now taken to religious psychology with far too little attention to the broader aspects of religion.

The future course of the psychology of religion lies, it would seem, in a profound conviction—a conviction that is part and parcel of the scientific spirit—that all life is of one piece and that there are fundamental and universal experiences and expressions which undergird all differences of symbols and behavior patterns. Human beings are fundamentally the same psychologically as they are physiologically. But environments differ with their bags full of tricks and influences, now to bring out one phase and now another, until men seem altogether different both psychologically and religiously. The greatest contribution which the serious study of the psychology of religion can offer, and will no doubt offer, is the increasing realization of the wholesome truth that though religions differ and though faiths separate, they have commen elements: because men everywhere are fundamentally the same; and because **Nature** is fundamentally One (a postulate of the scientific approach itself); and because religious phenomena *commonly* reflect man's grasping of his total environment which is so infinitely larger than himself. To understand this is to become tolerant of the variety of religious expressions and to appreciate the singleness of living. Religious psychology is a perennial testimony of man's getting on with the *total* business of life in a world that is fundamentally a unity both as to structure and function. As such, the serious student of the psychology of religion as a scientific discipline contributes an antidote to religious provincialism, the tempting sin of religious philosophers and theologians. See psychology, schools of.

*Bibl.* (Supplementary to Titles mentioned in the text.) G. M. Stratton, *Psychology of the Religious Life* (1911); James H. Leuba, *The Belief in God and Immortality* (2nd ed., 1921) and *The Psychology of Religious Mysticism* (1925); C. C. Josey, *The Psychology of Religion* (1927); H. S. Elliott, *The Bearing of Psychology on Religion* (1927); A. A. Roback, *The Psychology of Character* (1927); A. R. Uren, *Recent Religious Psychology* (1928); George A. Coe, *Motives of Men* (1928); Elmer T. Clark, *The Psychology of Religious Awakening* (1929); E. S. Conklin, *The Psychology of Religious Adjustment* (1929); W. B. Selbie, *The Psychology of Religion* (1929); Knight Dunlap, *Mysticism, Freudianism and Scientific Psychology* (1930); Henry H. Wieman and R. W. Wieman, *Normative Psychology of Religion* (1935); R. H. Thouless, *Introduction to the Psychology of Religion* (1936); W. L. Jones, *Psychological Study of Religious Conversion* (1937); Vergilius Ferm, ed., *Religion in Transition* (1937); L. P. Thorpe, *Psychological Foundations of Personality* (1938); G. B. Cutten, *Instincts and Religion* (1940); Paul E. Johnson, *Psychology of Religion* (1945); Knight Dunlap, *Religion, Its Functions in Human Life* (1946); G. W. Allport, *The Individual and his Religion* (1950); S. Doniger, ed., *Religion and Human Behavior* (1954).

**psychoneuroses:** A term used in psychoanalysis.\* Repressed complexes\* may manifest themselves in functional nervous disorders called psychoneuroses. Some examples of these are:

*anxiety neurosis* (symptoms: anxiety, palpitation, tremor, distress, excitability, sweating, terrifying dreams).

*neurasthenia* (symptoms: weakness, tiredness, although the sleep is ample, mental depression).

*conversion hysteria* (symptoms: paralysis, blindness, headaches, localized pains).

*psychasthenia* (symptoms: fear of crowds, obsessions).

*dual personality* (symptoms: split personality).

A few words about each: in *anxiety neurosis* the repression is not so deeply set. The self in imminent danger becomes anxious in the conflict. In anxiety one is aware of conflict, in anxiety neurosis one is anxious about something unknown, something within. In *neurasthenia* the complex is set deep and thus fully repressed so that expression in consciousness is absent. The neurasthenic person is tired and weak since he has spent his energy within. Mental depression and even physical fatigue become symptomatic. In moral living this type of person has no conscious temptations, has no interest in play, has no happiness but suffers moral neurasthenia. In *conversion hysteria* a substitute (even physical) symptom appears (by a kind of back door) for the inner conflict. A person, for instance, may suffer chronic vomiting which takes the place (and offers relief) of a mental sickness. Frequent handwashing may be symptomatic of inner stains of mind. In the case of substitution a mental symptom may occur, such as a fixed idea, obsession, a phobia, or sex perversion. In *psychasthenia* the condition takes on the form of loss of mental tension expressing itself in phobias, depersonalization and morbidity. In *dual personality* two distinct personalities appear in the same individual, usually without memory of the other, each well integrated.

Psychoneuroses reveal certain principles in their formation. 1) They are the result of conflict. Complexes even though repressed are dynamic and may conflict in themselves or with the self. An ambition complex and a sex complex may conflict with the assertion of the one (power and aggressiveness) and the loss of the other (impotence). Again, 2) conflicts are within the mind. Disorders attending psychoneuroses, therefore, are failures to integrate a person with himself rather than to some external situation. A person becomes his own problem rather than a problem of some external adaptation. To have harmony, conflicts must be resolved; "peace of mind" is more significant than an adjustment to some external circumstance. 3) Every psychoneurosis is an unconscious desire for deliverance. A person torn between an unconscious fear and urge to be brave may become psychically blind in a situation of danger. This psychical blindness is the deliverance since he is relieved of fear of the threatening danger which he has seen by removing himself from the situation and at the same time he is relieved of any anxiety of being considered a coward in the situation (since he is now not responsible in his predicament of blindness). The symptom, in other words, satisfies the conflicts in the neurosis. See analysis; criminal types; genius; neurosis; pastoral counseling: case studies; pastoral psychology: its governing limitations and qualifications; self.

**psychopath, the:** see criminal types.

**psychopathology:** The term for a study of mental disorders.* See emotion; motives.

**psychosis:** A term referring to any serious mental disorder.* See emotion; Esquirol, Jean Etienne Dominique; hypopituitarism; neurosis; old age; pastoral psychology: its governing limitations and qualifications.

**psychosomatic medicine:** see psychology of religion.

**psychosomatics:** Certain diseases are purely organic and physical (e.g., pernicious anemia, venereal infection, cancer). Other illnesses are held by many (though not all) to be psychogenic, that is of mental origin (e.g., dementia praecox or schizophrenia,* amnesia*). Between these groups there is a third class of afflictions which seem to be rooted in both physical and mental sources. It is not always easy to tell which came first. The term "psychosomatic" is used for this third group: *psyche*\* meaning mind and *soma* meaning body. These two intermingled play an important part in health and illness. An ulcer patient, for example, frequently finds no relief in diet and alkalis since psychic factors play into his condition. So also the victim of hives, the high blood pressure and cardiac patient *may* suffer his condition from mental difficulties (e.g., worry, frustration). Physicians today are realizing the importance of their patients' mental references and history in diagnosis. Digging up emotional conflicts* may initiate, in many unsuspecting cases, a cure for bodily illness. Psychosomatics, however, is no cure-all, especially where organic damage has been done through the years. See autosuggestion; Cabot, R. C.;

**psychogenic disorders;** somatogenic disorders; visiting the sick.

**psychotechnology:** see work and rest.

**psychotherapy:** *Psyche** is the Greek word for soul or spirit; *therapeia* is the Greek word for cure. Psychotherapy, thus, etymologically means the cure of soul or spirit. Thus psychotherapy is the term for the special inquiry into and discipline of any disorders* of the human spirit and the attempt to overcome them to promote a healthy state of the human personality. Usually this is done by personal counseling,* the use of suggestion, educational techniques, persuasion and sympathetic understanding on the part of the patient of his own difficulties which come out of his own conscious thinking or out of the subconscious memories latent or potent in his mind.

Usually these disorders are mild in the discipline called psychotherapy as distinguished from the special discipline called psychiatry which usually pertains to greater disorders of the personality requiring professionally trained counselors to carry on the diagnosis and cure.

All people need psychotherapy at one time or another in the rough business of living. "Soul cure" as it once was called has always been a major concern of religions. All the great religious leaders have recognized the need and offered ways and means to secure peace, poise and what the professional psychologist a generation ago called "integration."

Every minister as pastor is a psychotherapist. Basic qualification to success in this vital area is a full measure of common sense, first and last. This implies knowing people's basic interests and needs and the currents of frustration that block them. Professional psychology is of great help providing it never stands in the way of what mature experience and common sense may acquire in living through years of one's own difficulties and maturing in spite of adversities.

The cults of faith-healing have flourished in this area, partly because of successful accomplishment in bringing unity in some worthy aspiration to people who have been torn asunder, but very largely because of the hunger and hope which people possess of coming to terms with themselves. All vital religion is engaged in psychotherapy.

Recent schools of psychology such as psychoanalysis,* Neo-Freudianism* and depth psychology* offer techniques in this field. See cure of souls; emotional tensions, release of; flight into health; ministry; pastoral psychology: its governing limitations and qualifications; problem complex; psychology of religion; psychology, schools of; readiness, principle of; religion and mental health; structuring the counseling situation; therapy.

**psychotherapy:** Psychotherapy is the term which designates the work of a trained therapist with a patient who is troubled. Psychotherapy, in contrast to the technique of psychoanalysis,* does not attempt to probe into the emotional history of the patient but rather concentrates on the solution of surface problems. Psychotherapy does not require the time of psychoanalysis and may often be terminated at the time of a solution to the specific problem brought to the therapist's attention. While psychoanalysis involves a total reorientation of the patient, psychotherapy only strives to help the patient fit into whatever context he finds himself.

Psychotherapy is often recommended above psychoanalysis when the following things are true: 1) when the patient is sufficiently aged and the extensive reorientation of an analysis seems unnecessary and unwise; 2) when the problem of adjustment is a surface one and the patient can make a satisfactory adjustment without reorganizing his total schemata of responses; and 3) when the patient lacks sufficient insight to carry the bulk of his analysis. In this connection it may be wise to point out that psychotherapy is more often used with severely distressed mental patients when the prognosis for a total recovery is poor and where the most that can be hoped for is the alleviation of some of the more distressing symptoms.

Psychotherapy is a professional technique and may not be practiced by an untrained person. To some degree it is more available to the troubled in the forms of the trained counselor, the psychiatrist, the psychiatric social worker and the clinically trained psychologist. It is wise to make the distinction between the psychoanalyst and the psychotherapist in referring troubled persons to trained professional help. An able counselor will be capable of seeing the needs of the patient in terms of the type of therapy to be administered. See analysis; counseling.

W.W.B.

**psychotherapy, group:** see group psychotherapy.

**public speaking:** see sermon; social perception.
**pugnacious instinct:** see peace and war.
**pulpit technique:** see sermon; sermons, preparation of.
**punishment:** see child training; criminal types.
**puritanism:** see child training; displacement; resolution, the doctrine of.
**purpose:** see teleology.
**Pym, T. W.:** see psychology of religion.
**pyramid tract:** see Babinski reflex.
**pyrophobia:** see phobias.

# Q

**questionnaire method**: see Coe, G. A.; Leuba, James H.; psychology of religion.
**quibbling**: see fallacy of equivocation.

# R

**race psychology:** The concept of "race" is a highly vague and precarious category, both from the point of view of anthropology and psychology.

Sometimes the word is used to designate people of national or political groups: Dutch, Italian, German, etc.; sometimes along linguistic lines: Semitic, Aryan; sometimes religious: Jewish.

Again, the word is used to designate a series or composite of physical traits (independent of environmental factors apparent from several generations). Such physical characteristics are: facial angles, texture of hair, nose features, blood type, endocrine domination, pigmentation, constitutional differences, etc. These traits are not clean-cut and often overlap. A "race" in this sense is a general composite of selection of traits. An "average individual" (an abstraction) is taken to be a group characteristic—with a tendency to eliminate variability. There is always the temptation to disregard the individual by a class concept. In group psychology there may well be typical behaviors, socially conditioned, which in individual cases are not typical while, at the same time, the group characteristics though social are mistaken for fixed hereditary patterns. A Swede who has a neat home (characteristic of many Swedes) may have neatness conferred by social pressures of long standing rather than for any reason that is biological. So: sentimental French, stingy Scotsmen, humorless English.

Anthropologists and social psychologists, however, do tend to emphasize different mental and physical traits among groups

—giving grounds to their classifications based on the method of sampling. Sampling, however, is not a completely justifiable method for general conclusions. In race studies this method has been applied but the conclusions are precarious.

Group traits involving measurement of height, cranium, weight, sensory acuity, etc., have been established by anthropologists with some degree of impressiveness. Mental trait measurements are more difficult, involving cultural differences, the problem of sampling and the type of tests set up (some of which do not fit a given culture).

Cautious psychologists today refrain from admitting to the status of certain reliability the racial comparisons involving psychological tests which have been made. It is, accordingly, a justifiable conclusion that such psychological studies which claim to show "race" differences offer only limited usefulness. Until shown otherwise, a scientifically saner view would be to hold that between groups of people there are no differences with respect to innate mental abilities—until more reliably acceptable methods of comparison have been set up.

*Bibl.* For a Bibliography see article "race psychology" by C. W. Mann in *Encyclopedia of Psychology* (1946), ed. by P. L. Harriman.

**races:** see human genetics.

**racial past:** see Jung, Carl.

**racial prejudice:** see pastoral counseling and case studies.

**racketeers in psychology:** see popular applied psychology; pseudopsychology.

**rage:** see emotion; tantrum.

**rapport relationship:** see analysis.

**rationalization:** see fallacy of rationalization; motives.

**rating of personalities:** see personality; tests and measurements.

**rationality as a role:** see role playing.

**raw material of behavior:** see drives.

**Raven, Charles:** see sermons, preparation of.

**reaction:** see heightened reaction.

**reactions, native:** see drives; synapses.

**readiness, principle of:** It is not true that every troubled person wants help in dealing with his problems. The concept of readiness is important in the outcome of counseling. The man or woman who seeks help without prompting and who does so at a realization of his or her own inability to solve problems is more likely to move through the counseling situation with meaning and without delay. A disgruntled parent, e.g., who sends a child for psychological help when that child sees no reason for it (save as the punishment which may be implied in such a case) can hardly expect the child to embrace the need for such therapy. One large counseling center in New York City which deals with young children in therapy sessions will insist that when a parent brings a child for counseling, the parent also meet with a counselor at the same time. This presents a difficult counseling situation for in it you have a parent who has not come to discuss his problems but those of an offspring and you have a child who may have no desire to share his problems with anyone.

In the cases such as this counseling center handles, it is interesting to note that "readiness" for therapy comes first to the children. The parents often will talk to a counselor for dozens of sessions without being willing to talk about their own problems. It may be the case in any new counseling situation that the degree of readiness can be judged in terms of the initial reaction of the patient. One patient may go on for months in a counseling situation and be enthralled by the sessions. Another patient may have some acute anxiety as the result of simply having had one session. We could judge the readiness of these two patients readily by their reactions to a counseling situation. See learning. W. W. B.

**reading:** see minister, the, and his books.

**reading performance:** This is a highly complex performance involving a high degree of training and a variety of stimuli and responses. Adjustment to the printed page involves muscle movements of the eye—the eye moving not steadily but by jerks and pauses, with the pauses alone furnishing the important element in seeing. The return to the next line, however, is done by a continuous sweep.

When a person attends to a stimulus he responds to it as a whole not in piecemeal fashion. He can read three short words as easily as three or four letters. The reaction time for reading aloud unrelated letters is about twice that for reading aloud letters which form words. The present day "word method", of teaching children to read is based on the principle that the whole word often is grasped more easily than the component letters. A child is often able to read simple words in sentences before he knows his alphabet.

The motor side of reading is speech (whether loud or silent). This moves from infancy training to long established channels of habits of articulation. Reading sets off the habits of speech of the reader. It also touches off meaning responses which also follow habit patterns (thus, frequent misreading by false interpretation or lack of understanding).

Readers of familiar material (e.g., a theologian reading a new book in the particular area of his training and experience) will scarcely read each and every word of a page. He gets his cue from a few words which suggest larger patterns of meaning and he is thus able to integrate the whole page into the chief argument in which his discernment required only half-reading. This performance comes by training and familiarity.

This writer often reads a new book in his field (having done hundreds of book-review articles) by sampling a few beginning pages, turning to the concluding chapter and then sampling the middle pages—until the general plot unfolds. This, of course, is not always effective to understanding, particularly when there are many important small patterns of thought to be observed in the over-all point of view.

Habitual readers of the familiar local daily newspaper do not read consecutively nor word for word to catch the drift of the day's news. Bad reading habits include those which spell out the words thus bogging down the travel over the highway. Words, thus, are like the ties which hold the rails together; reading is itself the traveling over the rails.

Exception to all this is where a piece of writing is studied to be remembered in preparation for an examination on minute material. This varies, of course, with the subject matter and its familiarity (mathematical formulae, book titles and date of publication, etc.). Even so, the practice of exactness in reading and recall can develop speed, even as the continued application of motor responses on a musical instrument (without affecting the accurate performance indicated by the notes and their time-value). See fatigue.

**reality feeling principle:** This principle (enunciated by William James* and J. B. Pratt*) is this: that which concerns us from day to day will psychologically become real to us; on the other hand, that which does not concern us from day to day becomes unreal. A theologian would be expected to be warm toward any discussion about God and probably not so concerning automobile parts. An auto-mechanic would have reality feeling in reverse: warm toward automobile parts and cool towards theology. It follows then that if some noted physical scientist should express agnosticism about God this would not be surprising. He probably has had little time, opportunity, interest or disciplined thinking in that direction of his thought. His agnosticism would not be significant as a conclusion. It would be expected that symphonic music would be extolled by an accomplished musician and frowned upon by one whose daily routine offers no such appreciation for fine music. Judgment of people's estimation, then, must be considered in terms of their reality-feeling, their day to day concern. A disbelief often is not so much disbelief as it is the lack of reality feeling. See Leuba, James H.; occupational prejudice; psychological frames of reference; symbols.

**reality principle:** see juvenile delinquency; psychology, schools of.

**reason and intuition:** see intuition.

**reasoning:** see aging process; creative thinking; dogmatism; intuition; thinking.

**recall:** see memorizing; memory.

**recapitulation theory:** see children and religious beliefs.

**receptor:** A sensory nerve ending which is stimulated. A receptor may have a low threshold for one kind of stimulation and a high threshold for other kinds. It is the dendrite* of an afferent nerve cell.* See sensations.

**reciprocity in counseling situations:** see counseling periods; readiness, principle of.

**recitation:** see memorizing.

**recreation:** see emotional tensions, release of; pastoral counseling and case studies; relaxation; work and rest.

**recreation centers:** see clubs; old age.

**redirection:** see psychology of religion.

**reference, professional:** see professional reference.

**reflective autosuggestion:** see autosuggestion.

**reflex:** The direct and immediate response of an effector* (muscle or gland) or group of effectors to the stimulation of a sense organ. This term sometimes is used to refer to any automatic response. See Babinski reflex; conditioned reflex; patellar reflex.

**regeneration:** see psychology of religion.

**regression:** see libido.

**rehabilitation:** see criminal types; social maturation.

**reification of abstractions:** see fallacy of the reification of abstractions.

**relaxation:** see autosuggestion; creative thinking; emotional tensions, release of; Freud, Sigmund; intuition; religion and mental health; sleep.

**relearning:** see experimental extinction.

**release of emotional tensions:** see emotional tensions, release of.

**religio-therapy:** see cure of souls; pastoral psychology, its governing limitations and qualifications; prayer and autosuggestion; psychotherapy; religion and mental health; therapy.

**religion:** see psychology of religion; psychotherapy; religious response, the, nature and origin; sancta of religion.

**religion and environment:** see psychology of religion.

**religion and mental health:** Religion, of course, is a broad term. Here (in this article) religion is used in the rather conventional sense of a commitment to a God (theistic religion). (Theism is the viewpoint of a belief in a personal God.) The question here is: does such a religion have any value toward the achievement of mental well-being? Freud's* answer was negative. Religion magnifies illusion and it tends to foster weaklings. Jung,* however, (another psychoanalyst) expressed the view "that the increase in the number of neuroses has paralleled the decrease of religious life." (A statement before a group of Protestant ministers at Strassbourg in 1932.)

In 1948, under the auspices of the National Committee for Mental Hygiene,* a group of psychiatrists and representatives of various churches met to discuss the question of the relationship between religion and mental health. The following points were made by members of this group. 1) A theistic religion, in teaching a purpose and meaning to life, provides a motive for living. Such a motivation produces in its adherents patience, contentment and a spirit of endurance in the face of emotional crises, frustrations and the monotony of life. Even suffering is given meaning and thus has a constructive purpose. Lacking this kind of motivation an individual falls easy prey to despondency and serious depression when hardships come. 2) A theistic religion, seriously taken, elevates and fosters the ideal of inner poise which prevents hysteria in times of adversity or crisis. 3) Theistic religion has emphasized regard for others so that relationships with others tend to become smoother to the degree in which the individual is committed to it. The self is idealized as out-going rather than turning upon itself. 4) In theistic religion others are regarded as equally valuable in the sight of God and thus a stable and healthy interrelationship is strengthened on the basis of a foundation more solid than passing emotions or moral platitudes. 5) Theistic religion undergirds moral standards furnishing confidence in their pursuit and consummation.

All of these points are on the side of the ledger for mental health—and there are others.

Dr. James Vanderveldt of the Catholic University, Washington, D.C., reporting on this exchange of views on religion and mental health (above mentioned) comments on the controversial debate on the influence of sin- and guilt-feeling (which theistic religion is claimed to emphasize) on good health. His own view (as a Catholic) he reports as follows: Sin is a conscious experience and to feel guilty of responsible misdemeanors before God is a healthy response since it inspires a sense of inadequacy, responsibility and a need for correction. A feeling of guilt, however, that arises from the deep wells of the unconscious (the unconscious cannot be said to harbor "sins" which, by definition, are conscious) is undesirable and may well provoke ill health. Theistic religion in respect to guilt plays its role only where guilt is due to conscious sin; as such the psychiatrist who enters this field with any preconceived code of morals is transgressing the area of the minister as a witness to codes higher than individual opinion. Sin as an offense against a Divine Being is a matter of the confessional and not a matter for the office of a counselor or psychiatrist. (A Protestant would agree, reserving the privilege of private confession to his God without a necessary confessional.) The psychiatrist's approach is limited to the psychological factors that make for illness or health and in that area lies his province—not, in questions of metaphysics. Moreover, an analysis of conflicts is no automatic cure. Mere understanding is no sure road to recovery. A psychiatrist, knowing the area of psychological behavior may well (and should) give advice for a better plan of living—but he may well step beyond the borders of his knowledge and wisdom in giving advice if he assumes to say how, in detail, his patient may be helped religiously (religion being the undertone of life). The psychiatrist or a therapist may revive in his patient the values of a religion latent there and "lost" which, if revived, could help—even though the psychiatrist may not know that religion sympathetically. Some patients may profess no religion but the profession may belie their condition. There may well be a deep desire for the very thing that is needed and not acknowledged. This thing may well be the religion that once was powerful and lost and the underlying cause of real conflict. Here the psychiatrist may well join hands with the minister, the rabbi or the priest—the latter more skilled in the profession of showing the broad way back to religious recovery and through it to mental health.

Theistic religion stands as an anchorage to the tossing perplexities and shiftings of life. Psychiatry can of itself furnish no anchorage comparable to it. If the psychiatrist is ignorant of religion as an anchorage and prefers to call it "an illusion" he has no right to impose his personal view under the aegis of his profession. For many people theistic religion is a real thing with powerful increments to mental health.

The conviction that here is a supporting Power greater than ourselves—even to sustain us—even in our greatest depressions—is a therapy that reaches down deep.

Prayer has a reassuring effect and is an incalculable aid to mental health. The mental catharsis involved in prayerful relaxation tends to loosen the strains of inner conflict and to bring truer perspective. The aspirations, the hopes offered in prayer, may be tremendously tonic in quality; the trust in a Higher Power is the opening of the valve for the possible insurgence of energy. Theistic religion regards all these contribu-

**religion, theistic**                           **270**

tions to mental health as more than autosuggestion; prayer involves an ontological reality without which the effects themselves would be spurious.

Mental health is a fruit of a vital theistic religion. But in broken mental health a psychiatrist like the medical man contributes disciplined knowledge in finding the way back while the minister of a theistic religion stands ready to point the way to a long-range dynamic. See belief in God; confession; hospital chaplain, the; prayer and autosuggestion; psychology of religion; religio-therapy; religious response, the; success.

    *Bibl.* James Vanderveldt, "Religion and Mental Health" in *Mental Hygiene* (April, 1951).

**religion, theistic:** see belief in God; psychology of religion; religion and mental health.

**religious beliefs and children:** see children and religious beliefs.

**religious complex:** see complexes.

**religious cults:** see visions and hallucinations.

**religious education:** see children; children and religious beliefs; deceit (and character); teaching.

**religious humanism:** see positivism.

**religious instinct:** see children and religious beliefs; instinct.

**religious psychology:** see psychology of religion.

**religious response, the, nature and origin:** The religious response may be defined as the concern man has for that wider area of life of which he becomes seriously aware as affecting his ultimate destiny. "That wider area" may be his gods, his God, Fate, his Utopia, Nature or anything that is for him of ultimate significance. To this he may react in many ways (e.g., fear, joy, reverence) but always with the natural psychological responses.

Why are people naturally religious? In the first place, man as a psycho-physical organism adapts himself to his environment. Man is an adjusting organism like any other organic form. However, he becomes aware of *more* in his environment than do lower creatures. He adjusts with anticipation (dread or joy) to things far away and unseen, to far-reaching horizons; and he adjusts also in memory, to events forever gone in time (enjoyment or regret). The religious person is always one who is aware of wider horizons (however unclear they may be). In the second place, the environment presented to man is infinitely greater than man's day-to-day experiences, a world baffling and strange—evoking, naturally, some response to it.

It is this interchange of environment and response that forms the basis of the religious response—in the case of religion it is the awareness of the wider area of life which is involved. To it he responds as best he may naturally, even though intermittently.

How he reacts depends on circumstances, occasions, moods, specific needs and/or felt experiences. It is not *how* he reacts that makes man religious but *that* he thus responds (in whatever way).

The faith element in religion has always been strong because the awareness of and response to the Beyond are characteristically *more* than the day-to-day accruements of knowledge or manipulation.

"Religions" would never have arisen without people having been religious. All religious people are psychologically the same (as per the nature of the religious response); but religions differ since these reflect the habit-patterns of culture (mores, geography, economic circumstances, etc.) and are always a step removed from the response itself. A person may respond to God as he conceives God but the god of the religious response is more to him than his conception. In "religion" the conceptions (and behaviors) are crystallized into form and related with others and thus are representations of the real rather than the direct response to it. See children and religious beliefs; dispositions; instinct; psychology of religion (J. C. Flower and *passim*); sentiments.

    *Bibl.* Editor's Preface *Forgotten Religions* (1950), ed. by Vergilius Ferm.

**religious symbols:** see symbols.

**religious tolerance:** see psychology of religion.

**religious visitation:** see visitation.

**repetition compulsion:** The tendency to repeat patterns of reaction and behavior until they are spontaneous and automatic is a fundamental trait of organisms including humans. This tendency is called "repetition compulsion" by psychologists. This explains conservatism in religion or forms of worship or even the liberal type of reactions. See autosuggestion.

**repressed complexes:** see complexes; projection.

**repression:** The term employed by Freud\* for the unconscious tendency to exclude painful or unpleasant ideas from consciousness. Psychoanalytic psychology makes much of this concept. One common cause for repression (Freud's later view) is the state of anxiety. See analysis; anxiety states; censor; complexes; defense mechanisms; emotion; exhibitionism; genius; juvenile delinquency; projection; psychology of religion; psychoneuroses.

**repugnant experiences:** see complexes; repression.

**repulsion:** see sociometry.

**resistance:** see analysis; repression.

**resistance of neural impulses:** see synapses.

**resolution, the doctrine of:** "Every day, in every way, I grow better and better" was the self-suggestive therapeutic for generations of persons. It is the well-meant New Year's resolution made daily as a warranty against backsliding. "Today I will not smoke a cigar" may serve to prevent the consumption of tobacco for a twenty-four hour period but it may not eliminate the driving desire to do so. Actually, the open denial of a desirable satisfaction may create frustration of a high order. Psychoanalysis\* has not been totally free of a subject's gold star for good behavior. A patient or client may, indeed, refrain from committing an act of aggression or hostility for a period of years. If the virtue of avoiding that act is the end of analytical work then more of us could be analysts. However, the goal of the analyst is not to eliminate the manifestation of symptomatic behavior of a personality disorder but to eliminate the need for this disorder's existence as an answer to the fundamental problem. The puritan personality may be one who has only "pure" thoughts, to be sure, yet it is entirely possible that the puritan is a person fraught with "non-pure" desires which are submerged and denied in a daily statement of critical appraisal of desires in others. Denial of sexual desires may result in an overt record of sexual purity. At the same time the desire frustrated and the covert record may not be so "pure." The goal of a psychoanalysis is not to detach the individual from his "self" but is, rather, an attempt to make him come to terms with himself and reconstruct that pattern with the self's permission. Psychoanalysis does not provide an exercise of self suggestion intent upon eliminating the factors which mar the image that others have of us, or the image of ourselves, imposed upon us by others. It does attempt to ferret out the image we have of ourselves and construct upon that the kind of personality adjustment essential to human happiness. Couéism (see autosuggestion) may serve to eliminate the overt acts which are guilt-creating but it brings the reciter no closer to solution than the average resolution couched in "I should not." See analysis. W. W. B.

**respiration and deception:** see deception.
**response, group:** see morale.
**responses:** see projective techniques; S-R; synapses.
**responsibility, social:** see social responsibility.
**rest and work:** see work and rest.
**rest periods:** see work and rest.
**restitution:** see confession.
**restorative process:** see autosuggestion; confession.
**restraint:** see complexes; sex differences, psychological.
**retention:** see memory; memorizing.
**retirement:** see adult, the; aging process; in-laws; old age.
**retrograde amnesia:** see amnesia.
**revelation as discovery:** see creative thinking.
**reverence, the social media of:** see sancta of religion.
**reverie:** see autosuggestion.
**reversed effort, law of:** see autosuggestion.
**revivalism:** see psychology of religion.
**Rhine, Joseph B.:** see psychical research and parapsychology.
**rhythm, biological:** see efficiency and time of day.
**rhythmic vocalization:** see memorizing.
**Richet, Charles:** see psychical research and parapsychology.
**ridicule:** see catagelphobia.
**right and wrong:** see conscience; morality and psychology; motives.
**right handedness:** see dextrality.
**ritual:** see symbols; worship.
**Robertson, Frederick:** see sermons, preparation of.
**role playing:** This psychological concept is so widely misunderstood by our society that its employment for psychological health is widely limited. Role-playing is the device whereby we meet the various demands made upon us as per-

sonalities in the various levels of society. The child plays one role at home as he makes demands for food and love. This role is altered as the home response is that of authority. This same child plays another role as he meets his playmates and denies the authority at home. He learns to exploit as well as be exploited. He is one person to his first girl friend and another to his sceptical buddies whom he deserts as he relates to her. He affirms and denies. It is the concept of role-playing which teaches the young to exercise all the facets of the personality. He learns to love, hate, win, defy, lose and all the elements of his personality are brought to light and he learns to arrange them as he needs them. Wherever one role is developed at the expense of all others, the personality is crippled in a very literal sense. Modern educators have insisted too strenuously upon a rational man's having only one response to the world in which he lives. Rather than teach adaptive responses we have taught one wisest response. The rational man may, indeed, know only one role of response to life. The chances are that he is not a well adjusted man. (By not well adjusted we here mean he does not meet problems well.) Just as the child who cannot meet his playmates on a different ground from that upon which he deals with his parents is a lost person, so is the person who has but one role to play. Politeness on the baseball diamond may not lead to success just as razzing the cook at home may not produce much in the way of a good meal. The unhappy man more often than not will search for one solution to his problem. What role-playing teaches is that what the unhappy man needs is not a solution but, rather, a problem-solving procedure. It is easy to see why old authoritarian values have cried "heresy" when the John Deweys and the William Jameses came along and suggested role-playing as a philosophical concept. For it does indeed equate the ball diamond and theology when it speaks of salvation. See self.    W.W.B.

**Roman Catholicism and counseling:** The very nature of the Roman Catholic authoritarian theology seems to suggest a limitation to the degree of counseling that can be done by a psychoanalyst with a member of this theological group. It was the experience of one psychoanalyst who spent several years working with Roman Catholic patients that the degree of authoritarian regard on the part of these patients either excluded or limited the degree of a "cure." It was his opinion that the Roman Catholic Church need have no fear of psychoanalysis* as practiced by competent professionals as the patients were sufficiently psychologically crippled to prevent the possibility of their walking on their own feet. To extricate an individual from the realm of fear (where that fear is real) when his very training for love and life has been at the hands of a teacher whose position of authority is maintained by fear seems too difficult a task for those with the best training so far devised. See ministry, the, and counseling. For an interesting article in the same vein as this commentary, see the following: Bertrand Russell's *The Impact of Science On Society* (1951) and his *Authority and The Individual* (1949). W. W. B.

**romance:** see marriage, disharmony in.
**Rorschach, Hermann:** see projective techniques.
**Rorschach ink blot test:** see projective techniques.
**rotation:** see emotional tensions, release of; routine.
**rote memorizing:** see memory; memorizing.
**routine:** see creative thinking; fatigue; religion and mental health; rotation.
**Royce, J.:** see psychical research and parapsychology.
**Russian question, the:** see peace and war.

# S

**sacrament:** see confession.
**sacred and secular, the:** see minister as a person.
**sacred things of religion:** see sancta of religion.
**sacrifice, a psychological concept:** While not every person finding himself in the role of counselor may be trained to the degree that he or she may legally exact a fee for such work from those seeking help, the principle of "exacting" is one well worth looking into. In psychoanalysis* the analyst will often exact a considerable fee for each hour that he or she spends with a patient. This is discussed elsewhere but it will be of value to discuss here the concept of exacting something for help given. The fee paid to the psychoanalyst is partially a professional fee. But in part it is designed not to be an easy fee. The fee paid is usually determined to work a partial hardship on the counselee. Were this not the case he would 1) postpone dealing with many problems, 2) see no need for ending the counseling situation, and 3) treat lightly something which is so readily accessible. Remembering that the concept of sacrifice is not so much a theological concept as a psychological one, we can proceed to draw upon it as a "help-giving" concept. By sacrificing (in the case of the seemingly high fee of the analyst) the patient is able to emerge from the analytical situation having no feeling that he has not done "more than his share" in meeting the demands of the help-giving. He can always maintain that element of independence whereby he can see readily that he owes the analyst nothing for what has taken place. He will not emerge feeling "grateful" for something he

has achieved by hard work and by hard-come-by capital. The counselee who feels that the counselor wants him to be grateful for the help given should rightfully resent this impingement on his freedom. Just so with the minister who wishes to play the limitless with those he helps. For the good counselor will not exact gratitude; in fact, he will make every attempt to avoid receiving it. This concept of sacrifice is a sound one and can be employed in the counseling situation wherein no fee is permissible. By making the sick get up and walk to help is to make them take some responsibility for their cure and thereby not be crippled by gratitude. The teacher who does too much for a class, and the minister who carries too many of his parish's burdens will dilute the help he may be able to give. Somewhere between unavailability and ready accessibility lies the position of the counselor. The counselor who demands gratitude is not a free man himself. It would behoove the theologians to look at sacrifice as a means whereby a deity gives man his freedom and not in the usual sense of man's eternal insignificance and eternal bondage to the deity's authority. Robert Frost, in his *Masque of Reason*, God's speech to Job, expresses the idea that Job could find issue from his suffering only as he gave God His freedom. God and Job could find a meaningful relationship only in so far as they could maintain their respective freedoms. In this case God's freedom also demonstrates the sacrifice concept. God suffered loss of authority and pride by refusing to demonstrate total independence of man. As Robert Frost indicates, both man and God found freedom. W. W. B.

**sadism:** A term referring to cruelty, pain or suffering inflicted upon the person or object loved. Such cruelty gives pleasure. It is a form of sex perversion and the term was coined by Freud* from the name of the French novelist de Sade.

**saintliness:** This is, in the words of William James* "the collective name for the ripe fruits of religion" by which he meant a "good" religion. Psychologically, saintliness is an achievement by which the drives and emotions nourish behavior patterns commanding moral respect. According to James there are four psychological characteristics of saintliness universal in all religions: 1) a feeling of belonging to an ideal world-order that is far beyond a person's little interests or even the interests of "this world's selfish little interests"; 2) an awareness of a friendly companionship with this ideal world order; 3) a feeling of satisfaction mounting to elation as the individual merges himself in this "divine" order; and 4) a shifting of emotional focus away from self towards others and towards positive commitments.

The practical fruits of these inner conditions of saintliness, James has pointed out, express themselves 1) in self-surrender mounting to asceticism; 2) in a sense of the enlargement of life in which personal preferences become insignificant enough to make for patience, boldness and equanimity; 3) a cleansing of expression of those elements in the person which bring discord and the increase of expression of those elements which lead to harmony and purity; and 4) the increase, similarly, of the tender affection and outgo of the person to his fellows as in acts of charity and brotherliness.

Saintliness, however, may lead to excesses; devoutness when unbalanced may lead to fanaticism; purity when magnified to self-negation may lead to unsociability or social anaesthesia or uselessness; tenderness and charity may lead to spineless acquiescence where the situation may demand the more masculine virtues; and, saintliness may lead to untempered asceticism which breaks both body and spirit and renders the saint a liability both to himself and society. See confession; virtues.

*Bibl.* William James, *The Varieties of Religious Experience* (1902).

**salt taste:** see taste.

**salvation:** see ministry, the, and counseling; therapy.

**sampling, method of:** see race psychology.

**sancta of religion, the:** "Sancta" means the holy things. In religion there are many items which are considered holy: places, people, events, a special church, the Scriptures (for the Jew the Torah), certain festival days, ritual, baptism, candles at an altar, cross, consecrated water or wafer, communion wine, Lord's prayer, etc.

All institutions have their sancta. For example, a good American feels deeply about the Stars and Stripes, Declaration of Independence, the national anthem, etc.

Sancta are the social media of reverence. Group life finds

in these sancta unification which on mere theoretical grounds would be flimsy or lacking. People never argue their sancta, nor do they ask too many questions about them.

Religious groups differ (even as institutional and other social groups) in what they consider sancta. Sancta are evolved over many years. They may be reinterpreted but they tend to persist; they are the steel bonds to a past. Gradually new sancta are evolved, but only gradually. Even the sancta in family life (birthday customs, reunions, modes of eating) endure deep in the memories of its members.

A minister will find it difficult to overcome the peculiar sancta of a parish and he is wise who respects them. To attempt to change them over night is like trying to change deep sentiments at a command. They are not so changed. Only by patience may newer sancta be created—should such need to be created. (New sancta in religion should be fostered to express changing ideas, a changing order—but this takes time.)

People will take lightly criticisms of ideas in their religion but they will not take lightly proposed revisions of their sancta. Sancta once had value; many still function. To outsiders they seem artificial and superficial; to those on the inside they are real and deep.

Two churches alongside each other in a village or city will pray for the unity of the churches but fail to join together or even worship together. Both memberships may be sincere about "unity" but the sancta at the core of each church prevents their willingness to give up what is most deeply cherished: memories associated with a specific church building, a pulpit, a bell that tolled reverently on a Sunday, an old organ that has done service there, and a thousand other concrete evidences of sancta. This is why it is necessary to consider the sancta of religion in any attempts at church unity. While the old operate, the new must be developed along with the old.

A young minister will handle carefully the sancta of the church to which he is called—lest he find himself no longer its leader in that portion of the vineyard. See sentiments.

**sanguine temperament:** see temperament.
**Santa Claus:** see children and religious beliefs.
**Sapphism:** see Lesbianism.
**satisfaction and learning:** see learning.

**savings method, the, in memorization:** see memorizing.
**scepticism:** see disbelief; James, William.
**Schauffler, R. H.:** see visiting the sick.
**Schiller, F. C. S.:** see psychical research and parapsychology.
**schizophrenia:** Formerly called dementia praecox* this type of mental disorder is characterized by dissociation, particularly between the intellectual and the emotional processes (the latter also being, to a great extent, disorganized). Clinical symptoms are: loss of emotional rapport with the environment; automatic obedience; hallucinations;* fantasies; and (normally) disorganized throught processes. Types often mentioned are: dementia simplex (simple); catatonia;* paranoid;* and hebephrenia.* Freud* held that schizophrenia was the result of unconscious homosexual trends. Some hold that it is the result of conflicts revolving about a loss of self-respect; while others hold that it is not psychogenic but rather of organic pathology. See dreams; hypopituitarism; Jung, Carl.
**Schneider, H. W.:** see psychology of religion.
**scholastic psychology:** see psychology, schools of.
**schools of psychology:** see psychology, schools of.
**sciences, the:** see minister, the, and his books.
**scientific method:** see methodological naturalism.
**scientific method, limitations of:** see Leuba, James H.; psychoanalysis, limitations of; psychological frames of reference; reality feeling principle.
**sclerosis:** A hardening of nervous tissues or a thickening of the walls of the arteries.
Multiple sclerosis is the term for the hardening process occurring in various parts of the nervous system. Latter symptoms include weakness, monotonous talk, spastic gait and tremors when voluntary actions are attempted. See aging process; arteriosclerosis.
**scopolamin:** see deception.
**Scriptures, the:** see minister, the, and his books; ministry, the, and counseling; visiting the sick.
**second childhood:** see learning.
**second nature:** see dispositions; sentiments.
**secrets of the unconscious:** see analysis; projection.
**secular and sacred, the:** see minister as a person.
**security, economic:** see in-laws; success.

**seelsorge:** see cure of souls; pastoral counseling: case studies; pastoral psychology; pastoral psychology: its governing limitations and qualifications; psychotherapy.

**self:** All of us reveal ourselves as more than one self: the self we are, the self we think we are, the self we present to one group (our family), the self we present to the organization we serve, the self we present to our parish priest—these are only some among the many.

The real self (as we are) may be inconsistent with any of the others. It is particularly so in the efforts we make to impress others. The mask (the *persona*) we wear is not the *psyche*.* All of us often behave in a way opposite to our inner drives. An uncouth individual, given to loud words and bully manner, may be a sentimentalist and a lamb within his real self. We continue—all of us—to "cover up"—hence the occasional slips, inconsistencies and even "blow ups." It is frankly difficult to express the integrity of one's real self—since the real self is so often at odds with social mores and even with conscious ideals. Language is often a "cover up" of thought, a concealer of true meaning. We like to wear masks to make an impression of possession of something we lack; we turn on an oracular preacher-voice to cover up our incompetence; we turn on an "English accent" to impress by a culture something we do not really possess. How common!

But it is a fact of human psychology that the mask weakens the self. Whenever we try to cover-up and appear other than we are or think we are we fail to tap the greatest dynamic we possess—our true self. The wearing of many masks weakens the total impact of the unitive power of integration. Diffusion is one thing and powerful concentration another.

It is one of the greatest virtues in all living to dare to understand and expose one's real self. People, in the long run, respect integrity and despise, with deepest feeling, hypocrisy. The strains brought upon people in attempting to cover up themselves are open roads to mental ill-health and ultimate maladjustment. "The happiest day of my life" said a woman (in paraphrase) "was when I ceased trying to be beautiful."

To be one's self means to admit one's true self to oneself and to express it with control and not with phantasy and to direct it into a character* of worth. See dispositions; personality; psychoneuroses; role playing.

*Bibl.* J. A. Hadfield, *Psychology and Morals* (1923). Chap. XXIV.

**self, the divided:** see divided self; split personality.

**self centeredness:** see talents.

**self direction:** see children and religious beliefs; social maturation.

**self discipline:** see child training.

**self display:** see exhibitionism; role playing; sublimation.

**self evident truth:** see truth.

**self help:** see social maturation.

**selfishness:** see talents.

**self preservation:** see children and religious beliefs; libido.

**self prohibition:** see Alcoholics Anonymous.

**self reliance:** see adult.

**self respect:** see minister, the, and money; schizophrenia; teen-agers.

**self surrender:** see prayer and autosuggestion; saintliness.

**self torture:** see visions and hallucinations.

**senility:** see menopause; old age; social maturation.

**sensations:** The state of awareness of a specific qualitative type associated with some specific end-organ which gives the stimulus.

It was long held that there were but five senses: sight, hearing (auditory), taste* (gustatory), smell* (olfactory) and touch (tactual). (Popular language admitted a "sixth sense" as a plus avenue of awareness [clergymen were wont to speak of it as intuition, faith, etc.]. But this is discredited by scientific psychologists because of its indefiniteness.) More sense organs have been discovered to increase the number beyond the traditional five. For example, psychologists now speak of a temperature sense referring collectively to "cold spots" and "warm spots" (receptors) located on the surface of the skin; of kinaesthetic senses, those awarenesses of movement of any part of the body which are stimulated by receptors* (proprioceptors) in joints, muscles, tendons (sometimes to include the sensations arising from the semi-circular canals of the inner ear); pain sense (the term nociceptor referring to any sensory nerve-ending which mediates the awareness of pain); pressure sense (spots on the hair follicles). They also speak of touch sensations to include the "cutaneous sensations" (skin surface spots) of warmth, cold, pressure and pain. See brain; organic sensations; perception; projection; symbols.

**sense of pitch:** see talents.

**sense organs:** see sensations.

**senses, mediate and immediate:** see symbols.

**senses, sensations:** see anoetic; drives; extra-sensory perception; hallucination; sensations; sleep.

**sensori-motor arc:** The functional unit of the nervous system establishing a connection between receptor and effector, between situation and motor response to it. See afferent-efferent fibers; neuron; synapses.

**sensorium:** A term referring to the sensory mechanism in general; also to those areas of the cerebral cortex which carry the awareness of sense stimulation from sense organs. Psychiatrists employ the term as referring to the subject's degree of orientation to the immediate environment.

**sensory nerves:** see afferent-efferent fibers; neuron.

**sensory threshold:** The degree at which a sense stimulus provokes a conscious reaction.

**sentiments:** A sentiment arises out of a deep attachment of emotional response to certain objects, ideas, events or persons and is accepted consciously by the individual. (*See* disposition which is similar although accepted unconsciously.) An individual is aware of his sentiments and tends to identify himself with them.

The object to which a sentiment is attached characterizes the kind of, or particular sentiment. If it is one's native land, then we speak of patriotism as a sentiment; if it is devotion to an object that is taken to be of importance to one's ultimate destiny (*e.g.*, God) then it is a religious sentiment; if it is directed to parents it is a parental sentiment; etc. The dominant sentiment in one's life shows our aims and ideals.

Sentiments are good or bad depending on the character of the object of devotion and how, or to what extent, the devotion is given.

It would be of importance to any teacher that he should guide his student to good and proper sentiments. Learning a lesson is one thing; but having sentiment for the subject is another. No really successful teacher is a mere teacher; he is an inspirer of sentiments for his subject, assuming that he himself has sentiment for the subject taught. Once a sentiment is aroused, a deep momentum has been set which will affect the future course of interest and action. One must like a subject if one is to be enriched by it; and liking is a sentiment. (On the contrary, one may dislike a subject which, too, then becomes a sentiment.) Education is not merely a process in the growth of knowledge but a building of sentiments for subjects worthy of one's emotional commitment.

Sentiments build up into dispositions which become responses that have taken rootage in one's subconscious life and thus become spontaneous and "second nature." See emotion; motives; sancta of religion.

**sermon:** A sermon may be defined as a public religious discourse which is motivated toward action. It is not a mere lecture with accumulated points of information nor is it a discourse to initiate the response of enjoyment or mere appreciation. Its end is to arouse commitment and renewal.

It belongs to the subjective aspect of worship.*

Whatever skills belong to effective preaching belong to the effective art of public discourse.

First and foremost among such effective ingredients is the capacity to bring to focus the attention* of those to whom it is directed: by a topic of genuine and living interest, by a beginning which promises something worthy of attention *at the very start* and by a kind of continuation and conclusion that makes the listeners wish there were more of it to come. An audience that goes away hungry for more is the kind of audience that will return for more. A "finished product" is like a meal that has lost interest when the appetite has gone. A sermon should provoke a sustaining interest that will carry beyond the limitations of its delivery.

Like all public discourses the sermon should not be up in the clouds but move at the level of contact. Pictures hung high on the wall are of little interest—unless ladders are furnished. And who would stop and ask for a ladder? Puerile discourses are like pictures hung below eye-level, of no interest as pictures. One should in discourse meet people at eye-level. A sermon is no exception.

Theology may be very interesting if it is presented at eye-level. Undisciplined anecdotes and cheap and unrealistic illustrations are set at the level of baseboards.

Humor is always the tool of interest and it has its place in a sermon provided it is genuine. Humor does not equate itself with jokes or "funny stories"; rather, it is a subtle and surprising way of serving up the familiar, that provokes mirth. Humor is never humor where familiarity is absent since it cannot be discerned.

It is of great assistance to an audience's attention if it knows about how far the trip of the sermon will carry. If there are three major stops along the highway of discourse, known beforehand, the audience will be spared the horror of wondering where, when and if a destination will ever be attained. It will do no harm and certainly much good to announce a skeletal outline to provide a sense of integration for the length of the discussion.

To maintain attention it is a psychological law that things must move on. One does not pay attention very long to one focal point. Attention requires variety, motion, change. If the sermon moves—not, however, with the rapidity of unintelligible hops—it has the better chance of conscious response of those who listen.

Abstract ideas may form the subject matter but abstract ideas may have to wear concrete apparel—stockings, dresses and collars—to be looked at and recognized. A good preacher is an artist with the brush of the concrete—even though his subject-matter moves into the fundamentals of less concrete thinking.

He will be aware, as he delivers his ideas, of the faces which look up at him: to catch the inspiration of some appreciative eyes, to warn himself of the chasm that may exist between him and a mind that is being tempted by the invitation to the unconscious state, and to know when it is proper to pull the stops that properly call for pianissimo, fortissimo or even broken silence. Never shall the preacher pretend to be effective without noting the effects upon the living laboratory in front of him. The lights must burn brightly upon the faces he sees.

He does well to be himself rather than the second or third rate copy of someone else. Each personality is unique and uniqueness always invites freshness of approach. Language must be understood as only a conveyance; it is poor technique to shine up the brass of fine words or exquisite diction (conveyances) at the expense of going places and seeing the scenery.

If possible the sermon must wear the air of the spontaneous—otherwise it is doomed to be stale. A canned sermon however well prepared and delivered is still more like a blurred recording than a fresh living presentation.

Manuscripts seem permissible for formal occasions but much out of place for Sunday-to-Sunday use. To chain oneself to a manuscript is to develop a habit or handicap not easily overcome. Better would it be to make mistakes of grammar (to begin with) and develop the poise of natural spontaneity (which comes by habit of self assurance).

The elements of imagination and surprise are essentials to a good sermon but these are tools to be used without ostentation. Delivery will vary with one's physical stature, bodily grace and the voice that has developed out of the physical voice box. But never should there be any suggestion of professionalism: such as the preacher voice, preacher posture or the pretense of a piety that is absent. The eyes should come to focus in the place where worship is conducted and not upon some ethereal non-existent gallery of Mt. Olympus. Words should be pronounced as they are on the streets of the village and not as they may be spoken in some oasis.

Nothing in a sermon should be artificial or forced—not even in the prayer that either precedes or follows. When the spirit does not move, it is wiser to accept the situation and count the day as one of those harvests where the weather has been less favorable. There will be other and better occasions when the lips may be touched by a presence greater than the words which are spoken. One should not unduly worry about the effects of a sermon—some judgments may be left to the secret counsels of human hearts who, on the whole, recognize jewels or spurious coins, without voicing opinions.

It is the great Protestant tradition to emphasize the pulpit in worship. Any lessening of the importance of this function, whether by a crowded schedule, elaborate ritual or ornate music, is but a confession of bankruptcy in a high calling. The sermon is the most difficult and at the same time the most rewarding service that a minister of religion can perform and it is an act that requires psychological insights as much as depth of religious persuasion.

Possession of poise makes for great psychological effect. It spares the audience of worry and gives halo to the presentation, creating the atmosphere of authority. This is an achievement that comes only after many years of practice. Poise may be more easily attained if the speaker is in possession (even in his notes) of more ideas than it is possible to deliver at the time. There can, then, be no concern of "running dry" while the pump is working. There is no point in "giving out" everything that is on paper; it is better to get the main message across and save the unused pieces for another assembly. It is a good rule to carry a surplus so that there will always be the assurance of possession. The preacher with an "overflow" possesses power unmatched by any other. See creative thinking; fallacy of oversimplification; fiction; minister, the, and his books; preacher, the; social perception; sublimation.

**sermon, its healing function:** see funerals; pastoral psychology: its governing limitations and qualifications.

**sermons, preparation of:** Preaching is an art. The methods and techniques used in the preparation and delivery of sermons vary as widely as types, styles and methods of painting among artists. In painting, there are the classicists, the traditionalists, the surrealists, and almost as many others as there are individual artists. In preaching there are the traditional three-point theological sermonizers, the philosophical, the expository, the emotional, the scholarly, the poetic preachers—and then there are the windbags. Each according to his abilities and temperament and situation tries to preach what he understands to be "the gospel." (This article is wrtiten from the point of view and experience in conventional Christian Churches.)

Dr. George A. Gordon, for forty-two years minister of the Old South Church in Boston, describes his preaching techniques in his autobiography, *My Education and Religion* (1925). Throughout his ministry Dr. Gordon had three speaking appointments each week—a morning sermon, an evening sermon, and a mid-week prayer-meeting talk. His method was to select a theme for a mid-week talk, work on it conscientiously and present it. He would then file it in his "incubator" and a year later would re-work it and preach it at an evening service. Again he would file it in the incubator and a year later work on it some more and preach it at a regular morning service of worship. He read widely in the field of philosophy and theology, history and biography, and most of his preaching content came from his reading in these various fields.

Across the square from the Old South Church in Boston was the famous Trinity Church, and Dr. Gordon's neighbor in that famous pulpit was Phillips Brooks. Brooks preached "from the heart." He wrote his sermons carefully, paragraph by paragraph, and memorized them, and delivered them without manuscript. He usually selected a single theme, and had one point, and developed that one point from various angles. He was six feet four inches tall, and probably it was inconvenient for him to bend down to read a manuscript. He gave the impression that he was speaking extempore, when actually he had prepared his sermon carefully in writing, and then fixed it indelibly in mind so it was unnecessary for him to use his manuscript.

The late Dr. Alfred Barr of Baltimore used the same method, although he inclined toward the three-point technique, and always carried his fully prepared manuscript into the pulpit in his hip pocket. Without the manuscript in his hip pocket he would become panicky.

Dr. Harry Emerson Fosdick usually chose his sermon theme from what he called "life situations"—by which he meant that he took some common difficult human situation and preached to it. One point, approached from various angles. His method was to go into his study on Tuesday morning at nine o'clock and stay there until 1 p.m. He would take pencil and paper and begin to write,—and continue to write and rewrite until he had an outline and a sermon. The hours from nine to one, Monday through Friday, were sacred,—he could be reached only through four secretaries and then only in case of extreme emergency. By Friday his sermon would be written. Saturday he would "mull it over continuously," and Sunday morning he would take a small slip of paper with him into the pulpit on which were written the first sentences of each paragraph just as a reminder, and then deliver the sermon in a manner that appeared to be extemporaneous.

The late Dr. Frederick Shannon of Chicago would write suggestions for sermons on a folded paper, 8½ x 11, and place it on his desk. He usually had from one to two hundred of these incubating sermons on his desk. He would write suggested outlines inside each folded sheet, also insert in them poems, clippings, illustrative material and anything else of appropriate sermonic value. Then on Sunday morning between six and seven o'clock, he would go into his study, shuffle through these folders and pick out one that seemed to strike his fancy and go to work on it. He would work on it, making notes, outlines, and arranging the subject matter until 10 o'clock: then to the church to preach the sermon. He usually preached from 45 minutes to an hour, and it was my impression that he might have saved much time for his congregation had he prepared more carefully. However, he was a great pulpiteer, and was worth listening to. He kept up with scientific developments, and tried to enable his listeners to understand something of the life they had to live in the kind of world in which they had to live.

Dr. Charles Raven, canon of Liverpool Cathedral, a brilliant teacher and preacher, preached several times each week. He said he never wrote anything but books, and just made "a few mental notes" by way of sermonic preparation.

Thus it is clear that each man has his own methods and techniques in the preparation and delivery of sermons.

It seems to this writer that he has had to learn everything the hard way. Claiming for himself no special gifts, he has studied all sorts of methods and techniques of others and has tried especially to study his own disposition, weaknesses, and limited abilities. Out of many sources there has developed a method and a technique which perhaps may be worthy of consideration by those younger in the profession.

His chief interest has been in the field of philosophy—for the simple reason that a sound and right philosophical foundation is the first essential to a sound and right life. He has been concerned about the "social gospel"—since really there is no other kind of gospel. Both by background and experience he has "burned slowly" through the years over the social injustices which have become socially respectable, and has found himself almost unwittingly a "champion of lost causes." His reading thus has naturally gravitated toward the fields of history, biography and the social sciences as well as philosophy. He has tried to understand the incomparable Sacred Scriptures, the fountainhead of inspiration for every preacher, the great creative minds, such as William Shakespeare, Dante, Oscar Wilde, Alfred Tennyson, Frederick Robertson, William Ernest Hocking, William James, Halford Luccock, and the biographies of such men of great stature as Thomas Jefferson, Abraham Lincoln, Benjamin Franklin, Lord Ashley, seventh earl of Shaftesbury, and other pivotal figures in history.

The tendency of any preacher with a dominant concern (unless he is committed to the traditional pericope texts) is to pluck continuously on a single string of the sermonic harp. As a precaution against this weakness, several men, a number of years ago, collaborated on a list of themes they felt ought to be considered and presented each year—every year—from the pulpit. This list included the following themes:

1. The Pre-eminence of Jesus.
2. The Way of Love.
3. The Kingdom of God: Ethical and Social Implications; Christian Internationalism; Christian Implications of Labor and Industry.
4. Some Aspects of God: His love, mercy, peace, power, forgiveness, etc.
5. Evil and Its Mastery.
6. Immortality.
7. The Nature and Development of Personality.
8. Truth-seeking and Sound-thinking in Religion.
9. The Culture of the Spiritual Life—Prayer.
10. The Treatment of Historical Religion—The Bible.
11. The Function of Fellowship—The Church.

There are, of course, a number of other lists of themes. *The Pulpit* for January 1935, for example, contained a "Syllabus of Major Life Situations" which suggested an excellent basis for building a year's program of preaching.

Another list of "Central and Basic Ideas to be Kept in Mind" in the preparation of sermons (source beyond recall), is the following:

    I. The Growing Interdependence of Races and Peoples.
        1. The rapid rise of nationalism and race-consciousness.
        2. The penetration of Western industry and commerce

into all the world.
   3. Changing standards of family life.
   4. The philosophy of secularism and the scientific spirit.
II. The Christian Message for the Modern World.
   1. The Christian Conception of God.
   2. Jesus Christ—the Dynamic of Life.
   3. The Christian Conception of Personality.
   4. Christian Ethics and Society.
   5. Christian Experience and its Validity.
III. The Christian Approach to the Modern World.
   1. The Missionary Imperative.
   2. Evangelism.
   3. Christian Education.
   4. The Church—a Christian Fellowship.

The writer has tried to keep these general themes in mind in the preparation of his sermons. He has built up a file of these and many other subjects, including such special themes as Mother's Day, Great Biographies, Music, a series on the Commandments, the Beatitudes, etc. In his reading he has made notes and filed them under the various appropriate subjects.

It has been a habit, developed over the years, early each week, to select a theme or subject which seems to "strike fire" —usually Tuesday and not later than Wednesday, and outline and amplify the theme. Usually on Thursday or Friday the sermon is carefully written out in full—usually three pages of 8½ x 11 single-spaced. On Saturday the written sermon is taken into the pulpit and preached to an empty church. Notations are made and often the material is re-arranged. Often the preacher sits down in a pew and in his imagination "listens" to the sermon as it might sound coming from the pulpit. Usually an hour or two and often three are spent in giving the sermon this "finished treatment."

Then on Sunday morning the sermon is delivered—without extemporizing, or diversionary excursions. Every effort is made to simplify the material until a child might understand it. Frederick Robertson used to say that once each year he preached a sermon over the heads of his congregation, just to let them know he could do it! The rest of the time he aimed directly at them, and in his case it was not necessary to aim too high.

The average worshipper, accustomed as he is to hearing sermons, and hearing all sorts of speeches by all sorts of men via radio, television and community clubs, can invariably tell whether or not a man knows what he is talking about, or whether he is just "beating the air." He can also tell whether or not a speaker has carefully prepared his material for the particular occasion. An experienced speaker can tell in a few moments whether or not another speaker is giving an old address, given many times before—known in the trade as "cold tongue"—whether he is giving something of his own or "borrowed" from another, whether he is speaking out of a deep sense of mission and conviction, or just posing.

Years ago a beloved teacher gave the writer some never forgotten advice: "Preach what you know and believe, and preach it as sincerely as you know how." Out of a quarter of a century of experience in the Christian ministry, and after more sermons, speeches, addresses and talks of various kinds than I shall ever be able to enumerate, it is my conviction that the Church today needs men in the pulpit, perhaps as never before, who know what they are talking about and who are genuinely sincere and conscientious in their mission. J. R. W.

**serum for the aging process:** see adult, the.

**sessions in counseling:** see counseling periods.

**sex:** see Adler, Alfred; Adlerian approach to therapy; autoeroticism; character; child training; dreams; drives; exhibitionism; Freudian approach to analysis; glands; heterosexuality; homosexuality; Jung, Carl; marriage, disharmony in; masochism; menopause; old age; pastoral counseling and case studies; psychology of religion; psychology, schools of; psychoneuroses; resolution, the doctrine of; sadism; sex and the counselee; sublimation.

**sex and the counselee:** It is often the case that a sexual problem or conflict will manifest itself in the counseling situation. In dealing with the sexual components of the neurotic personality it is often wise to remember that sexual conflict, while often present, is seldom the problem to be tackled. We note briefly at this point that the purely Freudian approach to analysis has overstated the sexual elements of the personality conflict and thereby emphasized the detours around the basic problem rather than sought solution for those problems *per se*. Sexual conflict is then, more often than not, a symptom of a disorder rather than the fundamental problem.

The adroit counselor should have sound physiological understanding of sex as well as of the ability to meet the sexual components of the neurotic personality without conflict, derision, or lack of understanding himself. Belaboring in conversation the sexual elements may serve to deemphasize the underlying anxieties. Often as the basic problems approach solution the sexual conflict will be relegated to a rather insignificant place in the personality structure. The counselor will work to determine in the initial stages of his meetings with the counselee the elements of dependence and hostility that prompt sexual conflict. The acceptance of sexual conflict as a means of alleviating anxiety* may be a surface solution. The counselee, however, when oriented to the nature of his problem complex will undoubtedly find sexual expression compatible with his physiological sexual development and parallel with the degree of maturity represented by a personality free of conflict and anxiety.

In general, it is probably neither wise nor advantageous to label the sexual manifestation of a personality conflict other than to note the healthiness of the response and expression of sex. For example, it is well known that the "over-sexed," and we assume this means a high degree of sexuality, often indicates an inability for adequate sexual expression rather than preoccupation with sex. On the other hand, the personality which seems incapable of sexual response may not be giving full description to actual sexual capacity. It would seem the cardinal rule in counseling is to treat sex, sexuality, and sensitivity with proper respect. Should the sexual manifestation of a neurosis be overly complex it would behoove the counselor to recommend a well trained psychological counselor. See professional reference.

W. W .B.

**sex complex:** see complexes; psychoneuroses.

**sex crimes:** see criminal types.

**sex differences, psychological:** Women are said to be more personal and emotional in their interests than men. Floyd H. Allport (*Social Psychology*, 1924) states that this is the only significant psychological difference in sexes. But such difference is not congenital but environmental (early). A girl is not encouraged to do what a boy is expected to do and vice versa. She is taught to react to people rather than to center interests on the manipulation of things (play ball, build boats, etc.).

Dolls are her play toys and dolls are more than things. She is schooled in the area of emotions. Sexual interests in children are held in check by parents. These problems are regarded by parents as parental. Custom, thus, protects the girl who is in the most hazardous position and especially "needs protection." Inhibitions by parental over shielding are set up which reach into maturity. Women continue to look for personal rather than impersonal responses in others by reason of social conditioning, becoming more "sensitive" in human relationships. Conversations among women gravitate toward people and home ("men, clothes and decoration").

Feminism as a movement is a psychological as well as a political phenomenon (according to Allport). It is an assertion of freedom from past social restraints and the urge to self expression.

Sex interests of women operate "none the less powerfully" than in men—with this difference (Allport): love for women is a "perpetual theme" (home, children, husband); love for man is more aggressively ardent and more intermittent and less sustained. Men are less restrained in such interests (biologically and through early training or through social standards). Chivalry toward women has its psychological basis in possession on the part of the male and in jealous fear of losing that possession. Women, thus, are surrounded by barriers of possession which may pass as "honor" or even as "moral" (Allport). The ennobling of women may not be unmitigated chivalry but the result of jealous possession which confines the female role to restrictions of convention (reaching back into parental concern in childhood).

**Shannon, Frederick:** see sermons, preparation of.

**Sheen, F.:** see psychology of religion.

**shell-shock:** see psychology of religion.

**Sherman, M.:** see emotion.

**shift-eye test:** see deception.

**Shock, N. W.:** see aging process.

**shock (physiological):** A precipitous fall in the blood pressure below that of normal. (See hypertension.) This may be due to various causes among which are: a loss of a large amount of blood, severe pain, emotional causes, severe bodily injury, etc.

V. H. F.

**shocks:** see amnesia; trauma.

**shock therapy:** This consists of the use of convulsant drugs and electric shocks as therapy in certain conditions of psychoses.* Meduna initiated the use of convulsants (metrazol) in 1928; Sakel in 1936 reported the use of insulin shock; and Berkwitz in 1940 initiated the use of electric shock. See old age.

**sibling jealousy:** see juvenile delinquency.

**sickness:** see Cabot, R. C.; hospital chaplain, the; illness; visitation; visiting the sick.

**sick-soul:** William James'* term—the opposite of healthy mindedness—for those people who dwell on the fact of evil, for whom difficulties are too burdensome to be tossed aside, for whom the discords in life are loud, for whom there is some anguish of spirit which outweighs life's passing joys. Examples given by James: John Bunyan (*Grace Abounding*), Tolstoy (*My Confession*) and various expressions of Buddhism and Christianity. See divided self; healthy-mindedness; psychology of religion.

**Sidgwick, Henry:** see psychical research and parapsychology.

**signs of delinquency, first:** see juvenile delinquency.

**simile:** see figurative language.

**simplification:** see fallacy of over simplification; law of parsimony.

**sin:** see confession; conscience; hamartophobia; ministry, the, and counseling; original sin; projection; psychology of religion; religion and mental health.

**sincerity:** see children and religious beliefs.

**Sinclair, Upton:** see psychical research and parapsychology.

**sinistrality:** Preference for the use of the left hand in motor activity. This term is also used for the left preference in the use of such double organs as eye or foot. See handedness.

**situation:** see deceit (and character); structuring the counseling situation.

**situational criminals:** see criminal types.

**sixteen-year old, the:** see teen-agers.

**sixth sense:** see sensations.

**skill transfers:** see learning.

**skills:** see juvenile delinquency; learning.

**skull, human:** see phrenology.

**sleep:** Sleep is a biological necessity. Without it, human efficiency* is impossible and even life itself. Animals deprived of it (experimentally shown) will die in a few days even though well fed and otherwise cared for.

Sleep is a period when nearly all our sensory functions cease as well as nearly all our overt muscular activities. Sleep may be as deep as consciousness may be intense—with grades between.

If a person abstains from sleep for fifty, sixty, or more hours, experiments have shown that there is no psychological impairment (steadiness, computing, color naming, aiming, etc.) even for sixty hours. However, tasks calling for sustained attention show marked decrease in performance. Prolonged loss of sleep also initiates illness (headache, buzzing noises, burning in the eyes) and subjects tested become irritable and disorganized (e.g., laughing at anything). The fact that single tasks may be done successfully but prolonged tasks fall short is explained psychologically by the mode of compensation. Extra energy is necessary for the subject to do any single task because of the weight of sleepiness; since this extra effort cannot be maintained there is loss in sustained attention.

A person deprived of sleep cannot easily redirect his activity. He becomes sluggish in turning from one task to another. He performs now like a drunkard or one suffering excessive fatigue—not easily diverted!

People differ in their sleep requirements. They differ at a significant point: the depth of their sleep. The value of sleep is a function of its depth multiplied by its length. A person may "catch up" on his sleep after a prolonged absence from it in shorter time if it is profound and undisturbed. There are sleeping habits. One may learn to sleep at a certain time or even at any time by closing the eyes or lying down; on the other hand, one may not be so easily conditioned and suffer extreme difficulty in falling asleep. For those suffering such difficulties many devices have been set up (taking a hot bath, counting sheep, looking at a blank square, etc.). The relaxation of muscles (dropping the jaw, opening the hands, etc.) and the elimination of as much sensory stimuli as possible—these seem to be the simplest devices for falling asleep.

During sleep a sleeper does not lie still. Typically healthy subjects change their positions radically between twenty and forty-five times (two and one-half minute intervals) during an eight hour night span. Muscles seem to become fatigued by one long-continued position. Each shift of posture provides a specialized rest for the muscles. See anxiety states; autosuggestion; creative thinking; efficiency and time of day; egregorsis; fatigue; insomnia; noise disturbances.

*Bibl.* E. Jacobson, *You Must Relax* (1934).

**sleeplessness:** see insomnia; sleep; visions and hallucinations.

**slips of the tongue:** see Freud; psychology, schools of (psychoanalysis).

**slogans:** see fallacy of over simplification.

**sloth:** see organic sensations.

**sluggishness:** see sleep.

**smell:** This is usually referred to as the olfactory sensation.* Stimulation must be in the form of gaseous (possibly liquid) particles and must be in contact directly with the olfactory membrane in the nose. The membrane here is small (smaller size than a dime) and is located in the upper part of the left and right nasal passages. The receptors are simple (consisting of afferent nerve cells with dendrites running out to the surface of the mucous lining and bearing fine hairs which project into the air passage of the nose). It is difficult to say that there are different kinds of olfactory receptors (since stimuli cannot be applied to separate parts of the end organs).

Woodworth* has listed six elementary odors: 1) spicy; 2) flowery; 3) fruity; 4) resinous; 5) foul; and 6) scorched. There are many compound odors (roasted coffee, a compound of resinous and scorched; peppermint, a compound of fruity and spicy).

Smell acts as a warning to the organism of harmful conditions (bad air, bad food). Its aesthetic value is capitalized by the perfume industry.

**smoking:** see tobacco smoking and psychological efficiency.

**smooth muscle (unstriated muscle):** A specialized type of muscle cell which is under control of the autonomic nervous system* and is not under voluntary control. This type of muscle cell is found lining blood vessels, the alimentary tract, the reproductive tract, and in areas of the respiratory tree.

V. H. F.

**Soal, S. G.:** see psychical research and parapsychology.

**social approval:** see morale; motives; sociometry.

**social gospel:** see sermons, preparation of.

**social maturation:** Measurements of mental age* have been of increasing concern of psychologists in the last fifty years. J. McKeen Cattell (1860-1944), American psychologist, with his studies in individual differences helped to lay the ground for this inquiry. Binet* in 1905 offered a satisfactory method of measurement of intelligence and initiated the widely popular concept of mental age. Later studies have developed these results into wide acceptance.

The measurement of social competence as a special psychological inquiry is of recent development. Perhaps the most notable work is the formulation of the Vineland Social Maturity Scale which offers indices of the maturing process.

The V.S.M.S. is an attempt to measure overt social responsibility, independence and initiative. Levels of performance are correlated with certain categories, such as self-help, self-direction, occupation, communication, locomotion and socialization. Maturation in social competence moves through stages which are distinguished as age levels. The scale is made up of 117 items reflecting progress in social performance—birth to prime of life—which, in turn, reflects the deterioration of senescence or decline in social competence. Year scales are made to conform to make possible comparisons with mental age. Social quotients (S.Q.) thus are comparable to I.Q. Intelligence is taken to be the principal determinant of social competence. Interviews provide supplementary information.

Studies here reveal that social competence is influenced by limitations of individuals and by stimulations they experience. Deafness is found to place a limitation of about twenty per-cent on normal social maturation; blindness imposes limitations of about thirty per-cent. Untrustworthiness and misconduct are taken to be specific limiting influences.

Juvenile delinquency* has come in for special studies. One study reveals that social incompetence here parallels mental capabilities—including young adults. Social rehabilitation thus is aided by results of the S.Q. studies. See mental deficiency.

> *Bibl.* Edgar A. Doll, "Maturation" in *Encyclopedia of Criminology* (1949), edited by V. C. Branham and S. B. Kutash.

**social memory:** see sancta of religion.

**social motives:** see motives.

**social orientation:** see Jungian approach to therapy.

**social perception:** An important capacity of a person is his ability to "size up" people and situations. To do the right thing at the right time and to say the right word—these constitute the ability to "see into" a situation. Tactlessness is here the word for failure.

There are visible cues in a situation such as facial reaction patterns which are important in conversation, public speaking and social relationships in general. Experiments on perceiving facial expressions have been made chiefly with photographs of faces showing a variety of facial attitudes. Results show that people have a marked ability to judge correctly the intended emotions from pictures. The coarse types, such as pain, anger, fear and hatred were the easiest to judge; jest and earnest expressions (more difficult to determine) brought satisfactory results; half-crying and half-laughing (still more difficult) also showed some success. Individuals, of course, vary. Best success came to those who judged the "total ensemble" of expression rather than some part of the face.

Social perception is an acquired performance of many conditionings. Children very early show such capacities—as, for example, appropriate reaction to frowns, smiles, fears portrayed by facial expressions.

There are, of course, other kinds of social stimuli which affect "social perception." Gestures, movements of the body, visible postures, vocal cries are among such. See personality; postural response; sociometry; visitation.

**social prejudice:** see peace and war.

**social propaganda:** see peace and war.

**social psychology:** see criminal types; ecology; group psychology; group psychotherapy; marriage, disharmony in; peace and war; psychological frames of reference; psychology of religion; sancta of religion; sociometry.

**social responsibility:** see social maturation.

**social stimuli:** see emotion; peace and war.

**society:** see group mind; sociometry.

**society, economic:** see pastoral counseling and case studies.

**Society for Psychical Research:** see psychical research and parapsychology.

**sociology:** see juvenile delinquency; sociometry.

**sociology of religion:** see psychology of religion.

**sociometry:** This is a study of the patterns of interrelation of people in terms of the psychological factors involved. To understand society there must be a knowledge of the psychological structure at work within groups. Sociometry looks upon the process of feeling of attraction or repulsion between people as *tele*: *tele* in the words of the founder, J. L. Moreno, is "a feeling which is projected into distance; the simplest unit of feeling transmitted from one individual to another" (J. L. Moreno, *Who Shall Survive? A New Approach to the Problem of Human Interrelations* (1934). An individual's personality is thus viewed in the midst of interpersonal relationships, the center of numerous *tele* relationships with other individuals. Other individuals, in turn, are linked with other persons more distant psychologically from the given individual; yet through his indirect connection with them he may receive or exert influence and thus his personality is felt. Many psychological networks are thus involved in the area in which the person lives.

Moreno devised the so-called sociometric test. It discloses the feelings which individuals have with reference to each other in the group of which they are members. His test involves participation on the part of subjects, etc. He finds that the psycho structure of groups is related to the way a group functions; that individuals in general seek to relate to other individuals regardless of the response made by other individuals toward them; that in the dynamics of social change leaders come about not haphazardly but as expressions of needs and desires, leaders who are felt to be sensitive to the responses of others and thus are most successful in interrelating. Communities thus produce varieties of leadership depending on manifold needs. In a democracy, thus, there appear to be sociometric techniques that are helpful toward smoother functioning. See social perception.

*Bibl.* For a bibliography see Helen Jennings' article "Sociometry" in *Encyclopedia of Psychology* (1946) ed. by P. L. Harriman.

**solace:** see pastoral psychology: its governing limitations and qualifications.

**somatogenic disorders:** Disorders which originate in the body. The opposite is psychogenic.* See psychosomatics.

**son-in-laws:** see in-laws.

**soul:** see cure of souls; Descartes, René; Dewey, John; divided self; personality; psyche; psychology of religion; psychology, schools of; self; sick-soul.

**Soule, Mrs. Minnie:** see psychical research and parapsychology.

**sour taste:** see taste.

**span of life:** see life expectancy.

**Spearman, Charles:** see creative thinking.

**speech:** see figurative language.

**speech, incoherent:** see polylogia.

**speech, public:** see sermon; sermons, preparation of; social perception.

**speech and reading:** see reading performance.

**speech disorders:** see speech pathology.

**speech pathology:** This rather recent discipline has to do with speech disorders and correction.

Stuttering (dysphemia) is a functional disorder which shows abnormal hesitations of speech, repetitions, prolongations, and struggle with fluency. Stuttering usually begins during the pre-school age with noticeable prolongation of the initial sound of words and an automatic repetition of syllables—particularly under the stress of communication. Anxiety states* develop and devices to avoid speech are resorted to. More males than females are subject to stuttering. No single cause for stuttering is given as reliable. Among the factors stressed are: stuttering heredity, birth injuries, severe fevers during the time when speech is learned, a shift of handedness, emotional conflicts* brought on by parental criticism of normal hesitation in expression, etc. The treatments of this disorder are: the influences that are disturbing are sought out and removed; the child's good periods in speech are fostered and its bad periods respected by subjecting no stimulus to communication; more relaxation in intercommunication encouraged and more sense of security engendered. No one treatment has been found to cover all cases.

Defective speech sounds (dyslalia) constitute another type of speech disorder. Sometimes this phenomenon appears as a distortion of sounds, substitution of one consonant for another, omission of consonants, etc. Sometimes this is a case of difficulty in hearing, sometimes low intelligence (at the age of seven normal children acquire good speech), sometimes severe illness during speech learning, slow physical growth, poor motor coordination, difficulties of perception, sometimes isolation of the child, sternness of parents, etc. Speech improvement comes by training in identifying and emphasizing consonants and their sounds, analysis of words into their component parts, etc. There is less emphasis on drill and more upon meaning.

Again there are the disorders of the voice itself (dysphonia), e.g., pitch, intensity, quality. Excessive nasal sound, excessively high pitched voice, monotonous tones, etc., are common instances. Causes are various: cleft palate (organic), vocal cord abnormalities, inflammation, overstrain, emotional conflicts, etc. Improvements vary in terms of organic or functional causes. Usually a long period of retraining is required for functional cases. Hypnosis, relaxation techniques are sometimes needed.

Aphasia (dysphasia) is a more difficult form of speech disorder involving difficulties of comprehension and expression of meanings. There are problems of deficient memory, irritability and other severe impediments. Injury or disease is often the basic cause. Medical and surgical treatment, or psychoanalysis form the type of therapy in certain cases. Sometimes a shift of handedness helps therapy. Certainly mental therapy is a condition for relief in specific cases. See laliphobia.

*Bibl.* Charles Van Riper, "Speech Pathology" in *Encyclopedia of Psychology* (1946) edited by P. L. Harriman.

**speed in reading:** see reading performance.
**Spinoza:** see healthy-mindedness.
**spirits:** see psychical research and parapsychology.
**spiritual concern:** see success.
**spiritual healing:** see pastoral counseling and case studies; pastoral counseling: case studies; visiting the sick.
**spiritual life:** see saintliness; success.
**spiritualistic naturalism:** see naturalism.
**split personality:** see divided self; psychoneuroses.
**spontaneous autosuggestion:** see autosuggestion.
**S.Q.:** see mental deficiency; social maturation.
**S-R:** see psychology of religion; psychology, schools of.
**stages in creative thinking:** see creative thinking.
**staleness:** see boredom; emotional tensions, release of.

**Stanford-Binet tests:** see I.Q.

**Stanford revision of the Binet-Simon test:** see mental age.

**Starbuck, Edwin D.:** (1866-1947). Pioneer in the field of the psychology of religion in the use of the questionnaire method. His *Psychology of Religion* (1899) was a study in conversion. (See psychology of religion.) His doctor of philosophy degree was taken at Clark University. From 1906 to 1930 he was professor of philosophy at Iowa University where (from 1923 on) he directed an Institute of Character Research which was continued (1930-1939) at the University of Southern California. His *Character Education Methods* (1922) became widely and favorably known. After 1939 he continued as professor of psychology. His later volumes dealt with character training. He guided many students into careers of professional academic teaching. For an autobiographical account see *Religion in Transition* (1937), edited by Vergilius Ferm.

**statistical method:** see psychical research and parapsychology.

**stealing:** see deceit (and character).

**stereognosis:** The recognition of objects by handling them (not seeing them). Astereognosis is the term for the indication of a lesion in the parietal lobe suggesting the need for an exploration of this sensory process in a neurological examination.

**sthenic:** (Greek word meaning strength.) An adjective employed in psychological vocabulary to those feelings or emotions which are marked by excitement or increased nervous energy. Asthenic feelings or emotions, on the other hand, are those marked by depression. See anxiety states.

**stimulus, stimulation:** see adult, the; alcohol and efficiency; caffeine, psychological effects of; S-R; success; synapses.

**Stratton, G. M.:** see emotion.

**strife:** see peace and war.

**structuralism in psychology:** see psychology, schools of.

**structuring the counseling situation:** While it is readily pointed out that the counselor does not simply offer solutions to the counselee and that advice-giving is not counseling, this does not mean to say that the counselor does not enter into the counseling situation. This he does as he structures the situation. This means that he attempts to keep the counselee's attention focused on the basic problems as they emerge. E.g., it may be that the counselee has given indication of hostility or anger toward the counselor. The counselee may, having expressed this hostility in part, wish to avoid all the implications of his anger and therefore goes to every length to avoid expressing it again. The counselor will structure the situation by bringing the counselee back to the hostility. He may simply say, e.g., "The last time we met you expressed anger. Shall we look more at that anger?" At this point he says no more. He has structured the situation. This can mean *to some extent* playing the role of a central figure in the patient's experience in order to draw the fire of a response. It does not mean playing games with the counselee for a person who has been clever enough to avoid his troubles will be clever enough to see through a trick. Structuring must always be sincere and the counselor must always maintain his own identity and personality as he attempts to structure a counseling situation.

W. W. B.

**struggle:** see children and religious beliefs; peace and war.

**students:** see atmospheric conditions and work capacity; efficiency and time of day; learning; memorizing; memory; minister, the, and his books; noise disturbances; pastoral counseling and case studies; sentiments; sermons, preparation of.

**study:** see students.

**stuttering:** see dysphemia.

**style:** see minister, the, and his books.

**subconscious, the:** see unconscious mind.

**subjective worship:** see worship.

**subjectivism:** see psychology of religion.

**sublimation:** A term used by Freud\* and neo-Freudians for the deflection and direction of a drive into socially acceptable expressions. The purpose of sublimation is to produce harmony, profit, happiness and relief to tension.

Fear may be sublimated into readiness to meet emergencies of one's work. The sex drive may be sublimated in creative expressions in work. Self-display may be sublimated in some artistic expression such as a musical profession and even in philanthropic work. A preacher may conduct his worship service with great flair, his sermon with great eloquence and his hand shake with enthusiasm and warmth all the while sublimating his own vanity. See genius; motives.

**subnormal, the:** see mental deficiency.

**substitution, a symptom:** see heightened reaction; psychoneuroses; psychology, schools of (psychoanalysis).

**sub-vocal talking:** see psychology, schools of.

**success:** The factors involved in the attainment of success in a life work have been the subject and concern of many counselors of youth. Speculations on the topic have now emphasized this or that factor or even prescribed simple formulae. Survey studies (sociological and psychological) at several American universities (e.g., Columbia, Kansas, Ohio, Illinois Institute of Technology, Indiana) have come up with some findings among which the following factors seem determinative: 1) The vocation that affords the greatest degree of personal satisfaction and expresses most fully the subject's abilities and personality is the one most likely to bring success. Conversely, failure is most likely where these factors are not present. Of men who have distinguished themselves in their fields (nation-wide survey) 94% were in a field of their genuine interest. Misfits thus are potential failures. 2) A high IQ does not assure success, nor outstanding talent* and ability. Rather, the trait common to men who achieve is the quality of persistence, the willingness to give one's self and one's time—even to withstand discomfort and frustration. There is a definite relationship between ability and persistence; ability, standing alone, is not the factor which brings achievement. Persistence itself is the drive not only to survive disappointments but to find the vocation most suitable. 3) The earlier a person gets on with a career to be followed, the more likely is achievement his. 4) A correlation has been found between a successful father and the chances for success of the son. Fathers of successful sons (in a survey) were found to have had the traits of mental alertness, ambition, energy and desire to improve their conditions and that of their families. Thus success is more likely if the parental traits of success are there to inspire success. Being born with a silver spoon tends to nourish ambition (rather than, as many believed, to be a handicap). 5) It has been found (a study of young men between ages of 20 and 31) that a change of vocations is more likely to bring success than remaining at one particular assignment or with one establishment. Men willing to change positions until they find the situation that offers more stimulation and opportunity are the ones who, for the most part, have succeeded. Eminent people (another survey) have had more frequent changes of positions than those less successful. 6) The greatest hindrance to success is laziness. Psychologists have found that a person possessing a good vocabulary plus a mediocre achievement record, gives positive proof of laziness. The good vocabulary indicates good ability. Mediocrity spells some other contributing factor—the lack of application (laziness) for one reason or another.

7) Studies have suggested that people engaged in professions (research, teaching, etc.) reach their peak of productivity and creativeness between the ages of 30 and 40. In the case of business executives the peak is between the ages of 50 and 60. Taking into consideration all age groups, the peak of earning power is the highest of men in their middle 50's. 8) Studies suggest that most people tend to be happier during the days of their struggle to achieve rather than at the time their success has been reached. People who have the lowest or highest incomes are the ones most likely to be the unhappiest groups. Enough income to provide economic security (without wealth) is the economic promise of the greater chance for happiness.

9) People who are openly and avowedly dissatisfied with their work, their employers, their accomplishments and the accomplishments of their establishments are more likely to be successful than the complacent. The dissatisfaction reveals the very characteristics for success: drive, ambition, concern. 10) Studies reveal that the incidence of nervous disorders is higher among men who fail to succeed (both prestige and income) than among those whose success is moderate. To achieve personal goals is more likely to bring about mental health than frustration and failure.

11) Studies suggest that success and longer span of life go together: success tends to lengthen life and failure to shorten it. Morale* thus is conducive to physical well being and morale is conditioned by success. The more a man has to live for the more likely is he to live longer. 12) Success (according to a research organization) tends to bring more interest in matters of spiritual concern than otherwise. Among Americans, the percentage of church members is highest among the successful

and the lowest among the least successful. This indicates a correlation of success to an awareness of the higher virtues and values which in turn give expression to social commitments and spiritual concern. See creative thinking; learning; role playing.

**suffering:** see anxiety states; illness; masochism; pastoral counseling: case studies; religion and mental life; sacrifice, a psychological concept.

**suggestion:** see autosuggestion; peace and war; personality; psychotherapy; talents.

**suicide:** see pastoral counseling: case studies.

**sulci:** see brain.

**summer camps:** see teen-agers.

**Summers, W. E.:** see deception.

**Sumner, W. G.:** see psychology of religion.

**Sunday-Sabbath school:** see moral conduct and teaching; religious education.

**super-ego, the:** see Id, the, the ego, and the super ego; psychology, schools of.

**superiority:** see Adler, Alfred; Adlerian approach to therapy.

**supernaturalism:** see naturalism.

**suppression:** see complexes; conscience.

**surrender:** see self surrender; prayer and autosuggestion.

**survival, personal:** see personal survival.

**Swedenborg, E.:** see psychical research and parapsychology.

**sweet taste:** see taste.

**symbols:** see censor; dreams; Freud; Jung, Carl.

**symbols:** Religion is crowded with symbols. Symbols are the vicarious expression of experience lived or sought or the promoters of such experience. Sir Winston Churchill's two fingers raised in glorious gesture constitute the symbol of anticipated victory—V as in victory. The dimly lit vaulted arches of a cathedral suggest the transcendental aspect of Reality and man's outreach beyond his limited self. The cross represented to the early Christians suffering at Calvary, an event of awful significance. The altar shrouded in mystery and aloofness represents the holy presence which is the perfect beyond the attainable.

Aristotle held that we possess two types of senses: mediate and immediate. The mediate communicate distance: hearing, sight; the immediate: touch, pain, taste (and we may add warmth), without distance. The latter (he said) are more fundamental.

The senses may be said to furnish the raw material for live symbols. As we look back upon our earliest recollections we remember most vividly the ideas or events most intimate with *immediate* sensations. We shall never forget how wonderfully tasty was the certain dish which mother made. No one can ever duplicate it. Tactual impressions have a way of lingering in memory, far surpassing some striking school lesson. Our probable likes and dislikes which carry on in life may have had their genesis in some pleasant or disagreeable contact or taste.*

Now symbols which recreate for us the memory of these sensations are not easily shoved aside. They give us a vivid awareness. Those ideas, beliefs, prejudices, which come closest to our elemental sensations have the best chance for survival.

Indeed, it has been pointed out that for most people all deeply felt beliefs stem from association with the senses; and conversely those which are less vital and real are the ones most remote from the life of sense experience. Convictions are thus psychologically rooted in the intimate sense-life of experience. Sheer conceptual argument has less persuasive power for most people.

Symbols, thus, which provoke the stirrings of our sensation responses are to lay claim to longevity in spite of their apparently non-rational and even irrational appeal. Statues of the Virgin, holy water, incense, ethereally floating angels, may thus possess power even beyond words. Images which provoke realistic imagination are conducive to appeal.

As maturity comes and we learn to think less with concrete imagery we require less use of symbols in religious worship. It is characteristic of "intellectuals" (those dealing from day to day with abstract concepts) to feel less the need for attachment to concrete symbols. Churches which cater to this type will probably be plain in architecture, less ornate and more simple in appointments. Conversely, churches which go in strongly for pictures, statues, decorative arts and the like will betray their clientele: those whose thought molds are closer to the concrete and those less disciplined to the philosophical and metaphysical approach. (Exception here would be those reflective people who have grown tired of reasoning about the Beyond.) This same principle explains why mystics seek solitude and simplicity—their world is the world of ideas and much less the space-time world of tangibles. A mystic is in less need of symbols.

Symbols in worship are thus not accidents but revelations of the psychological stage of those devotees who enjoy them and for whom there is realistic meaning. Hymns reveal the principle vividly: those, for example, which give concrete imagery of the sanctified life or of heaven as over against those which appeal to the inner states of the spirit. Not only does this hold for the lyrics but for the musical structure as well. A swing-time tune is one type and a Lutheran chorale is another; the one more vivid to the senses and the other to the depths of emotion. See belief in God; children and religious beliefs; psychology of religion (J. C. Flower); psychology, schools of (psychoanalysis).

**sympathetic nervous system:** see autonomic nervous system.

**sympathy, attention for:** see attention for sympathy.

**symptoms revealing mental conflicts:** see psychoneuroses.

**synapses:** The points of junction of neurones* which end-to-end form the sensori-motor arcs.* At the synapse some kind of resistance is set up against the passage of the neural impulse from cell to cell. The minimum intensity to make a transit of a given synapse of an impulse is called a "threshold." Neural excitements tend to reduce original resistances. Thus the kind of reaction a person will make to a stimulation will depend on the various degrees of the thresholds in the nervous system. With acquired forms of response the pathways of transit are said to be different according to lines of least resistance. There are an enormous number of synapses and variability in intensities among people; behavior thus will be extraordinarily variable among different people and even within the person himself.

**synoptic reason:** see intuition.

**systolic blood pressure and deception:** see deception.

**systolic pressure:** see hypertension.

# T

**tabloid thinking:** see fallacy of over simplification.
**taboo:** see motives.
**tactlessness:** see social perception.
**tactual sense:** see aphia; sensations; symbols.
**talents:** It is a widespread belief that we are born with certain natural dispositions or talents which make certain accomplishments relatively easy and performances above the average. There are, it is believed, special talents for music, art, engineering, creative writing, etc.

The whole subject raises the controversial problem which educators and psychologists have long discussed—how far people are pre-determined to achieve in proficiency by the equipment which biologically has been passed on to them from "heredity" and how far environment—particularly earliest years—has fashioned their proclivities.

The minister is likely to be involved in making judgments or passing an opinion on this issue. In dealing with children and parents (their concern over their children) and particularly with young people, he may exert, as a respected counselor, tremendous influence in the shaping of lives. He would do well to treat this subject of talents with the greatest care and with a sense of responsibility.

It is true, of course, that heredity plays an important role in determining destiny. We are born with physical determinants, pigment of skin and eyes, stature limits, predisposition toward over- or normal-weight, weakness of susceptibility toward certain possible diseases, etc. But by far, the larger determinants in our destiny—larger than many people are given to realize—are the accumulations of subtle influences in our earliest contacts. Why does a child walk like his father or speak like his parents? Is it inheritance? Most assuredly, many traits are conditioned by unconscious imitation early acquired and hardly overcome. Our likes for certain foods, or our dislikes of foods prepared in other ways than those with which we have been accustomed, are surely not congenital. Our shyness, our disposition toward introversion* or extraversion,* our social behavior (which is personality*), our frugalities or our generosties, our over-selfishness or our unlicensed altruisms, our self-centeredness or our diffidence—surely all these come upon us through the subtle influences of home, of early companions and contacts. Once formed as habit patterns they are not so easily altered. When frozen or set they appear to be innate and impossible to change. When children enter school they already are grown oak trees in their habit patterns and not little twigs so easily bent into altered forms.

It is true that there are psychophysical endowments such as a more or less ease of coordination, and a type of temperament* (emotional reactions) which play an important role in what way or manner achievement may be made or hindered.

But—all said and done—it is dangerous to speak indiscriminately of talents as inborn determinants where achievements are due to environmental factors and lie in the area of responsibility.

A child's proclivity to music may—aside from general and normal acquisitions of hereditary—well arise from parental influence, from companions held in high regard, from hero-worship and even from the accidental influences of environment. A sense of pitch, easy for some, may, however, be acquired for many—given, of course, the ability to hear. But a sense of pitch is not musical talent.

Many so-called geniuses will attest to the fact that their success was due primarily to persistent effort. Add to this the elements of interest (however acquired) and ambition (drive) and the result is that what mistakenly was taken to be special talent turns out to be but the end result of a trait acquired rather than a trait bestowed.

A minister will be wise in his counseling to stress the environmental factor in the shaping of destiny. Even if a person had the "endowments" which make for achievement and lacked interest, drive and proper environmental stimulation, it is unlikely he would achieve work of any outstanding quality in any field. A good family tree and family environment plus a serious interest in some field will pave the way for success. It is precarious to suggest that a person is endowed with a special proclivity when many fields are, in fact, open to his successful accomplishment.

To tell anyone that he lacks talent is dangerous—since it fosters by suggestion the stark reality of failure even before any serious attempt has been made to learn of possibilities.

An instance may here be cited to show how easily the idea of inborn talent is employed to account for the lack which a person feels in a given accomplishment. A young man said he knew he had no musical talent because his wife tried in vain to teach him to play the accordion. He failed to realize, in the first place, that he had no basic background in the fundamentals of scales, that an accordion is one of the most difficult of instruments (requiring three co-ordinations at once —a pushing of the bellows with both arms, the pressing of the keys with the right hand in a sequence that is different from pressing of the buttons with the left hand) and further, that a series of lessons from a member of the immediate family may not be as fruitful as those taken from a professional teacher whose patience may be more generous by the promise of a fee.

It is better to regard the concept of talent with great reservation. A child told that he has no talent for art is encouraged to shy from any serious attempt in that direction. It may well turn out to be a misguidance of tragic proportions. Rather, the encouragement should be in the direction of emphasizing the importance of interest, of ambition to achieve (in whatever area), of the principle of dogged persistence which even Charles Darwin once said was the only manner by which the scientific approach to problems will ever come and the achievements in connection with that approach.

Even the familiar Biblical reference to ten talents, to one talent, is no reference to a specific hereditary trait of accomplishment in a specific field, although mistakenly quoted.

See early environment; genius; human genetics; success.

**talking:** see conversation.

**tantrum:** violent rage.

**taphephobia:** see phobias.

**taste:** A gustatory sensation. To stimulate taste a substance must be in soluble form and must be in contact with the "taste buds" which are found principally on the tongue and, to a lesser degree, on the soft palate and the lining of the pharynx. Taste is generally considered to be a chemical sense; the receptors are called "chemoreceptors."

Tastes are classified into four groups: sweet, salt, sour and bitter (with many combinations). Sensitivity to sweetness is greatest near the tip of the tongue, to sour along the sides, to bitter toward the back and to salt in a more general distribution. Drugs may abolish the functions of the four different kinds of receptors.

Taste is commonly confused with other modes of stimulation. Preference for foods may be thought to lie in their taste whereas the preference may, in fact, lie in the kinaesthetic or even visual or auditory stimulation. See sensations; symbols.

**tea:** see caffeine, psychological effects of.

**teaching:** see child training; counseling period; deceit (and character); learning; reading performance; sacrifice, a psychological concept; sentiments.

**techniques of suggestion:** see autosuggestion.

**technological revolution:** see pastoral counseling and case studies.

**teen-agers:** Dr. Arnold Gesell (1800-    ), founder-director of the Yale Clinic of Child Development, has, for many years, been a scientific student of the behavior characteristics and maturity traits of infants and children, well known for his published studies, e.g., *The First Five Years*—A Guide to the Study of the Pre-School Child (with collaborators, 1949); *The Child From Five to Ten* (with Dr. Frances L. Ilg, pediatrician, 1946); and for many other important publications.

In 1950 the Gesell Institute of Child Development was incorporated with the purpose of continuing as a clinic and teaching and research center for studies of wider ranges of child development. Many of Gesell's subjects have been followed through their early life spans—(largely middle-class New

Haven public school children who attended his Yale nursery school and clinic).

Recently, studies have been made on adolescents or teen-agers (incomplete). Teen-ager trends from the ten to the sixteen-year old stages have been marked out as patterns. It is, of course, not claimed that each child moves through the pattern stages in identical manner nor at the same rate (individuals differ in temperament,* body types, and environmental influences). But, most teen-agers (adolescents) show the following sequences of trends:

Trends are given in terms of yearly intervals.

A ten-year old is in an age of relative calm and equilibrium. A child at this age level trend may be expected to get along well with his playmates, follow parental guidance, be intensely moral, and emulate his father's interests (hobbies, sports, etc.). This repose is offset, however, by certain expressions of tension (fidgeting, stuttering and muttering, wiggling, biting finger nails, etc.). There is no inclination to neatness or cleanliness. Radio and TV programs are enticing, with definite preferences asserted as self possessions.

An eleven-year old is apt to be tempestuous and even obnoxious. It is a stage when appeal to reason draws blanks. Arguments do not follow logic but a tempestuous will. A child here tends to be against whatever is asserted as for his or her good. It is freedom asserting its springtime vigor. Few demands on eleven year olds rather than many—these few being firmly insisted upon—such should be the parental technique. A firm handed father (rather than a mother) appears better to handle an eleven year old. It is the ideal age for a youngster to be sent to a summer camp!

A twelve-year old is at an age of more pleasant attitudes. There is more concern for parental approval, more concern for attention, greater zest for living, a yen for flashy wearing apparel. It is an age of sensitivity ("conscience") and embarrassment. An uneven keel of maturity is also characteristic: manhood or womanhood vs. babyishness. Boundless energy for everything with a foaming optimism may be expected.

A thirteen-year old is at an age of withdrawal, an age of moodiness. Long periods of silence are usual. Seclusion is sought in his or her bedroom. There is even a resentment against an inquiry as to health or state of well being. The gap between children at this level and their parents widens. The thirteen-year old has special friends and does not easily adjust to the adults' companions. It is a time for parents to be patient and not intrude too much. Such undue intrusion may bring on resentment.

A fourteen-year old begins to overcome his introversion and is more sociable. It is a time of bursting enthusiasm: in intellectual inquiry, in great causes, in school activities. Such children or youths find themselves busy and like it. At this age they are not grown-up nor are they children—even to themselves. The exuberances are desultory: swinging legs, shouting, waving arms and, in general, difficult. There is a tendency to criticize elders as old fogies, to complain of their parental inhibitions as out-moded and artificial, and an inclination to evaluate standards from their own vantage point of view.

A fifteen-year old is argumentative, standing on his or her own convictions—accentuating the growing psychological chasm between him or her and the parents. Parents do well to be patient, giving advice discreetly.

A sixteen-year old is in an age of calmer seas. Some of the storms have been passed and the voyage with those of the family circle becomes smoother. There is a self-consciousness in the child of self improvement—although he or she may well be unaware that it may only be the first steps.

The above patterns may not be as marked in some children as they suggest, although "superior" and normal children are apt to reveal them even in their striking forms. Some subjects studied were not "laboratory" cases but those in the immediate circle of the family of the investigators.

The Gesell adolescent studies point to certain conclusions which relate to parental guidance: 1) Fathers rather than mothers have a greater influence on sons—more than is realized. 2) A teen-ager in open rebellion (overtly or by seclusion) can receive little in the way of advice and is not helped by a combative attitude of parents. The storm will pass. 3) The teen-age crises are not moral but stages in growth. There is no steady flowering of adolescence, but an unsteady rise and fall of growth. Parents do well not to expect springtime to issue easily from winter. There will yet be many storms and cold days before spring moves into summer. 4) A home atmosphere of good manners, courtesies and general good will and friendliness—certainly of comradeship—from infancy and through the early environment* stands the best chance in the rearing of well balanced individuals who, in their growth, must pass through the storms and stresses of adolescence. Each child must himself realize the possibilities of self-respect and be wisely guided in that direction by parents—not so much with a code of norms artificially fostered but by reasonable attitudes unconsciously taken over and possessed as their own by the children during the stage of transition to adulthood. See adolescence; child training; deceit (and character); juvenile delinquency; mental deficiency; morality and psychology; pastoral counseling and case studies.

**tele:** see sociometry.

**teleneuron:** see neuron.

**teleological character of life:** see aesthetic experience.

**teleological character of mind:** see Adler, Alfred; Dewey, John; instrumentalism; psychology, schools of (W. McDougall).

**teleology:** From the Greek word *telos* which means end or purpose. It concerns the forward look, the design of things, end-results. The mechanism has to do with parts and how they are put together; the use for which it is to serve, its ultimate goal—this is its teleological character.

**telepathy:** see psychical research and parapsychology.

**temper, bad:** see complexes.

**temperament:** A term signifying certain basic hereditary responses of emotional character which characterize an individual. (For another interpretation, see emotion.) People differ in their susceptibility to emotional stimulation, in their reaction time, the strength of their responses, by the moods into which they fall with more or less intensity and duration, by their emotional natures. Four basic patterns of temperaments have been recognized in psychological tradition: choleric (bilious, hot-tempered), melancholic, phlegmatic (sluggish, apathetic, composed), and sanguine (cheerful, optimistic, ardent). The first was associated by the ancients with yellow bile, the second with black bile, the third with phlegm and the fourth with blood.

In dealing with persons it is important to notice these emotional response patterns and to remember that they are matters which lie deep in the nature of the person and for which he is not altogether responsible. See dispositions; divided self; emotion; saintliness; sick-soul; talents.

**temperature conditions:** see atmospheric conditions and work capacity; drives.

**temperature sense:** see sensations.

**temptations:** see conscience; psychoneuroses.

**tendon:** An inelastic cord of fibrous connective tissue by means of which a muscle is attached to a bone.

**teniophobia:** see phobias.

**tensions, emotional, release of:** see emotional tensions, release of.

**ten-year old, the:** see teen-agers.

**Terman, Lewis M.:** see genius; mental age.

**test, sociometric:** see sociometry.

**tests, color:** see color blindness.

**tests, psychoanalytic:** see projective techniques.

**tests and measurements:** see race psychology.

**tests of age:** see adult, the; aging process.

**tests of deception:** see deception.

**tests of intelligence:** see adult, the; I.Q.; mental age; race psychology.

**tests of word association:** see Jung, Carl.

**thalamus:** A mass at the base of the cerebrum. Injury occurring on the ventral side beneath the thalamus (hypothalamus) brings on a pathological change in emotional response. W. B. Cannon believed that the thalamus is the center of control in emotions. See emotion.

**thanatomania:** Term for the neurotic obsession in reading obituaries, attending funerals and visiting cemeteries.

**thanatophobia:** see phobias.

**theism:** see belief in God; religion and mental health.

**theistic religion:** see religion and mental health.

**thematic apperception test, the:** see projective techniques.

**theocrasy:** (Gr. *theos*, God; *krasis*, mixture)
   a) A kind of worship involving a mixture of different gods.
   b) The intimate union of the soul with God, as for example, in deep contemplation.

**theological training:** see hospital chaplain, the.

**theology and theologians:** see ministry, the, and counseling; pastoral counseling and case studies; psychology of religion.

**theophany:** (Gr. *theos*, God; *phaino*, appear) The manifestation of God to man by actual appearance.

**theosis:** The ultimate absorption of the soul into Deity.

**therapy:** See Adlerian approach to therapy; Alcoholics Anonymous; analysis; autosuggestion; cure of souls; diagnosis; emotional tensions, release of; free association; Freudian approach to analysis; group psychotherapy; hospital chaplain, the; Jungian approach to therapy; juvenile delinquency; ministry, the, and counseling; pastoral counseling: case studies; pastoral psychology, its governing limitations and qualifications; prayer and autosuggestion; problem complex; psychoanalysis; psychology of religion (Dynamic School of British psychologists); psychology, schools of (psychoanalysis); psychosomatics; psychotherapy; religion and mental health; resolution, the doctrine of; shock therapy; speech pathology; visiting the sick.

**thinking:** see "capsule thinking"; creative thinking; Dewey, John; emotive language; fallacy of over simplification; "grasshopper thinker"; ideas; instrumentalism; intuition; law of parsimony; learning; memory; "potted thinking"; psychology, schools of; reasoning.

**third degree, the:** see deception.

**thirst:** see drives; organic sensations.

**thirteen-year old, the:** see teen-agers.

**Thomson, J. A.:** see minister, the, and his books.

**Thoreau, Henry:** see visitation.

**Thorndike, Edward Lee:** (1874-   ) Columbia University professor (emeritus) of psychology (Teachers College) who has contributed conspicuously to studies in the fields of animal psychology and to the whole field of education. See instinct; learning.

**threshold:** A term used to designate the point at which one state of mind passes into another. The threshold of consciousness would indicate the amount of noise, pressure or any other stimulus needed to arouse attention.*

**threshold, neural:** see sensory threshold; synapses.

**thyroid gland:** An endocrine gland* which lies anterior to the trachea, so called from its resemblance to a Greek shield.

Hypofunctioning of this gland leads to cretinism (a mental deficiency associated with this glandular dysfunction; cretins being short-armed and short-legged, sallow in complexion, large faces, protruding abdomens, etc.) and to myxedema (a condition of muscular weakness, dullness, slow reaction time, general lethargy). Hypertrophy of the thyroid gland brings on the disorder of exophthalmic goiter (enlargement of the thyroid gland). See hyperthyroidism; parathyroid glands.

**tic:** A regular spasmodic contraction of part of, or an entire skeletal muscle. The etiology of this condition is largely psychogenic* but certain organic abnormalities may cause it.

V. H. F.

**time, dissipation of:** see boredom; minister, the, and his books.

**time, fear of:** see chronophobia.

**time element in counseling:** see counseling periods.

**time of day and efficiency:** see efficiency and time of day.

**timidity:** see fears; motives.

**tithing:** see minister, the, and money.

**tobacco smoking and psychological efficiency:** There is much present-day discussion of the ill effects of the use of tobacco, pro and con. Scientific evidence is not in a conclusive stage (other than the question of over-indulgence). Although experiments have been conducted on the psychological effects of tobacco smoking it has not been easy to set up controlled experiments eliminating the operation of suggestion in the subject's reactions.

In one experiment the subjects were blindfolded and permitted to believe that they were smoking tobacco. On certain days they were given a pipeful of tobacco; on other days they were given pipes of exactly the same shape but without tobacco. In these tobacco-less pipes were placed electric heating coils that warmed the air drawn into the mouth. During the puffing, the subject smelled tobacco smoke given off in the room. One confirmed smoker continued the motions of blowing smoke rings during the smoking of a tobacco-less warm-air pipe! Tests before "smoking" and at separated periods after were given. No single conclusion as to the effect of tobacco smoking could be drawn from the experiments in so far as it involved *psychological* functions. Some psychologists hold that tobacco smoking has little if any definite effect upon *psychological* efficiency.

The functions tested included pulse (increase with use of tobacco), muscular fatigue (decreased with use of tobacco), reading reaction-time (gain in efficiency with use of tobacco), accuracy of adding (no change with use of tobacco), and so on. One factor which gave different psychological reactions was that of habitual smokers as over against non-smoking persons. Results were highly variable in either case.

One motivation to smoking not usually noted is the pleasure of handling and mouthing an object. An habitual smoker giving up smoking will be apt to acknowledge his diabolical urge to "reach for" a pipe or cigarette (a motor activity which in itself has nothing to do with actual smoking).

**toes:** see Babinski reflex.

**tolerance, religious:** see psychology of religion.

**Tolstoy, Leo:** see divided self; sick-soul.

**tontriphobia:** see phobias.

**touch sensations:** see aphia; sensations.

**toxiphobia:** see phobias.

**trades:** see juvenile delinquency.

**tradition:** see children and religious beliefs; conservatism.

**tragedy:** see emotion; motives.

**training:** see child training; early environment; home environment; learning; parents; talents.

**traits, racial:** see race psychology.

**traits of personality:** see dispositions; divided self; healthy-mindedness; personality; pseudopsychology; sick-soul; teen-agers; temperament.

**traits of success:** see success; talents.

**transference:** The term applies to the regard which a counselee, or psychoanalytical patient, has toward the counselor or psychoanalyst. It is patent that during a period of successful analysis, the patient will treat and respond to the analyst in the same manner as he would respond to those responsible for his developed patterns of response from childhood. Wherever the analytical sessions produce freedom, the patient will often regard the analyst as perhaps father one time, mother another time and even as a sibling at the next. Often the responses are "irrational" insofar as the analyst really has acted like one of these persons. As the patient develops, he will express hostilities and loves for these persons to the analyst; the latter, in fact, becomes the hated object, the loved object, the rejector, etc. at various stages in the relationship. This transference is to be expected and is, in fact, an essential element in a productive analytical relationship. If transference does not take place, it is likely that the movement in the analytical relationship will be slow, if there be movement at all. It is usually the case that this "transferred" object of feelings makes it possible for the doctor and the patient to see at first hand wherein the roots of these feelings are buried. If the transference is not utilized and permitted to establish a "block," e.g., where a patient regards the analyst so completely as the hated father that he cannot reach a close and understanding relationship with the analyst, then it is felt that transference may be a hindrance. Transference as a part of the successful counselor-counselee relationship must be looked forward to as essential to the outcome; it must, however, serve its role in a balance. See analysis; displacement; psychoanalysis. W. W. B.

**transfers of skills and training:** see learning.

**trauma:** The term means injury. In psychological literature it refers to mental shocks, tragedies and disappointments of serious consequence.

**triakaidekaphobia:** see phobias.

**Troeltsch, E.:** see psychology of religion.

**truancy:** see juvenile delinquency.

**trust:** see belief in God.

**truth:** There are two types of criteria of truth: 1) dogmatic and nonphilosophical and 2) philosophical.

1) A "truth" is said to be dogmatic when no argument is possible: only assertion. (See dogmatism.)

Non-philosophical "truth" is also not capable of argument since the appeal is such as to imply that reason has no place in its discovery. The following are instances of non-philosophical criteria of truth: 1) appeal to feeling as a criterion; 2) appeal to sheer intuition (defined by many as beyond or above reason); 3) appeal to general opinion (*consensus gentium*); appeal to some authority (e.g., Scriptures); and self-evident axioms (a thing cannot be and not be at the same time).

2) Philosophical criteria of truth may be one or a combination of the following three appeals: 1) coherence, 2) correspondence and 3) pragmatism. In coherence, that is taken to be true which fits into a harmony of ideas. In correspondence, that is taken to be true which agrees with a fact, situation, reality. In pragmatism that is taken to be true which functions well, is tested by workability and resolves a problem. See deception; Dewey, John; flight into health; instrumentalism; pragmatism. For an exposition and critical evaluation of theories of truth see *First Adventures in Philosophy* (1936), Vergilius Ferm, Chap. XXIII.

**truth serum third degree:** see deception.
**twelve-year old, the:** see teen-agers.
**twice-born, the:** see divided self.
**twins:** see human genetics.
**Tylor, E. B.:** see psychology of religion.
**types, criminal:** see criminal types.

# U

**ulcers:** see psychosomatics.
**unconscious, the:** see conscious, pre-conscious, unconscious.
**unconscious mind:** see analysis; autosuggestion; censor; conscience; creative thinking; defense mechanisms; dispositions; dreams; drives; Freud; Freudian approach to analysis; Id, the, ego and the super ego; Jung, Carl; juvenile delinquency; marriage, disharmony in; phantasy; prayer and autosuggestion; projection; projective techniques; psychology of religion; psychology, schools of; psychology, schools of (psychoanalysis); psychoneuroses; psychotherapy; religion and mental health; repression.
**unconscious morality:** see psychology, schools of (psychoanalysis).
**unhappiness:** see role playing; success.
**unity, church:** see sancta of religion.
**unity, psychological:** see aesthetic experience.
**unpardonable sin:** see conscience.
**unstriated muscle:** see smooth muscle.
**untrustworthiness:** see social maturation.
**urban dwellers:** see pastoral counseling and case studies.
**urges, elemental:** see Adlerian approach to therapy; dreams; drives; psychology, schools of (psychoanalysis).

# V

**value:** see axiology; success.
**values of religion:** see religion and mental health.
**Vanderveldt, James:** see religion and mental health.
**vanity:** see self; self display; sublimation.
**varieties of religion:** see psychology of religion.
**verbal learning:** see learning.
**vertigo:** Dizziness or fainting spells.
**veteran groups:** see peace and war.
**vicarious gratification:** see dreams.
**vices:** see children and religious beliefs.
**vices in war:** see peace and war.
**Viennese Psychoanalytic Society:** see Freud, Sigmund.
**Vineland Social Maturity Scale:** see social maturation.
**virtues:** see belief in God; self; success.
**virtues in war:** see peace and war.
**virtues of saintliness:** see saintliness.
**viscera:** see organic sensations.
**visions and hallucinations:** These belong to psychological phenomena of the abnormal type brought on by methods which destroy normal functioning. Fatigue, fasting, prolonged sleepless vigils and self-tortures are the usual deliberate methods of producing the desired effects. In many religious cults the "heightened experience" is preferred over any ethical insight or rational religious commitment.

Psychologically, these experiences follow the same pattern as a person who achieves exaltation by excessive drinking. Hallucinations are expressions of psychological disorganization, similar to the irrationalisms that are the effect of the taking of some powerful drug (such as opium, alcohol, and the rest).

Heightened mystical states belong psychologically to the same category.

In terms of larger significance and worth the old pragmatic principle holds good: by their fruits ye shall know them (whether of the Spirit). See hallucination.

**visitation:** A natural and integral part of the work of the parish minister is visitation in the homes of both parish members and those who are not in the circle of that membership.

The call may be with a definite purpose in connection with illness, on specific invitation for professional consultation, with the view of enlisting interest in the church or merely a social visitation. The minds of both the visitor and those visited upon may well be focused upon a specific purpose for which the particular visit is made. Whatever it may be, a minister will naturally, and without pose, be the type of person who knows that he is a public figure in the community and represents always a mission of dignity.

Henry Thoreau, American essayist and philosopher, once remarked: "If I knew for a certainty that a man was coming to my house with the conscious design of doing me good, I should run for my life." Many people feel this way about a visit from the minister. Thoreau's remark carries with it a kernel of wisdom. If a minister performs with a consciousness of religiousity he is probably wearing his religion on the outside of his shirt. Genuine religion is something one has without being acutely conscious of it. When one does good one hardly needs labels. A minister's casual visitation thus, if genuine, should be a normal affair in which frequently it may not even be necessary to discuss religion if the occasion does not naturally arise.

Dean Charles R. Brown of the Yale Divinity School used to tell his seminary students that when he called on the sick he never planned on what he would or would not say, whether he would speak about the weather or even read from the sacred Scriptures. His experience, he said, taught him the truth that religion is self-defeating like love if it is forced or artificial. Many times, he said, he sat at a bed-side of the ill without even saying a word. The fact that one is there at a time when there is trouble is sufficient.

A visitation should never be officious. Each situation, like people, is unique and should be met with common sense. People are quick to detect professionalism and artificiality and nothing is gained ever in promoting religion in that manner. We may find that even Christ in His ministry was never a member of "a profession." He did what came naturally to Himself and the occasion. He, no doubt, carried His carpenter tools without a copy of the Law and the Prophets and enjoyed the home of Martha, Mary and Lazarus without sermonic behavior.

Those upon whom the call has been made will suggest the type of service that is open and the acute minister will sense the cue. See hospital chaplain, the; pastoral counseling and case studies; pastoral psychology; pastoral psychology: its governing limitations and qualifications; postural response; social perception; visiting the sick.

**visiting the sick:** The effect of health upon one's spiritual well-being cannot be exaggerated. William James'* oft quoted reply to the question "Is Life worth living?" is very much to the point. He said "It depends on the liver." We might add, it depends on the condition of any or all other parts of the anatomy. For this reason, the ministry to the sick is of the highest importance inasmuch as their spiritual condition is always affected.

What the pastor does when calling on the sick depends on several factors, the most important of which are the age of the patient and the degree of seriousness of the illness.

If the patient is a child under ten years of age, one must use some imagination. Any barrier in the child's mind toward the minister or ministry must be removed and he must approach the child as a friend and neighbor. He must remove any cloak of professionalism, of pomp, and circumstance, for one cannot fool children. Once in a child's presence, the approach should be cheery and pleasant without trying to be funny. A small gift is often appreciated. The minister should never stay very long but should offer a brief prayer before leaving.

In the case of young people between fifteen and twenty-five years of age, the approach must be on the adult level. They must be encouraged. The pastor must not tell funereal stories or recite incidents of accident cases which have resulted in tragedy. The conversation must be pleasant and not dismal, avoiding all suggestion of a pious lecture or of morbid attitude. One of the best techniques is to divert their attention from themselves by discussing matters of interest to them. If the illness be prolonged such a booklet as Rufus Jones' *Finding the Trail of Life* (1926) makes excellent reading. It illustrates the indirect benefits which can come from the right use of a prolonged period of confinement.

People in the middle years, from 35 to 65, often need assurance and understanding. Theirs are the years of heaviest responsibility. Their business affairs and their domestic responsibilities are at peak loads. Illness for them is not only a great expense but a great worry inasmuch as there are others involved and dependent upon the patient. They need words of comfort and courage. Usually, if their condition permits, the pastor should visit as long as possible without tiring them. To be specific, it is inadvisable for a pastor ever to stay in a sick room more than approximately five minutes unless there is some special reason and a request for him to do so. There is an element of timing in visiting the sick which every pastor must develop; he can stay too long, and also leave too soon. He must use his own judgment and discretion and learn how to make an entrance into the sick room and how to take his departure without embarrassment or awkwardness.

In the case of the aged, the technique of a pastoral call differs in some degree. Usually the aged wish to visit a little longer than younger people. Invariably they wish the scriptures to be read and a prayer offered. They are most appreciative of any word of comfort or act of kindness the minister can convey to them.

In the case of Mr. "A," a bedridden cancer patient, the pastor called at the home, visited briefly with the family concerning the condition of the patient and the family situation before going upstairs to see Mr. "A." The pastor must make certain whether or not the patient knows the nature of his illness so as not to upset either the technique of the doctor or the family. After visiting briefly with the patient he offered a prayer and departed.

In calling at a hospital, the pastor first goes to the desk to check the name, room number, and condition of the patient. Before entering the sick room he speaks to the nurse on duty for any briefing she can give concerning the patient's condition. The patient's condition should determine how long the pastor stays and what he might say, the kind of prayer he should offer, and the scripture passage he should read if any.

Let no pastor underestimate the therapeutic value of the presence of a good man in a sick room, or the value of reading the scripture or of a prayer. Medical authorities say that more than half the patients hospitalized today have no physical or organic disease. Their trouble is psychosomatic.* "Psychosomatic medicine" is the field of promise today. Some years ago, Robert Haven Schauffler published a book he called *The Poetry Cure* (1925). In the introduction he writes this:

"An essay of mine called 'The Musical Pharmacy' appeared fourteen years ago. Its suggestions on the use of certain sorts of music for certain sorts of prevention and cure, were fortunate enough to play an influential part in the movement which soon installed music in hospitals, asylums, homes and sanatoriums as an accepted therapeutic agent.

"The success of this movement encouraged me to take up another long cherished plan. For it seemed that one thing was still more needed than musical therapeutics. This was The Poetry Cure.

"I had dreamed of a cheap and convenient pocket anthology of remedies for such troubles as fear, fatigue, swollen ego, ingrowing ugliness, the blues, pettiness, impatience, insomnia, torpid imagination, sorrow, hardening of the heart, sluggish blood, myopic vision of the inner eye, and other common ailments."

Another book of value to the pastor in his work with the sick is a volume called *Body, Mind, and Spirit* by Elwood Worcester and Samuel McComb. They are also the authors of a volume called *Religion and Medicine*. While the emphasis in these volumes borders on the psychiatric aspect of medical care, a word of warning may be in order to ministers concerning the danger in handling mental patients. Psychiatry and psychology are highly specialized fields. No minister can read two or three books on the subject and consider himself an authority in this area. The best advice is to try and do as little harm as possible and leave the patient entirely in more expert hands. The reading of the scriptures and the offering of prayer is the pastor's best service to the mentally ill.

One of the greatest services the pastor can perform for the sick is to listen to them. The Protestant Church does not have a confessional,* in the formal sense of that term, but the Protestant pastor probably listens to more honest and straight confessions than do most liturgical priests. William Blake has put it well:

> "I was angry with my friend:
> I told my wrath, my wrath did end.
> I was angry with my foe:
> I told it not, my wrath did grow."

The effect of the mind and the spirit upon the body can be nothing sort of miraculous. Very little is known to date concerning the possibilities of spiritual healing, but the life of Jesus gives us some intimation of the power of the spirit over the flesh. The wise pastor will discover in time that his ministry has a power and an influence over the sick far greater than anything he would dare claim for himself, and greater than he can begin to understand. About all he can say is that the power of God does work through man to bring healing to the sick. See hospital chaplain, the; visitation. J. R. W.

**vitamins:** see aging process; fatigue.

**vocabulary:** see success.

**vocation:** see careers; minister as a person; ministry.

**vocation and success:** see success.

**volition:** see will.

# W

**wakefulness:** see autosuggestion; insomnia; sleep.
**war:** see psychology of religion.
**war and peace:** see peace and war.
**watershed books:** see minister, the, and his books.
**Watson, John B.:** see emotion; fears, conditioned; psychology, schools of.
**weakness:** see glands.
**weakness in personality:** see Adlerian approach to therapy.
**weather, the:** see atmospheric conditions and work capacity.
**Weatherhead, L. D.:** see psychology of religion.
**Weber, Max:** see psychology of religion.
**wedding fees:** see minister, the, and money.
**weeping:** see emotion.
**Wertheimer, Max:** (1880-1943). German psychologist (came to the U. S.) who helped to initiate the Gestalt school of psychology. Perception* of movement he reported to be unanalyzable into discrete elements. His term phi-phenomenon suggests apparent movement occurring when two stimuli are presented in a certain temporal and spatial order. See deception; psychology, schools of.
**Westcott, bishop:** see psychical research and parapsychology.
**Whitman, Walt:** see healthy-mindedness.
**whole reading:** see memorizing; reading performance.
**whole thinking:** see creative thinking.
**will, the:** see autosuggestion; prayer and autosuggestion.
**wives and husbands:** see marriage, disharmony in; sex differ-

ences, psychological.

**Wolff, C.:** see palmistry and pedomancy.

**women:** see adult, the; age; aging process; climacterium; menopause; sex differences, psychological; wives and husbands.

**Woodworth, Robert Sessions:** (1869-    ) Professor emeritus of psychology at Columbia University whose published works have widely influenced the academic field of contemporary psychology. His viewpoint (somewhat conservative) is called dynamic psychology with special emphasis on the application of the principle of cause and effect. See memory; smell.

**Worcester, Elwood:** see Boisen, Anton T.; visiting the sick.

**Worcester State Hospital:** see Boisen, Anton T.; hospital chaplain, the.

**word association test:** see Jung, Carl.

**word commands in learning:** see learning.

**word method:** see reading performance.

**words:** see deception; emotive language; learning; reading performance.

**work:** see atmospheric conditions and work capacity; child training; creativity; deliberate effort; efficiency; efficiency and time of day; emotional tensions, release of; noise disturbances; occupational prejudice; sleep; sublimation; success; talents; work and rest; work inhibitions.

**work and rest:** Psychologists have given considerable attention to the relation of efficiency and manual labor. This phase of applied psychology is called psychotechnology. It has been found by careful observation that any increase in the number of working hours beyond an optimal point brings diminishing returns hour by hour, even reducing the total output of a whole day. Where work activity is uninterrupted fatigue occurs at a rate with positive acceleration—the longer one works without interruption the more rapidly do the effects of fatigue appear.

Rest periods are found to offset the drop in production providing they are properly placed. The proper place is not some arbitrary spot on the clock but, rather, that point where the decline in production first asserts itself. On the strictly psychological side, anticipation of a rest period, immediately before the rest, tends to accelerate production.

Mid-morning and mid-afternoon rest periods (pauses), in anticipation, contribute to efficiency.

It is difficult to measure mental output. Work requiring creative thinking will not follow the "work and rest periods" patterns of those engaged in manual work nor the similar patterns of those engaged in mental work of the type of repetition. Creative thinkers may find their efficiency in long stretches of application with corresponding long periods of dryness (pause). Individuals will differ on this score so much as to defy any set pattern. See atmospheric conditions and work capacity; creative thinking; efficiency; efficiency and time of day; fatigue.

**work inhibitions:** see atmospheric conditions and work capacity; boredom; noise disturbances.

**workability, test of truth:** see pragmatism; truth.

**worry:** Any undue concern over past behavior or undue consideration of anticipatory events or conditions. The term usually is restricted to specific anxieties. See anxiety, anxiety neurosis; anxiety states; fatigue; hypertension; learning; psychosomatics.

**worship:** J. B. Pratt* in his well known psychological study, *The Religious Consciousness* (1920) has called attention to two types of worship: the objective and the subjective.

In objective worship the emphasis is given to the Object of worship, of making some effect on God or effecting communication with Reality. In subjective worship the emphasis is given to the worshipper, of inducing in him a mood or an attitude or belief.

Catholic mass and other forms of ceremonialism are instances of objective worship. Here cathedrals, rituals, priests are outward symbols of this type. Protestant revivalism wherein the individual is appealed to to accept salvation or to give himself to the Lord is an example of subjective worship. Hymns (participated in by the congregation) devoted to conversion, sanctification, dedication are outward symbols of this type. So also church architecture fashioned for audience participation, social functions and the like portray this emphasis. Sermons to educate and arouse are people-centered.

Professor Pratt concludes that both forms of worship are psychologically desirable in a given worship. A subjective religious effect is best attained by a setting of objective validity. And conversely a real religious act of worship (worthship, reverence) of an Object of devotion cannot be real unless there is a mood and a response on the part of the participant. Either one without the other ultimately lacks vitality and lasting significance. See funerals; sermon; sermons, preparation of; symbols; worship and psychology.

**worship and psychology:** see funerals; pastoral psychology: its governing limitations and qualifications; prayer and autosuggestion; repetition compulsion; symbols; worship.

**writing:** see graphology.

**wrong and right:** see conscience; morality and psychology.

**Wundt, W.:** see psychology of religion; psychology, schools of.

# X

**xenophobia:** see phobias.
**x-ray, use of:** see human genetics.

# Y

**Yale Clinic of Child Development:** see teen-agers.

**Y.M.C.A. and Y.W.C.A. guidance groups:** see group psychotherapy.

**young, the:** see adult, the; aging process; character; child training; in-laws; juvenile delinquency; learning; mental deficiency; morality and psychology; motives; pastoral counseling and case studies; pastoral counseling: case studies; role playing; social maturation; students; success; talents; teen-agers; visiting the sick. See also: children.

# Z

**zelophobia:** see phobias.

www.ingramcontent.com/pod-product-compliance
Lightning Source LLC
Chambersburg PA
CBHW032032150426
43194CB00006B/241